# SCOTTISH HILL TRACKS

# Scottish Hill Tracks

## A guide to hill paths, old roads and rights of way

Fourth Edition  (revised) 2004

Edited by
**D J Bennet**
and
**C D Stone**
From the original compilation by
**D G Moir**

Map designed by
**J C Bartholomew**

Published in Great Britain by the Scottish Rights of Way and Access Society
and the Scottish Mountaineering Trust, 2004

First Edition  1947
Second Edition  1975
Third Edition  1995
Fourth Edition  1999
Fourth Edition  (revised) 2004

**British Library Cataloguing in Publication Data**
ISBN 0 9546735 0 6

A catalogue record of this book is available from
The British Library

Produced by Scottish Mountaineering Trust (Publications) Ltd
Colour separations by Digital Imaging, Glasgow
Printed by M&M Press, Glasgow and St Edmundsbury Press Ltd, Bury St Edmunds
Map manufactured by Collins Maps & Atlases
Bound by Hunter and Foulis, Haddington

Distributed by Cordee Ltd, 3a DeMontfort Street, Leicester, LE1 7HD
tel: 0116 254 3579, fax: 0116 247 1176, email (sales@cordee.co.uk)

# Contents

# Foreword

*By Tom Weir*

This handsome book, with colour photographs, a specially created map and revised descriptions of Scottish hill tracks, old highways and drove roads, combines the two volumes of the previous edition by D.G.Moir, published by John Bartholomew & Son Ltd in 1947, revised in 1975 and again in 1995, and now further researched in the light of recent changes of access and land use.

It was Government fear of the Highlanders that sent Field Marshal George Wade to Scotland in 1724 to build military roads with the aim of pacifying the homelands of the Jacobites who had threatened the peace in 1715 and again in 1719. By 1739 Wade had increased the number of his Highland companies to ten, had formed the Black Watch Regiment from clansmen loyal to the Westminster Government, and he and his successors carried forward a big programme of road building.

Thomas Telford (1757 - 1834), son of a Border shepherd, whose genius earned him the title 'Colossus of the Roads', achieved in his lifetime more than any single individual, pushing highways through 900 miles of mountainous and boggy terrain.

Balmoralism dates from the mid-1850s when the wealthy, made rich from the proceeds of the Industrial Revolution, were rapidly acquiring large Highland estates and building shooting lodges, bothies and well-made paths ideal for ponies and walkers.

By 1912 there were 203 deer forests occupying three and a half million acres. Cattle and sheep had been banished together with unwanted people. Owners and occupiers of these lands had become accustomed to purchasing privacy, but the introduction of the popular bicycle around 1885 brought a gentle breeze of change, coinciding as it did with the formation of the Cairngorm Club and the Scottish Mountaineering Club, just over 100 years ago.

In the Lowlands game-preserving and agriculture had gone hand in hand in the Border country with hedges, parks and coppice wood, integrating sport with farming. Walter Scott himself had channelled much of his vast wealth into tree-planting and beautifying his stretch of the River Tweed.

The Reverend A.E. Robertson, first completer of all 283 Munros in the original list, was a self-reliant user of old tracks on foot and by bicycle, without which he could not have achieved his marathon in the years between 1889 and 1901. He was an eager compiler of old tracks, coffin roads and cross-country routes. He became a director of the Scottish Rights of Way Society in 1923, Chairman in 1931, and after its reorganisation became its first President in 1946 - the same year that he was elected a Fellow of the Royal Society of Edinburgh.

To walk these ancient tracks demands not only sleuth work, but can be a contribution to history in noting changes and keeping this record of old routes up to date.

Carnoch, Knoydart.    Peter D. Koch-Osborne.

# Illustrations

# Acknowledgements

The Scottish Rights of Way and Access Society acknowledges with thanks the financial assistance of Tiso the Outdoor Specialist towards the production of the map which forms part of this book, and the co-operation of the Scottish Mountaineering Trust (Publications) Ltd in the production and publication of the book.

The editors acknowledge the willing help of the following members of the Society and others who have rechecked the majority of the routes described in this book, and notified changes necessary for this revised edition.

| | |
|---|---|
| Calum Anton | Alistair Lawson |
| Lorne Anton | Philip Lawson |
| Maureen Anton | Jenny Kett |
| Alastair Beattie | Mike Lewis |
| Margaret Beattie | Laurie Macaskill |
| Arthur Bennet | Donald Mackay |
| Cris Bonomy | Peter Mackay |
| Campbell Burnside | Catherine MacLeod |
| Irvine Butterfield | Duncan Menzies |
| Jean Bisset | Andrew Nelson |
| Janet Clark | Derek Purdy |
| Jim Clark | Mike Roberts |
| Neil Cook | Gordon Robertson |
| Alec Cunningham | John Snowdon |
| John Davidson | Bob Sparkes |
| John Duberley | Peter Starling |
| Mary Duberley | Jim Strachan |
| Muriel Dymock | Alex Sutherland |
| Harry Eccles | Euan Terras |
| Annabel Eccles | Tom Tokely |
| Pat Eccles | Sandy Valentine |
| Alan Eelbeck | Alan Wells |
| Bill Forsyth | Peter Wood |
| David Gray | Douglas Wright |
| Ken Hazelock | |

Many others have given assistance by correspondence.

The editors wish to express their appreciation of the help given by Janet Clark in undertaking the typescript of this revision and also to thank Bruce Logan for co-ordinating its production.

*Donald Bennet    Cliff Stone*

# Introduction

This book gives route descriptions for over three hundred cross country walks in all parts of Scotland, most of which can be accomplished in a day. The majority of these routes follow existing roads (some public and some private), tracks and footpaths. In places there are no such recognisable features, and the routes cross moors and hills where the walker must find his own way; in other places old paths and tracks may, through disuse, have returned to their natural state and now can barely be recognised as vague lines and erosion scars across grassy hillsides or heather moors.

Many of the routes follow ancient roads and drovers' tracks, and some are now regarded as rights of way. However, not all the routes described in this book are rights of way, and no claims are made about their legal status. In any event, the new access rights established under the Land Reform Act (Scotland) 2003 apply to most routes and some of these may in future be designated as Core Paths (see page 6). Where access rights are excluded and use of a route is objected to, it will usually be possible to by-pass the excluded section, and this may be signposted. Routes may also be diverted because of wind farm developments or for other land management reasons.

Although the main purpose of this book is to describe cross-country routes over open country, moors and hills, there are inevitably sections where the walker must go along public roads. The choice of routes has been made to reduce to a minimum the amount of walking on main roads with heavy traffic, but there remain many sections of walking along minor country roads which do not carry much traffic. This is inevitable and will not, it is hoped, detract from the quality of the routes as a whole.

It is to be hoped that not only will this book open the eyes of many readers to the great wealth of one-day cross-country walks in Scotland, but also stir their imagination to the possibility of any number of long-distance routes lasting several days. One has only to look at the map of Scotland at the end of this book to see the great network of routes covering the country which can be linked in literally dozens of different ways. Adventurous walkers can plan their own personal pilgrimages across Scotland; north, south, east or west, and thereby dispel criticism levelled at some of the designated long routes that they inhibit individual route planning and encourage walkers to follow paths that have become eroded. However, over the centuries some routes have evolved as described below.

## Roman Roads

The oldest known roads in Scotland are those made by the Roman soldiers between AD 78 and 185. Their three main lines of road can still be seen:

1. From the Cheviots to the River Tweed at Melrose and on to the Forth.
2. From the Solway Firth up Annandale and northwards to the Lower Clyde.

3. From the Roman Wall at Camelon by Stirling and Strathearn to the River Tay north of Perth.

The best remaining section of Roman road is the 20km stretch of Dere Street from the Cheviots to Jedfoot, which has been very little disturbed since it was made in the 2nd century. This stretch shows that the usual idea of a Roman road as being a long straight line is only partially true. The Roman engineer did prefer a direct line, sighted from skyline to skyline, but he chose his route with skill and on hilly ground found a winding road more practicable than a straight one.

Roman roads have endured because they were well constructed. Part of the Annandale road was found by excavation to have a 28cm layer of large stones and a 10cm layer of small stones, all bound with clay with a total width of 6½ metres. The standard construction was four layers, two of stones, a third of mixed material, and a top layer, sometimes of paving stones but more generally of gravel bound with clay.

## Mediaeval Roads

Some of our roads may be even older than Roman times, but we have no proof of this in Scotland. In England an extensive system had clearly been in use in prehistoric times, and there are some ridgeways in southern Scotland which may be either prehistoric or mediaeval, for example the ridgeway from Soutra to Melrose known as the Girthgate (route 38), the Minchmoor track (route 25) and the ridgeway from Peebles to Yarrow (route 22). The mediaeval traveller had the same ideas as his prehistoric ancestor. He wanted to avoid bogs, streams, ravines and forests, and he therefore climbed to the high ground as quickly as possible and kept along the ridges until he found the shortest crossing of the next valley.

The foundation of abbeys and churches, and the growth of villages and towns, resulted in the development of more roads, particularly in the valleys where the new settlements were growing up, but for more than fourteen centuries after the Roman period there was no proper road construction in Scotland. The word 'road' itself originally referred to riding, and it was not until Shakespeare's time that it was used for the road to travel on. The older name was way or highway, and in Scotland gate or gait. We find a Thirlstanegate mentioned in a charter about 1240, and there are numerous Gatesides still among our place-names.

Horseback and foot were the only means of travel in the Middle Ages, and except for waggons of a kind owned by some of the abbeys, all merchandise was carried by packhorse. For these a beaten track along the ground was sufficient, trodden out by the passage of many feet, without any properly made road.

In the course of time some of these tracks have been made into roads, whilst others have been left to revert to their natural state. Interesting examples are the tracks which cross the Cheviots into England (routes 1 to 11) and the old routes across the Eastern Grampians from Deeside to the south which still retain their old names - Tolmount, Capel Mounth etc (routes 166 to 176). One useful indication of an old road is when it forms a parish boundary, as most of Scotland was divided into parishes in the 12th and 13th centuries. This is not always conclusive proof that a road is quite so old, since there have been some more recent changes in parish boundaries, particularly in the 15th and 16th centuries.

## Drove Roads

The rearing of cattle and sheep was for centuries the mainstay of the Highland economy, and every autumn large droves of animals were taken from the Highlands to the cattle markets or trysts. The most important market was for long the Michaelmas Tryst at Crieff, where in the course of a week as many as 30,000 cattle were sold, besides a smaller number of sheep. The chief buyers were the English, and it was not uncommon for them to hire the sellers to drive the stock on to England.

By 1770 the Michaelmas Tryst was transferred to Falkirk. In a lawsuit in 1846 evidence was given that for centuries people north of the Grampians had been in the habit of driving sheep and cattle to the southern markets along two lines of drove roads:

1. By Drumochter, Atholl and Crieff from the northern and eastern parts of Ross and Inverness-shire.

2. By Glen Coe, the Black Mount and Callander from Wester Ross, Inverness, Argyll and the Western Isles.

The drove road by Glen Coe had been in use long before the military road was made in 1750 on the line of the old road, with occasional diversions. It was the practice of the drovers to travel ten miles a day, as that was the distance the animals could go without suffering serious harm, and to rest the animals at regular stances on the roadside.

Other markets on a smaller scale were held all over Scotland. In the action brought in the Court of Session in 1887 to preserve the Glen Doll right of way (route 175) it was proved that it had for long been used by drovers taking sheep from Braemar to the market at Cullow, near Kirriemuir. The long distances travelled by drovers is shown by a report to the Privy Council in 1598 concerning McKenzie of Kintail, who had 24 cattle stolen on his way to the fair at Glamis.

Many local drove roads owe their existence to the old Highland custom of families moving in early summer with their cattle, sheep and goats to the hill shielings, where they spent the summer in stone or turf huts, making the milk into butter and cheese. This custom died out as the higher grazings were converted into sheep farms. Other drove roads were in use in fairly recent years by sheep going to and from their winter grazings. Auction marts and modern transport have ended these old customs. A few drove roads still carry the name Thieves Road as reminders of the times when cattle lifting was practised on a large scale. (Further reading: *The Drove Roads of Scotland* by A.R.B.Haldane ISBN 187474 47 69).

## Kirk and Coffin Roads

These, as the names indicate, are local rights of way to churches and churchyards. In the Highlands many of them were quite long tracks, for example the route from Glen Lyon to Dalmally which was used by the Macgregors going from their homes in Glen Lyon to their clan burial ground at the foot of Glen Orchy. Coffins might be carried for many miles, all the local men taking turns. Osgood Mackenzie records, in his book  *A Hundred Years in the Highlands*, that when Lady Mackenzie died in 1830 five hundred men, taking turns, carried the coffin sixty miles from Gairloch to Beauly. When coffins were rested, everyone added a stone to a cairn on the spot, a custom that was responsible for many of the cairns still to be seen on some of these routes.

## Military Roads

In 1724 General Wade was sent to Scotland by King George I to report on the state of the Highlands and make recommendations for ensuring peace among the clans. One of Wade's proposals was to improve communications by making proper roads between the various garrisons which had been established some years earlier at Inverness, Fort William and Kilcumein (Fort Augustus), and in 1724 he began making proper roads to replace the old rough tracks, work which explains the old lines:

*If you'd seen these roads before they were made,*
*You'd lift up your hands and bless General Wade.*

By 1734 Wade's soldiers had made some 250 miles of roads:
1. Fort William to Fort Augustus and by Whitebridge to Inverness.
2. Dunkeld to Inverness by the Drumochter Pass.
3. Crieff to Dalnacardoch.
4. Dalwhinnie to Fort Augustus by the Corrieyairack Pass.
5. Ruthven Barracks (Kingussie) to the Corrieyairack road.

His last work was the erection of the bridge over the River Spey. General Wade left Scotland in 1740; he died in 1748 with the rank of Field Marshal, and was buried in Westminster Abbey.

The road work in Scotland was carried on by Wade's successor, Major Caulfeild, who had the title of Inspector of Roads, and was responsible for the construction between 1740 and 1767 of some 830 miles of military roads. These included:
1. Stirling to Crieff.
2. Dumbarton to Inveraray and Tyndrum by the Rest and be Thankful.
3. Stirling to Glen Coe and Fort William.
4. Coupar Angus to Fort George by Braemar, Tomintoul and Grantown.
5. Fettercairn by the Cairn o' Mount to Huntly and Fochabers.
6. Bridge of Sark (Gretna) to Portpatrick.
7. Fort Augustus to Bernera Barracks (Glenelg).
8. Aberdeen to Huntly.
9. Stonehaven to Aberdeen, Portsoy and Fochabers
10. Stirling to Dumbarton.
11. Contin (Ross-shire) to Poolewe.

Some of these roads were in time abandoned; others were transferred in the 19th century to the county authorities for maintenance.

## Modern Roads

Roads, as distinct from tracks, had their beginning in Scotland in 1617, when the Scottish Parliament made the justices of the peace responsible for "mending all highways". The old tracks were in bad condition through increasing traffic, and were quite unfit for coaches, introduced to Scotland in the early 17th century. Travellers commonly described these tracks as infamous, infernal, execrable, with deep pools and ruts of liquid mud, or with rocky channels worse than the bed of a river.

The statute of 1617 had little effect. A new Act in 1669 introduced the scheme of statute labour, whereby every man in the parish between the ages of 15 and 70 had to give six day's labour on the roads every year, and the highways were to be made 20 feet broad and fit for horses and carts in winter as well as in summer. There was a general reluctance to work, and the scheme was never a success.

From 1713 onwards it was gradually superseded by the turnpike system, under which the people using the roads paid tolls and the road trustees employed a staff of roadmen. The turnpike system was abolished in 1878, when the maintenance of roads was made the responsibility of the local authorities. For historical reference the most useful early maps of Scotland showing roads are the following:

1654   Blaeu's Atlas. The first map showing roads, but only some in the Lothians, Renfrew and Berwickshire.

1679   Rob.Greene. Scotland, with main roads. 13 miles to one inch.

1745   Hermann Moll's Atlas. With main roads. Scales from 4 to 7 miles to 1 inch.

1746   T. Willdey. Map, showing Wade roads. 5 miles to 1 inch.

1755   Roy's Military Survey. The first really detailed map with roads. In the British Museum, never published.

1775   M.I.Armstrong's County Map of Peebles and Tweeddale

Various county maps are mentioned in route descriptions. A complete list of maps is given in   *The Early Maps of Scotland*, published by the Royal Scottish Geographical Society.

## Rights of Way

Many of the routes described in this book are rights of way, but there are others which are not. Public rights of way have been recognised in Scots law for centuries and are a valuable part of our cultural heritage. A right of way must run from one public place to another public place along a more or less defined route (it need not be an identifiable path) and it must have been used openly and peaceably by the public otherwise than with the permission, express or implied, of the landowner, for at least 20 years. Many rights of way have been established for walkers only, but some have been established for use by horse riders and cyclists also.

**Access Rights and Core Paths**

The Land Reform (Scotland) Act 2003 established statutory access rights for everyone over all land and inland water in Scotland, subject to certain exclusions.   The rights, essentially for recreation and passage, and not restricted to linear routes, can be exercised at any time of the day or night but must be exercised responsibly.   Land managers must manage their land responsibly in relation to the rights.   Guidance on exercising access rights and on managing land responsibly is given in the Scottish Outdoor Access Code. We have printed on page 10 a short version of the main responsibilities of those exercising access rights.

Under the 2003 Act local authorities are obliged, within 3 years of the Act coming into force, to draw  up a plan for a system of Core Paths sufficient for the purpose of giving the public reasonable access throughout their area. The system may include rights of way, paths established under the 2003 Act or other legislation, or any route by means of which people cross land.   You will be able to exercise access rights over Core Paths even where those paths cross land otherwise excluded from the rights.

Public rights of way co-exist with the new access rights but are not affected by exclusions applying to those rights (eg through farmyards or near houses or over land where crops are  growing).   You are entitled to continue to use a right of way in those circumstances.   Although the new access rights do not extend to the use of motorised vehicles, you can still use a vehicular right of way where it has been established.

It is an offence for a proprietor or anyone else to create an obstruction across a right of way, and the local authority has the power to remove any such obstruction and re-instate the route.   Local authorities have similar powers in relation to access rights under the 2003 Act.

Much more could be written about the law relating to rights of way and access rights in Scotland, but that is rather outwith the scope of this book. Those wishing to learn more should read  *Access Rights & Rights of Way: A Guide to the Law in Scotland* published by The Scottish Rights of Way & Access Society.

# NOTES

### Equipment

It is assumed that the walker setting out on the exploration of hill tracks in Scotland is aware of the need for appropriate equipment and clothing. The routes described in this book vary from short low-level walks on dry, well made footpaths where strong boots and special clothing are not required, to long, rough and often trackless routes over high ground which is frequently wet and boggy, particularly in the west. In the latter case strong waterproof shoes or boots are needed, unless one is prepared to get wet feet, and suitable protective clothing, waterproof and windproof, should also be regarded as necessary.

It is also assumed that those who read this book and set out on the walks described in it will carry a map and compass, and be able to use them. Not all the routes described are visible on the ground as paths or tracks, and where there is no visible sign of a route, walkers will have to find their own way, and if the visibility is bad may have to use a map and compass for navigation.

### Tracks, Times and Distances

The numbering of the routes in this fourth edition of *Scottish Hill Tracks* has as far as possible been kept the same as in the third edition, otherwise serious confusion would be likely to result. To accommodate new routes in this edition, therefore, the letter X, Y and Z have been used. Thus a new route in the vicinity of existing routes 182 and 183 is numbered 182X.

The use of a symbol ↑ denotes places where a ScotWays signpost indicates the start or finish of a route which is a right of way. However routes not so indicated could also be rights of way.

Many of the upland areas of Scotland are now crossed by tracks made for shooting and estate management purposes. Some of these are old tracks made many years ago which are now blending with the landscape, others are recently bulldozed tracks which have created very obvious scars over hills and moors, and others are the tracks of all-terrain vehicles (ATVs) which have been more recently introduced, and which when used over soft grassy ground tend to leave dark muddy tracks. There are also many rough roads that have been driven into the hills as part of forestry operations.

Some of these tracks and roads are on the lines of existing paths, others are not. The existence of these tracks is sometimes helpful to walkers, but frequently they do not go in the direction that the walker wants. The Ordnance Survey maps, even the most recent Landranger series, do not show all these tracks accurately, so the walker must be careful when map reading to be aware of possible discrepancies.

The time required for any walk will depend on the distance, the weather, the state of the path and the amount of uphill climbing involved. In the west and north-west of Scotland more than in the east, routes are likely to be over rough ground, paths may be faint or non-existent and the ground wet and boggy. All these factors make for slower progress than on good paths, and the normal walking rate of 3 miles per hour (4½ km/hour) is likely to be reduced to about 2 miles per hour (3km/hour). Some of the paths in Knoydart and elsewhere are so rough that they might well be described as '2km/hour-walks', a self-explanatory description of really slow progress.

Another important factor to be considered in bad weather is the state of streams that may have to be crossed. If a stream is in spate and there is no bridge, then the crossing may be very difficult, dangerous or even impossible, and a long detour may be required to find an alternative crossing. It may even be necessary to turn back. These remarks apply particularly to the north-west Highlands where high rainfall and swollen streams are not uncommon. Take note of weather signs and forecasts before setting out.

Some of the walks described in this book go over mountainous country and reach heights over 1000m. In winter these walks become full-scale mountain days, and those setting out on them must be adequately experienced and equipped for winter hillwalking (see page 11).

### Transport

Information is available from offices of the various operating companies throughout Scotland – see Yellow Pages.

Public transport information is available from TRAVELINE, phone: 0870 608 2 608, www.travelinescotland.com

Some Councils publish guides for their own areas, for instance the Highland Council, Glenurqhuart Drive, Inverness, IV3 5NX, which also includes the islands.

The Royal Mail operate Post Buses which, in addition to delivering mail, have limited passenger seats useful to walkers in remote areas, but most services are in the mornings. Details are now obtained by phone: 0845 774 0740, www.royalmail.com/postbus

### Accommodation

Information about all types is published by Visitscotland in its book; *Where to Stay in Scotland*, available from 23 Ravelston Terrace, Edinburgh, EH4 3EU, phone: 0845 22 55 121, www.visitscotland.com, or through tourist offices and many bookshops.

The Scottish Youth Hostels Association, 7 Glebe Crescent, Stirling, FK8 2JA, phone: 01786 891 400, www.syha.org.uk has information about membership and hostels, many of which are well placed for walks described in this book.

In some of the remote parts of Scotland there are bothies which give basic shelter to walkers. The Mountain Bothies Association maintains many of these bothies about which details can be obtained from its Information Officer: Ted Butcher, 26 Rycroft Avenue, Deeping St James, Peterborough PE6 8NT, www.mountainbothies.org.uk. There are also increasing numbers of independent hostels and bunkhouses. Information about these is available in the advertising pages of walkers' magazines such as *The Great Outdoors* and brochures such as *The Highland Bunkhouses, Bothies and Barns*, published with the backing of the Highland Council. There is also a useful

*Independent Hostel Guide for Scotland*, published annually in March and available free (see A5) from: P Thomas, Portnalong, Isle of Skye, IV47 8SL

**Maps**

The most suitable maps for walkers are the Ordnance Survey Landranger Maps, 1:50,000 scale. In revising this book, the compilers have made use of the latest editions of these maps. As far as possible place names, spellings and heights correspond to the maps whose revision dates are mostly in the 1990's, with reprinted versions including selected changes ongoing. Users of this book are recommended to use up to date maps rather than earlier ones to depict such features as woodland and forests, tracks and paths. However, not even the most recent maps are entirely accurate in showing paths, some of which have long since disappeared yet still appear on current maps.

In each route description in this book, the relevant sheets of the Landranger series are listed. Six-figure map references are given in the conventional way, the first three figures being the easting and the last three figures being the northing. In the text the abbreviation m is used for metres height or vertical interval, while distances are quoted in metres and km (kilometres). Miles are only used for giving route lengths.

**Gaelic Place Names**

The following Gaelic words occur frequently in place names, and a knowledge of their meanings helps our understanding of the maps:

| | | | |
|---|---|---|---|
| a' an | *the* | eas | *waterfall* |
| abhainn, amhainn | *river* | garbh | *rough* |
| allt | *burn, stream* | geal | *white* |
| aonach | *ridge* | glas, ghlas | *grey, green* |
| ban, bhan | *white* | gleann | *glen, valley* |
| beag, beg, bheag | *small* | gorm | *blue* |
| bealach | *pass* | lairig | *pass* |
| ben, beinn, bheinn | *hill, mountain* | laogh, laoigh | *calf* |
| bidean, bidein | *peak* | liath | *grey* |
| braigh brae | *hill-top* | lochan | *small loch* |
| buidhe, bhuidhe | *yellow* | meall | *rounded hill* |
| carn | *cairn, hill, pile of stones* | mor, mhor | *big* |
| clach | *stone, stony* | na, nam, nan | *the, of, of the* |
| coille | *wood* | odhar | *dun-coloured* |
| coire, choire | *corrie, hollow* | ruadh | *red* |
| creag | *crag, cliff, rock* | sgurr, stob, stuc | *peak (usually rocky)* |
| dearg | *red* | | |
| drum, druim | *ridge* | srath | *strath, wide valley* |
| dubh | *black, dark* | uaine | *green* |

# SCOTTISH OUTDOOR ACCESS CODE

The Code provides detailed guidance on how to exercise statutory access rights responsibly.
In particular –
– Take responsibility for your own actions.
– Respect people's privacy and peace of mind.
– Help land managers and others to work safely and effectively.
– Look after your environment.
– Keep your dog under proper control.
– Take extra care if you are organising an event or running a business.

The Code also provides a practical guide to help people decide what best to do in everyday situations, including canoeing, cycling, deer stalking, farmyards, fields, fishing, forests and woods, golf courses, grouse shooting, horse riding, sporting events, wild camping and many other situations which space does not permit us to cover. For more information we recommend that readers consult the full text of the Code, a copy of which can be obtained from Scottish Natural Heritage or found on its website, www.outdooraccess-scotland.com

The Mountaineering Council of Scotland (MCofS) and the Scottish Rural Property and Business Association (SRPBA, formerly The Scottish Landowners Federation) have jointly published a useful booklet *Heading for the Scottish Hills* which lists many estates in the Highlands and gives addresses and telephone numbers of many owners, factors and keepers who can be contacted for information about stalking and shooting activities likely to affect walkers. MCofS also publishes annually a leaflet *Hillphones* (www.hillphones.info) which lists telephone numbers for recorded messages in the major hillwalking areas, giving daily information about deer stalking activities. The use of these publications is recommended to those who plan to walk across hills and moors during the stalking and shooting seasons.

**Mountain Safety**
Bearing in mind that many of the walks described in this book take one over high ground, in some cases to mountain tops, and that in winter the conditions can be very severe, an appreciation of mountain safety is important. The following points should be kept in mind, particularly if planning a long, high route in winter:

*Before you go:*
Plan a route within your capability
Know the weather forecast
Know how to use map and compass
Know the mountain distress signal (six whistle blasts at one minute intervals)
Know simple first aid and be able to recognise the signs of exposure

*When you go:*
Do not go alone
Leave information about your route and estimate of return time
Wear suitable footwear and take spare clothing
Take map, compass, torch, whistle, food and drink
In winter take an ice axe and know how to use it
Recognise dangerous snow and ice slopes
Be vigilant at all times!

# A Brief History of the Scottish Rights of Way and Access Society

By Douglas Lowe

## Early Days; the First Period 1845 - 1882

The Association for the Protection of Public Rights of Roadway in and around Edinburgh was formed in 1845. At the formation, Adam Black, co-founder of A & C Black, Publishers, who was then the Lord Provost of Edinburgh, delivered the founding motion:   "That it would prove highly beneficial to the inhabitants of towns, many of whom were employed in sedentary occupations and pent up in crowded houses in narrow streets and closes, were they to enjoy such facilities for taking recreation in the country as might tend to promote their health of body and vigour of mind". Archaic language, but carrying an important social message which is equally true today. The new Association was soon active and dealing with disputed paths around the capital, Roslin Glen and Corstorphine Hill being prominent.

Perhaps because of the cosmopolitan nature of the citizens of Edinburgh, the organisation began to look further afield, dealing with such diverse problems as access to the Field of Bannockburn and combating the attempts of early Victorian sporting estate owners to close many of the glens and hills to the walking public. It quickly evolved into a national organisation, and changed its name to The Association for the Protection of Public Rights of Roadway in Scotland.

The Association funded and organised the successful court action against the Duke of Athole's attempts to close Glen Tilt to the walking public. This court case in 1849 was widely reported and did much to increase awareness of public rights of way in Scotland. Despite being hampered by lack of funds following the Glen Tilt case, the Association continued its work during the 1860s, after which it appeared to become rather inactive.

## The Second Period, 1883 - 1922

In 1883 the Association was stung into action by an attempt to close one of the paths on its own doorstep in the Pentland Hills. It was reconstituted as The Scottish Rights of Way and Recreation Society Limited, and moved into arguably its most productive and influential period.

The Pentland paths were investigated and the first signposts were erected. The first guidebook to the Pentland paths was produced in 1885, and the first Bartholomew's map of the Pentland Hills appeared in 1890, John Bartholomew being one of the directors of the Society. Problems were reported from the North, and a small delegation, led by Walter A.Smith, set off in 1885 on an expedition to erect signs on many of the Grampian and Cairngorm paths, including the Lairig Ghru, the Lairig an Laoigh and glens Feshie, Tromie, Tilt and Doll.

The action in the last-named glen led directly to the celebrated Glen Doll court case in 1887 from which the Society emerged victorious, having successfully defeated an attempt to close the Glen Doll to Braemar route. Duncan Macpherson of Glen Doll had contested the action vigorously from the Court of Session up to the House of Lords and, having lost, had to bear costs of £5000, a substantial sum in those days. For a long period after this case there was a reluctance on the part of landowners to contest the rights of walkers to travel along these ancient routes. The costs of the Glen Doll case to the Society were £650-7-4d, a sum which came close to bankrupting it.

The substantial costs arising from the Glen Doll court case led directly to the Society's sponsoring of a Right of Way Bill through Parliament which saw important additions being made to the Local Government Scotland Act 1894 where, for the first time, direct responsibility for rights of way matters was imposed on local authorities. The Society's board, which at that time included three MPs, James Bryce, T.R.Buchanan and Peter Esslemont, felt that the Act was satisfactory but would not be complete until a simpler and cheaper method for resolving rights of way disputes had been found.

The Society had also supported James Bryce's Access to Mountains (Scotland) Bills, (1884, 1888 and 1892). Continuing their high profile, brought by the success and publicity of the Glen Doll case, the Society kept a watching brief of the various Railway Bills that were going through Parliament, seeking to preserve any rights of way that might be threatened by new railway lines. It was a very busy time for the Society: investigating, negotiating, erecting signposts where possible, and declaring in 1891 that they were "dealing with disputes in 17 of the 32 counties of Scotland."

The influence of the 1894 Local Government Act, whereby Local Authorities in the form of the Parish Councils took responsibility for rights of way, began to be felt and in the years 1904 to 1923 the Society's activities partially lapsed as its work overlapped with the Parish Councils. Indeed, the Society was warned on a few occasions not to interfere. It continued intermittently to deal with matters such as the Lochaber Water Supply Bill, where as a result of raising the level of some lochs for hydro-electric power purposes, paths would be submerged and lost.

**Modern Times, 1923 to 1945**
In the years following the 1894 Act the need for the Society should have diminished, but by the early 1920s it was apparent that the Local Authorities were not exercising their powers adequately. The Society re-emerged in 1923, doing much signposting work in the Pentland Hills and throughout the country, recognising that the Society's signs were important both in publicising and preserving rights of way paths.

From early days the Society had been assembling information and evidence on rights of way routes, indeed in 1891 one of the directors, John Blair, had suggested collecting evidence of routes from drovers and shepherds who in those days were still in the habit of taking their beasts to market on foot. The year 1924 saw the publication of Walter Smith's book *Hill Paths in Scotland*, which was a distillation of much of the Society's work. Smith had been on the Board since 1883 and was Chairman from 1904 to 1931.

The Society became involved in the dispute at Glen Tanar on Deeside, and also kept a watch over the growing number of hydro-electric schemes. It managed also to preserve for the walking public part of the Old Glencoe Road across the Black Mount, which continues to be heavily used to this day as it forms part of the West Highland Way long distance path.

## 1946 until the Present

At the start of the Second World War the Society's signs, together with all other road signs, were removed to avoid providing any useful information to an invading army. In 1946 the Society was reconstituted as the Scottish Rights of Way Society Limited and began systematically to re-erect the signs which had been removed. Disputes still arose, but modern times also brought modern problems. More hydro-electric schemes threatened to submerge and extinguish ancient paths, particularly in the great long glens of the western highlands; plans for large-scale road schemes and motorways had to be examined and the Society's role as public watchdog continued. Much work was done in liaising with Local Authorities on rights of way matters and, following the 1967 Countryside (Scotland) Act, in trying to get Local Authorities to list and record rights of way in their areas.

In recent years concern has been expressed at the loss of rights of way and other paths as a result of the rapid development of forestry in Scotland. Negotiation between the Society and the Forestry Commission a few years ago led to an Accord between the two parties which it is hoped will arrest the loss of rights of way as a result of forest planting.

Following the 1894 Act the Board had, as noted above, expressed some degree of satisfaction at the new legislative provision for rights of way, but said that matters could not be considered to be complete until a simpler and cheaper method for resolving rights of way disputes was found. In 1990 the Society, with the guidance of its then Chairman Professor A.E.Anton, submitted to the Secretary of State for Scotland a proposal for the reform of the law relating to rights of way which, if enacted, would have brought about this hundred-year-old wish. A few years later in 1994, Scottish Natural Heritage in its report *Enjoying the Outdoors* restated the need for reform of the law, and in doing so implicitly endorsed some of the Society's 1990 proposals. Unfortunately, the Society's 1990 proposals received little support from the civil servants of the Scottish Office, to whom they were originally addressed, and almost ten years elapsed before the subject of legislative change was raised again, as described below.

Anticipating forthcoming access legislation, the Society changed its name and objects in 1999 to The Scottish Rights of Way and Access Society and enlarged its remit to concern itself with all types of access and not solely rights of way issues.

In October 1997 the Government had asked Scottish Natural Heritage (SNH) to review the legal arrangements for access to the countryside with a view to giving the public greater freedom to enjoy open-air recreation in the countryside.

The task of advising SNH was passed to the Access Forum, a group representing recreation, land management and local authority and agency interests, which included the Society as one its members.   The Society played its part through all stages of the advisory and consultation procedures which led to the enactment of the Land Reform (Scotland) Act 2003.   With this Act the aspirations of Adam Black, James Bryce, and many others since then, have come to fruition.   The new Act gives the public greater freedoms than ever before and goes further even than James Bryce had proposed in his Access to Mountains Bills.   It established for the first time statutory rights of access to almost all land and inland water in Scotland, to be exercised responsibly, for recreation and passage.   Rights of way, which have been specifically safeguarded in the Act, will continue to be important especially where they cross land excluded from the statutory access rights: and they will co-exist with the new access rights and core paths to be set up under the new legislation.   Enshrined within the new Act is a means of judicial determination of the existence and extent of access rights and rights of way. The new procedure was originally intended to apply to access rights only, but the Society, which had long argued for the introduction of a simpler, quicker and cheaper procedure for determining the existence of rights of way, was responsible, during the passage of the Bill, for securing that the new procedure extend to those rights also.   It is satisfied that the new procedure should provide what has long been awaited.

Adam Black's words and actions were surprisingly forward-thinking for mid-19th century Edinburgh, but his forward-thinking was imbued into the ethos of the Society, and much of its quiet efficient work of the last 160 years has had a long-term effect that was not fully appreciated at the time.   The establishment of the Great Glen Way during 2002, for example, was the culmination of proposals made by the Society over 20 years ago.

The Society has gone to the courts where necessary, when all else has failed, but, as mentioned, much of its work over the last century and a half has been quiet and efficient.   By negotiation and agreement, by judicious signposting, and by taking a stand, where necessary, Scotland's great heritage of rights of way paths has been saved from the attrition that would otherwise inevitably have taken place.   Drove roads, old military roads, kirk roads, coffin roads; many of these trails that we now follow owe their continued existence to the Society's vigilance.   All of us who walk, hike or ramble amongst Scotland's hills and glens owe a debt to the Society, a debt that can be recognised through membership of the Society and support of its essential and continuing work.

# SECTION 1
# The Cheviots

Across the Cheviots run some of the oldest tracks in Scotland. The earliest that can be dated is the Roman road Dere Street, constructed and used by the Romans between AD 78 and 185. In 1296 Edward I travelled along the Wheel Causeway. The Redeswire crossing, now the Carter Bar road, is mentioned in 1375 in Barbour's *Brus*. A state paper of 1543 (*Henry VIII Domestic Series XVIII, part 2, No. 530*) gives the following seventeen crossings of the Cheviots:

White Swire (White Law) (route 1)
Pete Swire
Cribhead, Smalden Road and Roughside - crossing Auchope Rig between Auchope Cairn and The Schil. Another list of 1597 refers to one crossing as Auchope Swire
Hunt Road, apparently over Butt Roads (524m), 5km south-west of The Cheviot
Hexpethgate (route 3)
Maiden Cross (route 5)
Black Braes (route 6)
Hindmoor Well (over Lamb Hill)
Hewghen Gate (over Rushy Fell)
Gamel's Path (route 7)
Phillip's Cross (omitted in 1543, but included in a list of 1547) (route 8a)
Almond Road (route 8b)
Redeswire (Carter Bar road)
Carter - Carter Fell is 5km west of Carter Bar (a track crosses Knox Knowe on the west of Carter Fell, see route 9)
The Wheel Causeway (route 10)
Bells - the road by Deadwater
Kershopehead - east of Newcastleton

## 1 Kirk Yetholm to Kirknewton
*13km/8miles*            *OS Sheet 74. Start 827 282. Finish 914 303*
  Go E by road to the Halter Burn and cross this to continue by a section of the Pennine Way which goes over the south shoulder of Green Humbleton. Leaving the Pennine Way at map ref 853 268 strike SE between Madam Law and White Law to go E to Trowupburn and down to the College Burn, thence N down the valley by Hethpool to Kirknewton.
  Alternatively from Trowupburn a farm road goes N to the Elsdon Burn and down to Hethpool. Or, from Green Humbleton a shorter and more northerly track goes over to the Elsdon Burn and by Hethpool to Kirknewton (now part of St Cuthbert's Way).

## 2  Kirk Yetholm to Wooler by The Cheviot

*29km/18miles          OS Sheets 74 and 75.  Start 827 282.  Finish 922 280*
Follow the Halter Burn up to Burnhead, then go SE up the slope of Latchly
Hill to the col between The Curr and Black Hag, then SE to the Border. Follow
the Border ridge S over The Schil (601m) and round the head of the College
Burn to Auchope Cairn and The Cheviot (815m).
This is all part of the Pennine Way. From The Cheviot go due E down its
slope to Langleeford Hope and down the Harthope Burn to Wooler.
The walk can be shortened by omitting The Cheviot. From the south
shoulder of Black Hag descend E by the Fleehope Burn to Fleehope and
Southernknowe, then turn SE up the Lambden Burn to Goldscleugh. From
there continue up the burn for 1km and then turn N between Preston Hill and
Broadhope Hill to Broadstruther, from where a farm road goes E over Steely
Crag to the Harthope Burn road.
An alternative from Southernknowe is to go steeply uphill due E, then NE
over the moor to Commonburn House, from where a farm road goes E to
Wooler. This alternative is now a game bird area where the heather is heavy
walking. Notices are posted as to when it is suitable for walking access but
please respect the Country Code at all times.

## 3  Town Yetholm to Alwinton

*27km/17miles          OS Sheets 74 and 80.  Start 814 266.  Finish 922 063*
From Town Yetholm go S by the B6401 road to Primsidehill, then SE by
Clifton and up Kaim Rig and the east shoulder of Black Hill and through forest
to the col between The Curr and Blackdean Curr, then down to Auchope and
Schilgreen in the Sourhope valley. From Schilgreen go S over the hill to the
Dod Burn and further S over the hill to Cocklawfoot. (This point may also be
reached from Primsidemill by road up the Bowmont Water).
From Cocklawfoot go SE up Cock Law to the Border west of Butt Roads
(524m), and S by Hazely Law, across the Usway Burn and by Clennell Street
past Nettlehope Hill and Wholehope Knowe to Alwinton in Coquetdale. From
Hazely Law there are alternative routes by the Usway Burn or by Barrow Law
and Barrow Burn down the River Coquet.
This old crossing of the Border was known as Hexpethgate; the Cocklaw
was a regular meeting place for the Wardens of the Marches. On Roy's map
of 1775 this route is shown as a road, and marked 'Road from Morpeth to
Kelso'. South of the Border the track has the name of Clennell Street. Today it
is a very enjoyable walk and the forest roads when used are good.

## 4  Kirk Yetholm to Byrness by the Pennine Way

*43½ km/27miles          OS Sheets 74 and 80.  Start 827 282.  Finish 764 027*
The Pennine Way goes E from Kirk Yetholm across the Halter Burn and
up over the south shoulder of Green Humbleton to the ridge which forms the
line of the Border.  Then it follows the Border over White Law, Black Hag
(549m) and The Schil (601m) to Auchope Cairn (726m).

The Pennine Way diverges here to take in The Cheviot (815m) and returns to follow the Border ridge SW to Dere Street and the Roman camps at Chew Green. In another 1½ km the Pennine Way turns S over Ravens Knowe and Windy Crag to Byrness on the A68 road.

## 5  Kirk Yetholm to Byrness
*30½ km/19miles        OS Sheets 74 and 80.  Start 827 282.  Finish 764 027*
From Kirk Yetholm go by road up the Bowmont Water to Mowhaugh. Then go SW up the Hall Burn by a poorly defined track on the lower flanks north-west of Berry Hills to cross The Street between Windy Law and Craik Moor, and down to Greenhill on the Heatherhope Burn. Continue SW up the Capehope Burn past The Yett on an improved track to Buchtrig and by the east of Hangingshaw Hill to join Dere Street, 1km east of Towford. Finally, go SE by Dere Street, which is now well defined and signposted, to the Roman camps at Chew Green (route 7), and then W and S by the Pennine Way (route 4) to Byrness.

## 6  Morebattle (Hownam) to Alwinton by The Street
*21km/13miles        OS Sheets 74 and 80.  Start 778 192.  Finish 860 114*
From Morebattle, 7km south-west of Town Yetholm, a road goes S up the Kale Water to Hownam (7km). From there go E uphill by the track called The Street, which runs SE over Windy Law, Craik Moor and Green Knowe (415m) to the Border. This point may also be reached from Town Yetholm by road up the Bowmont Water to Mowhaugh, thence S by the Calroust Burn to join The Street less than ½ km north of the Border.

The fact that 7km of the parish boundary between Hownam and Morebattle runs along The Street shows that it is a very old highway. On Roy's map of 1755 this track across the Border is named 'Clattering Path'.

From the Border, The Street goes S over Black Braes and along a ridge to Hindside Knowe, then it drops down to the road in Coquetdale 1km north-west of Barrow Burn and 10km from Alwinton.

It should be noted that on the English side of the Border there is an extensive artillery range and danger area, marked on OS maps, which restricts especially the use of some alternative routes.

## 7  Jedburgh to Rochester by Dere Street
*35 km/21miles        OS Sheets 74 and 80.  Start 661 240.  Finish 834 979*
This is a splendid route for walkers over the Cheviots as Dere Street is mostly a broad grassy track. From the bridge at Jedfoot, where the A698 road crosses the Jed Water 3km N of Jedburgh, Dere Street runs SE and straight for 8km by Cappuck (Roman fort) to Shibden Hill; thence by Whitton Edge, Pennymuir (Roman camp), over the Kale Water at Tow Ford and SE by Blackhall Hill to the Border at Black Halls. It then goes S for 1km to the extensive Roman camps at Chew Green, thence SE by Outer Golden Pot (now as a road) to Featherwood, and then down a straight 5km S to Bremenium (camps) and Rochester, from where it is a further 8km by road to Otterburn.

The Roman Road can be reached at Tow Ford by road from Hownam.

From Chew Green southward the road lies within an artillery range and for that reason an enquiry about the firing is advisable and can be made at Redsdale or Otterburn Camp, (telephone number 01830 520569).

This was the main Roman road into Scotland; in use by the Romans between AD 78 and AD 185, it ran from Durham to the Forth and has been traced to Dalkeith. In the Middle Ages this road, where it crossed the Cheviots, was known as Gamel's Path. Today, some of the northern section of Dere Street is part of the revived St Cuthbert's Way.

### 7X  Jedburgh to Melrose
*22km/13½ miles*          *OS Sheets 73 and 74.  Start 661 240.  Finish 547 340.*
Going N from the bridge over the Jed Water at Jedfoot on the A698 road (see route 7), follow the waymarked link through Monteviot House to the B6400 road on the north side of the River Teviot. There, from map ref 647 250, a section of Dere Street ran N to the Eildon Hills. It is now signposted St Cuthbert's Way and it runs NW for 6km to Forest Lodge on the A68 road. Thence follow the St Cuthbert's Way to Melrose *via* the Eildon Hills.

Although the route described above is not entirely a hill track as such, it usefully links route 7 with Melrose where it is possible to join up with several other hill tracks.

### 8  Edgerston to Byrness
*11km/7miles*          *OS Sheet 80.  Start 690 089.  Finish 764 027*
Start from the Wooplaw road end on the A68 near Edgerston, 14km south of Jedburgh by road (bus). By a forest road it is a pleasant walk *via* Arks to Fawhope. Continue by the track along the north edge of Leithope Forest and at its north-east corner turn S and then towards cottages near Upper Hindhope. From there go SE over Whiteside Hill to join the Pennine Way at map ref 773 083 near Coquet Head, thence S over Windy Crag (490m) to Byrness.

### 9  Edgerston to Kielder
*22½ km/14miles*          *OS Sheet 80.  Start 665 077.  Finish 627 934*
From Edgerston go SW by road over Hareshaw Knowe to the Hawick Road (A6088),  then S from near Carterhouse Farm by an old road to the disused quarry and then a forestry road which ascends to the Border at Carter Fell and continues S to Limestone Knowe (549m). From there go by the march fence by Grey Mare's Knowe, then descend due S to Kielder Head and SW by a good forest road down the Kielder Burn to Kielder Village. In 1543 this was known as the Carter Route as the track crosses Carter Fell.

Re-afforestation affects this route and its alternative;  they are no longer feasible except for determined walkers. Some forest roads have not been kept up to even footpath standards and walking is difficult underfoot. Elsewhere paths have disappeared and only by map and compass can the route be navigated. Some of this area is for game birds only where the Country Code should be respected.

Alternative: On joining the Hawick Road , turn right for 1km and go SW beside a plantation, across the Carter Burn and up a track through forest to a point about 100 metres before the bridge at Burns Cottage.  There the track turns off left on the east  of the Black Burn and climbs uphill to Knox Knowe (499m), cairn on the Border.  Descend SE to the Carry Burn, then go up the slope of Grey Mare's Knowe, keeping to the high ground, and from the top descend as described above to Kielder Village.

## 10  Bonchester Bridge to Sauchtree or Kielder by the Wheel Causeway
*21km/13miles        OS Sheet 80.  Start 594 101.  Finish 562 967 or 627 934*
From Bonchester Bridge go S along the road by Braidhaugh to Cleuch Head where a track climbs SE to the east side of Wolfelee Hill and goes S over Wardmoor Hill.  The Wheel Causeway enters Wauchope Forest where the trees form a right-angled corner.  From there take the middle of the three rides (which is wider than usual and can become overgrown before being cleaned periodically) for 6km through the forest to a gate, a little to the west of Wheelrig Head (447m).

From the gate go SSW for 400 metres and follow a forest road down the east side of Wormscleuch Burn to Myredykes. (To follow the actual line of the Wheel Causeway south of Wheelrig Head is now quite difficult, being overgrown with only a narrow path).  From Myredykes it is 4km to Sauchtree and 6km to Kielder by minor roads.

In mediaeval times the Wheel Causeway was the road from Roxburgh (then the largest town in the Borders) to Annandale. Edward I travelled along this route in 1296.  On Roy's map it is named 'Road to Jedburgh'.  On Stobie's 1770 map of Roxburghshire it is marked as a road running from Easter Fodderlee by the east side of Abbotrule and Doorpool to Spar.

A Post Bus service operates to Bonchester Bridge from Hawick.

## 11  Newcastleton to Kielder
*20km/12½ miles        OS Sheets 79 and 80.  Start 529 922.  Finish 627 934*
From Newcastleton follow the B6357 road up the Liddel Water for 7km to Dinlabyre, then go SE uphill by a forestry road to Larriston Fells. (Take the right-hand fork at map ref  550 909).  Continue by the track to Bloody Bush on the Border, then down by the Grains Burn and Ackenshaw Burn to The Forks, and down the Lewis Burn to Lewisburn, from where it is 4km north by road to Kielder.

This is an old road used in the early 19th century for the transport of coal from Northumberland;  bridges on the road have the date 1828.   On the Border there is a monument giving distances along the road.

Alternatively, just past Ackenshawburn, cross a stone bridge and turn left up a forest road for 450 metres. At the point where this road bends right, go straight on uphill and descend NW. The path, 5km long, is waymarked for cycle route number 5, (see Border Forest Guide).

# SECTION 2
# The Borders

### 12 Hawick or Roberton to Newcastleton
*28km/17miles        OS Sheet 79.  Start 501 144 or 433 143.  Finish 483 875*
   (a) From Hawick go due S on the minor public road for 9km via Pilmuir
and Dodburn to map ref 473 059 at Dod. Then go due S uphill and along a
forest ride and edge by the Thieves Road over Dod Rig and down to join the
forest track crossing Priesthaugh Burn. Follow this track for 800metres to a
quarried scree slope at map ref 474 009 where, from the far top edge, a path
climbs ESE to a ride which leads S to open ground beyond the watershed.
Continue down Swire Knowe by the Queen's Mire to Braidliehope and
Hermitage Water (Mary Queen of Scots rode this way in 1556 from Jedburgh
to Hermitage Castle and back in a day to see Bothwell). It is then 12km by
road to Newcastleton. However, the alternative is to go uphill from Dinley,
then by Thief Sike and west of Hartsgarth to Redheugh at map ref 496 906
and 3km by road from Newcastleton.
   An almost parallel route to (a) above starts from the bridge at map ref 507
100 over Slitrig Water, 5km south of Hawick on the B6399 road. Go SW from
Barns by a broad track up the ridge between White Hill and Penchrise Pen,
then S by a forest track to Peelbraehope (cairn) and to just west of Hawkhass,
leaving it at map ref 489 027 to continue SE by forest ride ascending SE to
Scaw'd Law (503m). From there go down Sundhope Rig to Sundhope and the
B6399 road south of Whitropefoot, 11km from Newcastleton.
   (b) Starting at Roberton, go S by Plover Plantation and to Parkhill, then SE
by Whithope Moss (north of Branxholme Easter Loch) to Newmill (A7 road).
Continue SE up Allan Water, leaving it near Lochburnfoot (map ref 467 091)
to join the road to Dodburn (E of Southfield), thence to Dod and
Newcastleton as described in (a) above.
   Alternatively, take the road up Borthwick Water to the bridge at Muselee
(map ref 398 117), then go SE uphill by a broad track on the E side of the burn
on the old drove road to a section of the Catrail at map ref 404 104. From
there continue down over Commonside Moor by the Teinside Burn to the
River Teviot at Teinside Lodge. Cross the A7 road and take the quiet country
road from Northhouse to go via Priesthaugh to reach Dod from where there
is a choice of route to Newcastleton as described above.

### 13  Roberton to Teviothead
*11km/7miles                OS Sheet 79.  Start 433 143.  Finish 405 054*
   From Roberton go as described in 12(b) to map ref 404 104 and there
turn right by a track to Broadlee Loch. Keep it on the left and continue over
High Seat and Dryden Fell, descending by Dryden to the River Teviot and
Teviothead on the A7 road.

### 14  Eskdalemuir to Craik (and Roberton or Hawick)
*16km/10miles                OS Sheet 79.  Start 256 978.  Finish 349 081*
   In its first part this is an old Roman road, probably linking the Annandale

Roman road with Dere Street (see route 7). Eskdalemuir is 21km by the B709 road up Eskdale from Langholm. Leave this road at Eskdalemuir where it turns left to cross the White Esk and follow the minor road going N on the east side of the river to go over the hill to Raeburnfoot. (Roman fort on the left). From there go up the Rae Burn for 2km and at map ref 267 007 leave the forest road and go uphill NE on forest rides, where there is some evidence of the Roman road, to cross another forest road at map ref 278 024. The Roman Road is then close to and intersects other forest rides and careful map work is required here to avoid following the wrong ride. Continue over Craik Muir and Lamblair Knowe to Craik Cross Hill (449m), the highest point on the route. This part is through the extensive Eskdalemuir and Craik Forests where notices are displayed denoting sites of historical interest. Beyond the highest point keep NE on the top of the ridge by the forest cycle way, which does not coincide throughout with the line of the Roman road, then go down to Craik from where a road goes for 10km down Borthwick Water to Roberton.

To reach Hawick, 17km from Craik, leave this road at the bridge below Philhope and go E to the wood north of Broadlee Loch, then on towards the Branxholme Lochs road and Hawick. The walking distance may be shortened from Craik (see route 31b) by going S to Old Howpasley and then E to Lairhope and Teviothead on the A7 road 14km from Hawick.

R.P.Hardie in *The Roads of Mediaeval Lauderdale* suggests that this may also be the road referred to in a 13th-century charter as the royal road from the valley of the Annan towards Roxburgh.

### 15  Moffat to Eskdale by the Colt Road
*22¹/₂km/14miles        OS Sheets 78 and 79.  Start 092 050.  Finish 243 004*
From Moffat take the Wamphray road across the Moffat Water, then go left to Craigbeck (map ref 106 037) from where a forest road goes up the Cornal Burn to its source. Soon after the Southern Upland Way heads off N, the forest road turns SW down Wamphray Water and in about 400 metres a path leaves the road at map ref 155 041 and goes steeply uphill by Colt Rig and E over Cowan Fell. This faint path continues E to meet another forest road on the col between Dun Moss and Loch Fell. This road leads down the Cauld Law Grain and Garwald Water to the B709 road at Garwaldwaterfoot, 3km N of Eskdalemuir.

Part of this route coincides with the Southern Upland Way.

### 16  Moffat to Ettrick or Eskdale
*25¹/₂km/16miles*
*OS Sheets 78 and 79.  Start 092 050.  Finish 273 145 or 239 050*
(a) To go to Ettrick, follow route 15 to the Wamphray Water and go N up it to its source along the Southern Upland Way. At the watershed the path crosses to the Selcoth Burn at map ref 160 058 and goes NE to Ettrick Head, between Capel Fell and Wind Fell. From there it is downhill by the Ettrick Water to Potburn, thence by a minor road for 9km to Ettrick, from where it is 5km by the B709 road to Tushielaw Inn.

From the A708 road, 7km NE of Moffat at Shortwoodend, the walking distance can be shortened. Cross the Moffat Water by bridge towards Sailfoot and Selcoth. One hundred metres before Selcoth, at a bridge, take the signposted tractor track on the north side of the Selcoth Burn for 1³/₄km to a sheepfold and signpost. Cross the burn and join a faint track on its south side. At Cat Shoulder this track crosses a series of steep gravel screes. These can be avoided by heading uphill on grass, S and then W to another sheepfold near to where the previous route crosses the Selcoth Burn at map ref 160 058 and is joined to continue to Ettrick as described above.

(b) An alternative route is to continue from Shortwoodend by the A708 road up Moffat Water for 2km to Cappelgill. Near that point cross the water to Bodesbeck and follow the track going E uphill on the north side of Bodesbeck Burn, crossing the ridge and descending into the Ettrick Valley at Potburn and continuing as before to Ettrick by road. This was the original road from Moffat to Selkirk. On Ainslie's 1772 map of Selkirkshire the mileages are given and the pass above Bodesbeck is named 'Peneracross'. Roy's map of 1755 names it 'Road to Hawick'.

(c) To go to Eskdale from Potburn in the Ettrick valley, continue along the road for 2km to Broadgairhill and there ford the Ettrick Water or in another 600 metres cross it by the bridge at Nether Phawhope. Go up the forest track to the Steps of Glendearg, the watershed between two burns of the same name at the source of the White Esk (Esk Riverhead on Ainslie's map). The route continues down the west side of the burn which is crossed to Glendearg and its access road to the B709 road, just south of the Seismological Station, 8km north of Eskdalemuir.

### 17 Tweedsmuir to Ericstane (6km north of Moffat)
*16km/10miles      OS Sheets 72 and 78. Start 098 243. Finish 073 110*
From Tweedsmuir cross the River Tweed and take the road to Fruid Reservoir for 4km, where there is good parking at the dam. Follow the road along the north-east side of the reservoir. From Fruid a rough road goes round the head of the reservoir, past its end and towards Macrule Hill where a track can be seen slanting up its east slope. After about 1¹/₂km the track bends left and becomes indistinct. Keep uphill round the west slope of Ballaman Hill where two cairns (Resting Stone) can be seen at map ref 089 163. From there two routes are possible:

(a) Continue round the west slope of Ballaman Hill and watching the direction carefully (use compass) bear SSE across tussocky ground to cross the source of the Glencraigie Burn, which flows NW into the River Tweed. Continue SSW, keeping E of the Crown of Scotland (538m) and then S to cross the Whitehope Burn and reach the col east of Chalk Rig Edge. From there descend to the Annan valley and Ericstane and go 6km by the minor road to Moffat. From the bridge at map ref 075 104, just north of Annanwater Hall, a waymarked right of way leads in 2¹/₂km to Hartfell Spa, discovered in 1748.

(b) From the west side of Ballaman Hill strike SW across Barncorse Knowe to Earlshaugh (an old sheep and cattle station) where a path goes S to the top of the Devil's Beef Tub. This path, which continues down and along its west

side, can be dangerous.  Instead, at the march fence turn left and go along it
for at least 800 metres to turn S again and traverse down the hillside east of
The Skirtle to Corehead and on to Ericstane and Moffat as in (a).

## 18  Drumelzier to St Mary's Loch
*20 km/12¹/₂ miles          OS Sheets 72 and 73.  Start 135 341.  Finish 241 232*
From Drumelzier (south-east of Broughton) leave the village to go SE by
the track up the Drumelzier Burn and cross it to Den Knowes and over Den
Knowes Head.  Then go up by the west shoulder of Pykestone Hill and S
along the course of the Thief's Road to Long Grain Knowe and by Dollar Law
(817m), then SE to Notman Law, Shielhope Head and Greenside Law.  Continue
from there for 900 metres to join route 21 down  to Craigierig (Megget Dam
carpark at map ref 210 233) and St Mary's Loch.  This is a very fine ridge walk
over the 600m level.

From Dollar Law one can reach the Crook Inn on the A701 road, 11km
from Broughton, by going S to Dun Law then SW over Cramalt Craig to the
radio beacon on Broad Law, and descending the access road NW to the River
Tweed close to the Inn.

## 19  Broughton to Peebles
*19km/12miles          OS Sheets 72 and 73.  Start 112 369.  Finish 251 404*
From Broughton go NE through Broughton Place and keep straight on
along the old drove road which crosses Hollows Burn and climbs to the col
between Broomyside and Hammer Head.  On passing through the gate, keep
E along the drove road, rising slightly to cross the east shoulder of Hammer
Head at about 400m.  Then drop down, crossing the farm road to Stobo
Hopehead, and cross the Hopehead Burn by a bridge below a conspicuous
sheep fank.

Passing this, the drove road climbs SE to a col south of Midhill and descends
to Harrowhope (ruin), whence follow the farm road on the north side of Easton
Burn to Stobo Kirk.  Turn right along the public road for 400 metres, then left
across the River Tweed by the bridge to Easter Dawyck. Go up E to the col (400m)
and down to The Glack.  Take the public road downhill to cross the Manor Water,
turn S and 1km beyond Cademuir go NE over Cademuir Hill to Peebles.

## 20  Stobo to the Manor Valley and Craig Douglas (Yarrow Water)
*22km/14miles          OS Sheets 72 and 73.  Start 175 364.  Finish 292 246↑*
From Stobo, 11km south-west of Peebles, cross the River Tweed by the
bridge to Dawyck Mill and go SE over the hill by the Dead Wife's Grave,
following the old drove road between Hunt Law and Whitelaw Hill to the
Manor Valley.  Cross the Manor Water by a bridge to Glenrath and go up the
burn to the wood beyond Glenrathope, where a zigzag track climbs S up
Windy Neese.  When this ridge fades out head SE to the march fence gate at
map ref 242 303 and down to a forest track in Slate Cleuch, or go by Drycleuch
Law to Muttonhall and down the Douglas Burn by Blackhouse to reach Craig
Douglas on the Yarrow road (A708),  1¹/₂ km from the Gordon Arms Hotel.
(See also route 22).

*Dere Street to Whitton Edge across the Cheviots (route 7)*

*Ettrick Pen from Over Phawhope (route 16)*

*Looking up Glen Sax towards Dun Rig (route 22)*

*The Three Brethren cairns (route 25)*

## 21 Peebles to Cappercleuch (St Mary's Loch) by the Manor Valley

*30km/18¹/₂ miles          OS Sheets 72 and 73.     Start 250 403.     Finish 240 231*
From the south end of the River Tweed bridge in Peebles turn right and go along Caledonian Road, turn left at the end and go up Edderston Road to a gate with a 'Right of Way' sign, and cross Cademuir Hill to the Manor Valley road.   Continue up the valley and at the SRWS sign, 1km before Manorhead, cross the Manor Water and follow the track over Redsike Head and down to Craigierig near the Megget Reservoir Dam (carpark at map ref 210 233).

Alternatively, from the boundary fence beyond Redsike Head, go SE over the spur of Black Rig and down to Glengaber, 2km west of St Mary's Loch

Finally, go E along the public road on the north side of the Megget Water to reach the A708 road at Cappercleuch beside St Mary's Loch.

## 22 Peebles to Craig Douglas (Yarrow Water) or St Mary's Loch by Blackhouse

*21km/13miles     OS Sheet 73.    Start 260 393↑.    Finish 292 246↑ or 270 242*
For this fine ridge walk go SE from Peebles by Springhill Road and its continuation by path, and cross the Haystoun Burn at Gypsy Glen to the wide old drove road which steeply ascends the hill and runs for some distance along the ridge over Kailzie Hill, Kirkhope Law and Birkscairn Hill.   At the SRWS sign to Yarrow, cross the fence, go SSE before bearing SSW and, keeping to a height of about 500m, continue towards the forest west of Whiteknowe Head.   Cross the boundary fence at an iron gate at map ref 264 303 and go SSE, skirting a forest plantation on the right-hand side to reach a waymarker at map ref 268 293.   Then in 100 metres enter the forest by a fire-break and follow the waymarked route down SE to a T-junction, turning S to join a forest road and exiting at Douglas Burn west of Blackhouse (where James Hogg, the Ettrick Shepherd, was herdsman from 1790 to 1800).   From there it is 3km by farm road to the Yarrow Water at Craig Douglas. The Gordon Arms Hotel is 1½ km east along the A708 road.

At Blackhouse the drove road joins route 23 (now part of the Southern Upland Way) and strikes SW over the hill to Dryhope at the foot of St Mary's Loch.

For an alternative route from Peebles to Birkscairn Hill, go by Bonnington Road to Bonnington, turn left past this farm to the Glensax Burn and go up the burn to Glensax.   Then climb SE up the hillside to the ridge ½ km south of Birkscairn Hill.

This old drove road is a continuation of the one which used to go from Falkirk through the Cauldstane Slap in the Pentlands (route 51) and across the Meldon Hills (route 42). On Ainslie's map of Selkirkshire in 1772 it is marked 'Road to Peebles'.

## 23 Traquair (Innerleithen) to Tibbie Shiels Inn (St Mary's Loch)

*23km/14miles               OS Sheet 73.   Start 331 347.   Finish 241 205↑*
From Traquair take the B709 road S for 1km.  This route is now part of the Southern Upland Way and at a cottage immediately south of the churchyard go SW uphill following waymarkers to Blake Muir.  Continue by the east side of Deuchar Law to Blackhouse.  There, cross the Douglas Burn and go SW

over by the west of Ward Law to Dryhope at the foot of St Mary's Loch. Cross the Yarrow Water and continue along the south-east side of the loch to Tibbie Shiels Inn.

On Edgar's 1741 map of Peeblesshire this route is shown as the only road from the Tweed to the south. The original route from Edinburgh to the south is shown on Moll's map of 1725 as going by Dalhousie, near Temple, and over the Moorfoot Hills. It then went down the Leithen Water to Traquair. From the ford at the foot of St Mary's Loch the route continued by the Bridge Road over Altrieve Rig to Tushielaw, and on southwards. On Roy's map of 1755 the road is named 'Muir Road from Ettrick and Yarrow to Lothian Edge and Dalhousie'. A branch to Moffat went up the other side, ie. the south-east side of St Mary's Loch.

### 24   Traquair (Innerleithen) to Ettrick by Yarrow
*14¹/₂ km/9miles*                OS Sheet 73.  Start 328 343.  Finish 390 243
Go SE from Traquair by Damhead and up the ridge between the Fingland Burn and Curly Burn, over to Glengaber, then SE to the dip between Glengaber Hill and Peatshank Head and down to Deuchar and Yarrow.

Cross the Yarrow Water by the road bridge and go 2km up the road to its summit just west of Witchie Knowe.  Leave the road and strike SE across country, down to ford the Tower Burn and continue by the track to Ettrickbridge.

### 25   Traquair to Yarrowford or Selkirk by Minch Moor
*9km/6miles or 14km/8miles*
                OS Sheet 73.  Start 331 347.  Finish  407 300↑  or 457 287
From Traquair follow the Southern Upland Way by The Riggs SE up the hill along the old road to the Cheese Well (500m) and over the north shoulder of Minch Moor (567m).  Continue E over Hare Law, beyond which the route divides, the Minchmoor Road bending to the right and going SE downhill to Yarrowford and Broadmeadows Youth Hostel.

To reach Selkirk, keep due E at the junction after crossing Hare Law and go along the ridge and over Brown Knowe and Broomy Law to the Three Brethren (Cairns).  There, leave the Southern Upland Way and descend by the north side of Long Philip Burn to Philiphaugh Farm, close to Selkirk.

This old road between Traquair and Selkirk, now part of the Southern Upland Way, was in use in the 13th century as part of the road between Kelso Abbey and the Abbey lands at Lesmahagow. The original road kept to the north of Peat Law (it is marked on the map as 'Picts Work') and went to a bridge which once crossed the Ettrick near Bridgelands (Lindean).  Edward I travelled over the Minchmoor Road in 1296.

In 1305 the tenant of 'Westropkeliok' was bound to find a man at St James's Day for eight days during Roxburgh Fair to keep the road through Minche Moor from robbers (*Calendar Documents, relating to Scotland, Vol.2, No. 1675* ).  The later Minchmoor Road (as shown on Roy's map of 1755) is the one by Yarrowford. Dr John Brown describes it in his essay Minchmoor: "You go up the wild old Selkirk road which passes almost right over the summit, and by which Montrose and his cavaliers fled from Philiphaugh, where Sir

Walter's mother remembered crossing, when a girl, in a coach and six, on her way to a ball at Peebles, several footmen marching on either side of the carriage to prop it up or drag it out of the moss hags...".

Another track to Yarrowford, the Clattering Path, branches to the right 1½ km from Traquair, keeps to the right of Minch Moor and descends by the Lewenshope Burn to theYarrow Water at map ref 388 295, 2½ km west of Yarrowford.

## 26  Galashiels to Yarrowford (Broadmeadows) by Yair
*13km/8miles*                     OS Sheet 73.  Start 492 358.  Finish 414 300
From the Mercat Cross go upwards and round past the back of Galashiels Academy following Southern Upland Way guide posts SW over Hog Hill to Yair Bridge. Turn right and go uphill behind Yair House SW for 3km until the SUW turns NW on emerging from the forest north of Peat Law at map ref 439 312.

Leaving the Southern Upland Way there, the route continues W and after crossing the Long Philip Burn ascends the north shoulder of Foulshiels Hill, affording an exquisite panorama of the Yarrow valley before dropping to Broadmeadows Youth Hostel and Yarrowford.

An alternative is to start at the former Peel Hospital (now a housing development) and go from its west side (signposted: 'Williamhope') up the Glenkinnon Burn for 1½ km, then S uphill to the east shoulder of Broomy Law. Make for the prominent cairn just above the 380m contour, from where it is a short descent to Broadmeadows.

## 27  Ettrickbridge to Roberton or Hawick
*13km/8miles to 15km/9miles*
                OS Sheets 73 and 79.  Start 390 243.  Finish 433 143 or 501 144
There are four possibilities for this route:

(a)  Immediately south of the bridge at Ettrickbridge go up the track SW then S round Helmburn Hill to join another track from Howfordhill on the left. In 700 metres take the right-hand fork and bear SE passing between The Dod (364m) and Akermoor Loch to Langhope and Todrig. Going to Roberton, continue S over Whitslaid Hill and from Whitslaid go SE to Blawearie and then by a minor road for 4km to Roberton or by farm roads for 3km via Borthwickshiels and Glenburn. From Todrig to Hawick either (i) first go E to the col west of Leap Hill and down to the bridge over the Ale Water and up to cross the road by the Ogilvie Cairn.  Continue SE across the moor to the walled drove road just west of Whitehaughmoor (map ref 470 177), 4km by minor road from Hawick; or (ii), continuing east from Todrig, a minor road goes for 6km by Easter Essenside to Ashkirk (map ref 473 223) on the A7 (bus route).

(b)  Go from Ettrickbridge as in (a) for 600m and then, keeping SW across the burn, go uphill to Stobie Slack and Ettrickshaws, then S up by a wood to Shaws Mid Hill.  Take forest tracks to the east side of Shaws Upper Loch, then turn SW to Gildiesgreen (ruins).  Continue SW on a track and S to the crest of the hill (353m) at map ref 379 176 where a ride leads SW along Hurkle Rig and by Redfordgreen (map ref 365 167) to the B711 road, 8km from Roberton.

(c)  Go up the valley from Ettrickbridge for 4km and cross Hyndhope Bridge going S by the farm and cottages to Old Hyndhope  and continue S up the ridge beyond.  Take a 300-metre ride to cut the west corner of Dodhead Forest, passsing 300 metres W of Whitehillshiel (ruin), then over to join farm roads north of Drycleuchlea and on to Redfordgreen, 8km from Roberton; see (b).

(d)  From Ettrickbridge take the Selkirk road for almost 2km and just before Hulterburn turn right up Hungry Hill and go up the north shoulder of Hulterburn Hill.  Then go SE to Essenside Loch and Easter Essenside.  There cross the Ale Water to Burnfoot and in another 200 metres take the track SE uphill to a forest track and then across the moor to Whitehaughmoor, 4km from Hawick; see (a).

## 28  Yarrow to Ettrickbidge or Roberton by Delorainehope
*6km/4miles or 27km/17miles*
        *OS Sheets 73 and 79.  Start 337 256.  Finish  390 243 or 433 143*
At Yarrow Feus (10km up the Yarrow from Broadmeadows) cross Yarrow Water to Sundhope.  Go on a track SE climbing at first steeply to pass between Ladhope Middle (429m) and Scawd Law (436m), over the watershed descending west of Nether Hill to Kirkhope, 1km west of Ettrickbridge, from where it is 7km west by the B7009 road to Gilmanscleuch up the Ettrick valley.  A more robust walk from Sundhope goes S between Sundhope Height and Scar Hill directly to Gilmanscleuch.

There, cross the Ettrick Water to Easter Deloraine and go up the Potloch Burn to Delorainehope.  Continue up the Potloch Burn following a vehicle track to the ridge and turn SE down to Deloraineshiel to reach the B711 road at map ref 352 157, 9km from Roberton.

Alternatively from Delorainehope, go SE up a burn to the col between Dun Knowe and Wedder Lairs and  SE down to Drycleuchlea, Redfordgreen and the B711 road, 8km from Roberton (see also route 27c).

## 29  Gordon Arms Hotel to Tushielaw by Cadger's Hole
*8km/5miles*        *OS Sheets 73 and 79.  Start 308 248.  Finish 305 185*
Cross the Yarrow Water and go up the Hartleap road (B709) for 1½km to shortly beyond Eldinhope Cottage.  Then strike uphill on the left, climbing gradually S from the road to the col south-west of Meg's Hill.  Continue uphill S to the march fence and shortly after this go SE down over Crookedside Hill (444m).  Descend from the 'hole' by a steep track to Crosslee and Tushielaw in the Ettrick valley, 1km north of the Inn.

## 30  Tibbie Shiels Inn (St Mary's Loch) to Ettrick
*10km/6miles*        *OS Sheets 73 and 79.  Start 241 205↑.  Finish 273 145*
There are two distinct routes, with minor variations, over the hills from Loch of the Lowes to the Ettrick valley:

(a)  From Tibbie Shiels Inn go SE by Crosscleuch and uphill on the old road (now part of the Southern Upland Way) to Earl's Hill.  At map ref

254 100, diverge left from the SUW and go S round Fall Law.  Then E by the col (The Captain's Road) on the north side of Cowan's Croft and down the Hopehouse Burn to the B709 road, 1½ km south of Tushielaw Inn and 2 km north-east of Ettrick (Ramseycleuch).

(b) From Tibbie Shiels Inn go S along the east side of the Loch of the Lowes and then up the east side of the Riskinhope Burn and over Pikestone Rig (joining the Southern Upland Way) to the col east of Peniestone Knowe. At that point a signpost indicates two routes:

(i)  continuing by the SUW down the west side of Scabcleuch Burn to the road at Scabcleuch, 2½ km west of Ettrick,

(ii)  a more northerly route, leaving the SUW and going SE along the flank of Ramsey Knowe and over to the path (formerly known as the Kirk Road) on the south-west side of the Kirk Burn to the church where James Hogg, The Ettrick Shepherd, is buried.

One of these routes is probably the Thirlestangate (gate = way), mentioned in a Melrose Charter of AD 1214 - 1249.

### 31  Ettrick to Hawick or Teviothead
*21km/13miles*       *OS Sheet 79.  Start 273 145.  Finish 465 117 or 405 054*
From Ramseycleuch on the Ettrick Water take the B709 road S for 1km to Deephope (footbridge) where a forest track ascends steeply NE, before turning to go due S at the junction at map ref 287 142. In another 200 metres leave the forest track after crossing the burn which is then followed S upstream for 150 metres when a ride to the E winds uphill to a gate at map ref 295 139, south-east of the 469m top of  Gamescleuch Hill. Descend open ground SE to a forest ride then track between map refs 301 136 and 303 132 on Brown Knowe where a ride NE for 250 metres to map ref 305 133 joins the track from Meerlees (alternative route) and goes along the south slopes of Hazel Rig to Buccleuch (B711).

Alternatively from Deephope, continue 2km by road  to Meerlees. Shortly before the house take the forest ride S then SE, becoming a track to the junction at map ref 290 113 and turning N to cross the Crow Burn and NE to Brown Knowe, joining the Deephope route at map ref 305 133 along the south slopes of Hazel Rig to Buccleuch.

To Hawick from Buccleuch, follow the estate road (main drove road) from East Buccleuch over Little Bleak Law up into the forest to the south-east corner of Kingside Loch.  Cross a forest road, then follow rides E and SE over Mid Rig to the junction with a forest road at map ref 356 129 which is taken E for 100 metres before turning SE for 300 metres (rough felled in 1997) to cross the Ale Water at an old march fence corner at map ref 360 127. Turn E after 200 metres to pass about 300 metres N of Girnwood Loch on the line of an old drove road.  Cross the track to a dyke, which is followed past Hoscoteshiel (ruin) to the road-end east of Girnwood, then down to Deanburnhaugh on Borthwick Water. (By following the track west of the burn flowing out of Girnwood Loch SSW for 800 metres, another old drove road is met at map ref 361 118 also going E to the Girnwood road-end, but connecting from the west by a ride to a Craik Forest track at Henwoodie (ruin) at map ref 349 116). From there go S by the public road for ¹/₂ km to Muselee. Cross the bridge and head E for 1¹/₂ km to join and follow the Branxholme Lochs road (see route 14) S and E via Branxholm Bridge on the A7 road to Hawick.

To reach Teviothead from Buccleuch two routes are possible:

(a) Follow the route as described to Muselee and from there go by Broadlee Loch and Dryden Fell, see routes 12(b) and 13.

(b) Go S by the farm road from Buccleuch up Rankle Burn for 4km to Baldhill (ruin). Continue S for 1km beside dykes and fences to a ride leading through to join a main forest road. Turn left here and uphill for 250 metres to fork right just north of the source of Aithouse Burn which is followed down to Craik. On reaching the minor public road, turn right to its end opposite Howpasley. Continue by a track up the Howpasley Burn and in 700 metres turn uphill on the left and go E by the south side of Rashy Hill and down by the Lairhope Burn to the River Teviot and Teviothead, see route 14.

# SECTION 3
# The Lammermuirs and Moorfoots

### 32 Cockburnspath to Duns
*35km/22miles*          *OS Sheet 67.   Start 774 712.   Finish 786 540*
Some of the section of the original route between Cockburnspath and Lodge Wood has fallen into disuse and is not practicable. Instead, a part of the Southern Upland Way is substituted.

From Cockburnspath follow the waymarked SUW in its reverse direction going by Abbey St Bathans to Lodge Wood. From there to Commonside the original route and the SUW combine as far as map ref 733 578, where the route diverges to continue S and by the west side of Black Hill (no path) to the radio mast on Hardens Hill. Finally, go down by the access road to a minor road, 5km from Duns.

### 33 Dunbar to Lauder ('The Herring Road')
*45km/28miles*          *OS Sheets 67 and 73.   Start 683 786.   Finish 534 474↑*
The 'Herring Road' was used in olden times by country people bringing home a stock of salted herring for winter use. Only the first part to the Whiteadder Water is the original road; between there and Lauder the 'Herring Road' is shown on the old OS 6-inch map as going further north, over Hunt Law and Wedder Law. Roy's map of 1755 shows the road going over Meikle Says Law, Hunt Law and Wedder Law, and calls it 'Muir Road from Lauder to Dunbar'.

The present day route is better started from the end of the public road near Halls at map ref 654 723↑ (which is 6½ km from Dunbar). Go uphill on a good track, keeping west of Watch Law, to Dunbar Common, then SSW over upper reaches of Mossy Burn and West Burn, descending Spartleton Edge on its west side to the Whiteadder Water, 1km south of Johnscleugh. Continue by road SE to the Whiteadder Reservoir, round its northern end to Penshiel and S by track to cross the Longformacus road. Proceed by a diverted path, also a right of way (avoiding wildlife area near Killpallet) on the E side of Killpallet Burn. At the march fence an option is to go right for 1km then S by the Mutiny Stones (ancient burial cists) to Byrecleugh. However, from the fence the preferred way now goes by Dye Cottage from where the alternatives are:

(a) Go S by route 36(b) to Westruther, 11km by road to Lauder or from map ref 647 562 follow the SUW (passing *Twinlaw Cairns*) to Lauder *via* Braidshawrig.

(b) Go W on local road to continue from Byrecleugh. Shortly upstream of there cross Dye Water by farm bridge and go up Hall Burn, then SW over moor – no path, joining the SUW at map ref c.614 554 near Rutherford's Cairn, to reach Braidshawrig.

From Braidshawrig the direct and shortest route to Lauder is by an old track going SW across moor on the west side of Blythe Water. In 2km the

SUW (which has taken a different route from Braidshawrig) is rejoined, and the waymarked SUW now coincides with parts of the right of way and continues to the plantation ahead where the wall at the edge of the wood is followed to its south end. Turn right after a stile to enter wood and take the first turning left down to Wanton Walls and, continuing, cross the A697 road to follow the SUW through wood and over the Leader Water by Thirlestane Castle to Lauder.

An alternative from Braidshawrig is by the track NW over Edgarhope Law to Earnscleugh Water, then down the valley and by Edgarhope Wood to rejoin the SUW and reach Lauder.

### 34  Stenton (East Lothian) to Cranshaws or Duns
*18¹/₂ km/11¹/₂ miles or 36km/22¹/₂ miles*
                    *OS Sheet 67.   Start 621 741.   Finish 691 619 or 786 540*
From Stenton (bus service) take the road by Rushlaw West Mains to the foot of Duchrie Dod, then ascend by Duchrie SE to Dunbar Common. Keep between the Mossy Burn and the West Burn to Beltondod from where the waymarked track is followed down SW to the Bothwell Water. Continue alongside it SE to the road bridge below Crichness, thence by road to St Agnes and Cranshaws.

To reach Duns, branch off left 500 metres south of St Agnes by road up to Harehead and shortly before the farm a broad track rises in an easterly direction for 600 metres to join a right of way running NW to SE. Continue on it SE to reach Ellemford Bridge then by road for 1km to Lodge Wood and join route 32, following it to Duns.

### 35  Garvald to Longformacus
*22¹/₂ km/14miles*                    *OS Sheet 67.   Start 590 709↑.   Finish 693 573↑*
From Garvald church go NE by the track down Whittinghame Water to Stoneypath Tower and by minor road to Stoneypath, which can also be reached from Stenton (bus route). Then go uphill, due S at first and SE by Mid Hill to the highest point on Dunbar Common (399m) and down to Johnscleugh on the Whiteadder Water crossing it by the farm access bridge. Continue SE by road to the Whiteadder Reservoir, round its northern end to Priestlaw Farm and up over the east shoulder of Priestlaw Hill to the Longformacus road. Crossing Wether Law is difficult and the alternative is by road to reach Horseupcleugh, then go down the Easter Burn and by Dye Water to Longformacus.

### 36  Cranshaws to Longformacus and Westruther
*6¹/₂ km/4miles or 19¹/₂ km/12miles*
                    *OS Sheet 67.   Start 693 615↑.   Finish 693 573↑ or 634 500*
The preferred start to this variable route goes from the B6355 road, 400metres south of Cranshaws where a good farm track climbs SW towards a wood. The track (which is not completely shown on OS maps) continues along the edge of another wood directly to the junction of the Longformacus road with the Horseupcleugh road at map ref 674 595.

An alternative to reach this point from Cranshaws village goes W from there along a farm road to Cranshaws Farm (ruins of old church of historical interest down on the left). After passing a substantial pele tower and a steading, a track continues on the west side of Long Wood then down and round by its south end to go SSW to map ref 674 595.

From there a choice of routes is possible:

(a) Go SE by road 3km to Longformacus and from there either:

(i) go along the Watch Water Reservoir road until 400metres beyond Rawburn, then strike SW across moor on an old ROW (pathless for 2km) to reach Wedderlie, thence by road 2½km to Westruther. From Rawburn an option is to go by the SUW leaving it at map ref 646 555 to continue to Wedderlie, then to Westruther as above.

(ii) follow the Duns Road for 800metres and at the top of the hill go SSW on the west side of Dirrington Great Law to Kippetlaw. From there go south by intermittent path east of Dirrington Little Law to reach the B6456 road, 5½km from Westruther.

(b) To reach Westruther omitting Longformacus, follow the road to Horseupcleugh and Dye cottage (junction with route 33). From Horseupcleugh an option is to go down Easter Burn then west along the north bank of Dye Water and across Wester Burn (no footbridge) to reach Dye Cottage. After crossing Dye Water by bridge a good track is followed south over moor to join the SUW, shortly leaving it at map ref 646 555 as in option (a) (i) to Wedderlie and Westruther.

### 37  Gifford to Carfraemill by Lammer Law
*19½km/12miles            OS Sheet 66. Start 530 677. Finish 508 534*
From Gifford go S by Yester Mains to Long Yester, then SW by Blinkbonny Wood and up to the east shoulder of Lammer Law. Continue over Crib Law (509m) to Tollishill and by the Kelphope Burn down by the minor road to the Carfraemill Lodge Hotel at the junction of the A68 and A697 roads (bus route) which is1½km from Oxton (where route 38 can be joined). This is a very old route, forming both a parish boundary and the old county boundary on the top of Lammer Law. Now it is also a well used vehicle track through the moorland grouse estate.

### 38  Soutra Aisle to Melrose by The Girthgate
*35½km/22miles         OS Sheets 66 and 73. Start 452 583. Finish 547 343*
Soutra Aisle on Soutra Hill is reached by the A68 road to Soutra Mains and then by the B6368 road. Just beyond the Aisle an old grassy road is plainly visible as it goes S to cross the Armet Water. This was part of the Roman Dere Street, also in use in mediaeval times, and is well defined for 5km to the Roman camp at Kirktonhill (Channelkirk).

Beyond Kirktonhill, the valley crossing is not now practicable and it is necessary to go left round by public road to Oxton. There at the cross roads, turn right and go SW uphill by road to continue by a track west of Overhowden to a point (map ref 477 507) west of Collie Law; it is then necessary to go left uphill alongside a field dyke to the plantation on the ridge at map ref 485 501.

The line of the old road is to be found on the west side of this plantation, and the ridge is followed S to Inchkeith Hill. Watch the direction here after passing the farm buildings. This is The Girthgate. From Oxton the Roman Dere Street kept more to the east in the Lauder Valley. The dyke along the ridge is the line until in sight of the Stow to Lauder road, at which point strike left to reach this road near its highest point. Then go left along the road until a cart track is seen on the right going S towards the east end of a wood. The track ends at a road junction south-west of Threepwood. For a continuation to Melrose, in preference to following the road down the Allan Water, go E for 2½ km along a minor road to join route 39 at Bluecairn.

This route is shown on Armstrong's 1773 map of the Lothians as starting from Soutra Aisle and going S to Threeburnford, and then by Collie Law as described above. It is named on that map and on the old OS 6-inch map as the 'Girthgate', i.e.sanctuary road, from some tradition that connected Soutra Hospice and Melrose Abbey. As the road has been identified as the 'via regia' or royal road referred to in a Melrose Charter of 1180 (see R.P.Hardie, *The Roads of Mediaeval Lauderdale*), and Soutra was not founded until 1184, it seems that Soutra Hospice was founded because of the existing road. South of the Stow to Lauder road, the Girthgate formed the old county boundary for a mile.

## 39  Lauder to Melrose
*16km/10miles*                    *OS Sheet 73. Start 531 476. Finish 547 343*
This route is part of the Southern Upland Way, although going in the reverse direction to that followed by most SUW walkers. From the Square at Lauder go SW up a path by the Lauder Burn along the edge of the golf course and turn SSE uphill past a plantation on Woodheads Hill, crossing straight over the minor public road, to continue to Fordswell. Then go by a road for 1km to Bluecairn. From there a fine broad track goes S over Kedslie Hill to map ref 540 385 where the track forks. Take the left fork past Easter Housebyres and go down to Gattonside and the footbridge across the River Tweed to Melrose.

## 40  Leadburn to Heriot
*27½ km/17miles*                  *OS Sheet 66 or 73. Start 235 554. Finish 402 545*
From Leadburn take the A703 road towards Peebles for just over 1km to Craigburn (parking nearby), then go NE by a farm road to Kingside. There turn SE following a track to Cockmuir; then 150 metres past the farm, along the public road, take a field track going SE to Toxside. Descend by the farm to a minor road and continue on this road round the north side of Gladhouse Reservoir (formed in 1879) to Mauldslie. An indistinct old cart track goes off SE from between the cottages and the farm, and follows a burn.

The track then becomes a sketchy path for 400 metres, but becomes distinct again after it rounds a square wood to ascend the face of Mauldslie Hill to the col between it and Torfichen Hill. In another 1½ km the path descends to join a track and then the B7007 road. Cross this, go through a gate and continue directly over the moor (no path) to the Tathieknowe Burn. Follow this down on the right-hand bank, joining a track before Carcant, to reach the B709 road 5km from Heriot House, near the A7 road (bus route).

The amount of road walking can be reduced by 3km if the B709 road is left at Heriot Mill to follow the farm track N up to Heriot Cleugh, then E to go down by Shoestanes. This adds 1½ km to the total distance of the route.

This route is shown as a road on Armstrong's 1773 map of the Lothians, joining at Garvald the road from Edinburgh which went *via* Esperston and then S as the 'Traquair Road'.

From Heriot House, the old Galashiels road goes NW over the hill to Middleton, 3km of it now being a grassy track.

### 41  Leadburn to Lyne
*19½ km/12miles*          *OS Sheet 73.  Start 235 554.  Finish 203 410*
From the A703 road, 150 metres south of the crossroads at Leadburn, an access track leads to the dimantled railway line. Follow the Peebles branch S to Waterhead. Bypass the gravel quarry by going along the main road for some 800 metres, rejoin the old railway at the metal bridge and follow the line until it meets the road to Shiplaw. Go right along this road to the crossroads just west of Shiplaw. There turn left and continue S by Stewarton and between Black Meldon and White Meldon along the road to reach Lyne just north of the A72 road, 6½ km from Peebles.

It is not necessary to follow the public road at the Harehope Burn as a track continues S and uphill from the public road and through a break in the plantation to a picnic site from where a track leads to Lyne.

It is possible to obtain access to this route at various points, including the convenient carpark about 1½ km south of Leadburn on the A703 road and at Noblehouse (an alternative starting point) on the A701 road, 8km south-west of Leadburn. In the latter case (which has the advantage of joining the route south of the gravel quarry) follow the forest and farm road E to the crossroads west of Shiplaw and proceed to Lyne as above.

### 42  West Linton to Peebles
*20km/12½ miles*          *OS Sheets 72 and 73.  Start 173 492.  Finish 250 404*
Take the B7059 road SE by Broomlee to the Moffat (A701) road, cross and go along the adjacent farm road SW for 800 metres. Then go uphill by Romanno House Farm and SE over the hill to Fingland Burn by a broad grassy track. On the south of Green Knowe at map ref 186 462 take the lower track and at map ref 188 461 (where a track leads round the hill to Fingland) take the footpath through a gate into the forest, across the stream and E through the forest to Greenside (or Courhope). From there go uphill and in about 270 metres leave the main track by taking the right-hand fork to cross a forest ride and continue up over the hill, descending to Upper and Nether Stewarton. Go E to the Lyne road and S along it for about ½ km, then turn left on the road to Upper Kidston. There, take a farm track on the left and go round north and east of Hamilton Hill to a broad track leading to Peebles.

This route is the southward continuation of the drove road through the Cauldstane Slap (see routes 22 and 51). It is marked on Roy's map of 1755.

### 43  Peebles to Innerleithen (by Leithen Water)
*14km/8¹/₂ miles or 19¹/₂ km/12mls*

OS Sheet 73.  Start 262 403↑.  Finish 333 367

From the east side of Peebles Hydro, a farm road goes N up the east side of the Soonhope Burn to Shieldgreen. Another way to this point goes from map ref 242 510 off the A703 (Edinburgh) road by a farm track past Venlaw towards Whitfold Hill, contouring by a path round its south-east shoulder to join a forest track going N to Shieldgreen. Some 70 metres west of the house the right of way goes N and climbs steeply uphill past the ruin of Shieldgreen Tower, now only a mound. The route is a broad, well-defined grassy track which crosses two forest roads and continues upwards, now on an easier gradient, to the col between Makeness Kipps and Dunslair Heights. From the col take the track to Dunslair Heights, then go SE through a gap in the trees to the forestry road down to Williamslee. From there it is 2km by an estate road to the B709 road (parking nearby) and a further 5km along the road to Innerleithen by the Leithen Water.

An alternative route which follows the original line of an old right of way from the col down to Craighope (shown on Armstrong's 1775 County Map of Peebles and Tweeddale) has been obscured by forestry. To follow it from the top of the col, continue in a northerly direction to a gap in the old stone dyke, follow a break in the forest NE and then gradually downhill for 150 metres to a forest road. Turn left along this road for 25 metres, then down NE through a break in the forest (which becomes steep and slippery) to the upper end of the forest road and follow the burn down to Craighope from where it is 2km to Williamslee, thence to continue as above to Innerleithen.

### 43X  Peebles to Innerleithen (by 'The Tops')
*16km/10miles*                    OS Sheet73.  Start 262 403↑.  Finish 333 367

Take route 43 to Dunslair Heights and from there go by the track SE through a gap in the trees (which leads to the forestry road down to Williamslee) to the boundary of Glentress Forest. Follow this over the tops of Black Law and Black Knowe to strike across the summits of Mill Rig, Lee Burn Head and Lee Pen (good views). Descend S from there by a boundary wall to go left shortly before reaching the mast at the foot of the hill by a vehicle track leading to Innerleithen.

### 44  Stow to Clovenfords
*18km/11miles*                    OS Sheet 73.  Start 458 446.  Finish 448 364

From Stow cross the Gala Water to Stagehall and go S by a minor road for 1¹/₂ km, then W to Lugate. There turn left, go through the steading and take the farm road to Fowie. An alternative from Stagehall is to leave the minor road and take the farm road W from there to continue by a track over Stagehall Hill and down SW by the burn to join the farm road from Lugate to Fowie.

From there follow the line of an old right of way which goes W diagonally across fields, steadily rising to pass through a narrow wood and across moorland over the col between Dunlee Hill and Scroof Hill. Descend to Scroof and go down the Caddon Water past Caddonhead on a good track. Shortly after it turns E, leave the Caddon Water and take the right-hand road uphill SE over the north-east shoulder of Black Law to Blackhaugh to rejoin the Caddon Water and continue by a minor road down to Clovenfords.

# SECTION 4
# The Pentland Hills

### 45  Colinton to Glencorse (Milton Bridge) by Howden Glen
*10km/6miles*                    *OS Sheet 66.  Start 219 684.  Finish 248 625*
From the south end of Dreghorn Loan pass through a gate and along a driveway.  After passing Laverockdale House turn right along a path which follows the Bonaly Burn under the city bypass A720 road.  Thereafter bear left across a field to a gate and track which, after Green Craig Cistern, joins a distinct track up Howden Glen.  This crosses the pass between Allermuir Hill and Capelaw Hill and continues S over Fala Knowe and downhill across the east side of Castlelaw Hill.  The route continues past a prehistoric fort and *souterrain* to reach Castlelaw Farm and then  Crosshouse.  After crossing the A702 road, finally go by Glencorse Old Church to Milton Bridge near Penicuik on the A766 road.

The Ministry of Defence own much of the land covered by this path, (and others in the same area) and have a firing range south of Castlelaw Hill.  When red flags are flying (red lights at night) walkers are not allowed into the area marked 'Danger Zone' on maps.  This danger zone is clearly shown on Bartholomew's Pentland Hills Walking Map (Scale 1½ inches to the mile).

### 46  Colinton to Glencorse (Milton Bridge) by Bonaly
*10km/6miles*                    *OS Sheet 66.  Start 214 686.  Finish 248 625*
From Colinton go up Bonaly Road, over the city bypass and past Bonaly Tower to the entrance to Bonaly Park where there is a carpark.  Continue up the steep track past Bonaly Reservoir, over  the col between Capelaw Hill and Harbour Hill and down to Glencorse Reservoir. Go left along the access road to Flotterstone; at the A720 road, turn left then right and go by Glencorse Old Church to Milton Bridge.

### 47  Currie or Balerno to Glencorse (Milton Bridge)
*10km/6miles*        *OS Sheet 66.  Start 183 678 or 163 662.  Finish 248 625*
From Currie go uphill by the Kirkgate road, passing the church, and continue straight on up to the moor.  Then go SE through Maiden's Cleuch, between Harbour Hill and Bell's Hill, and descend to Glencorse Reservoir where route 46 is joined.  This route is shown on Roy's map of 1755.

Alternatively, starting from Balerno, go up Harlaw Road by Malleny Mills to the small track opposite Harlaw Farm (carpark).  Bearing away from Harlaw Reservoir, continue almost due E across the moor to join the route from Currie before the climb to the Maiden's Cleuch pass.

By turning right at Glencorse Reservoir, routes 46 and 47 can be linked with route 48 by way of the road along Loganlee Reservoir.

#### 48  Balerno to Penicuik by the Kirk Road
*12km/7¹/₂ miles*                    *OS Sheet 66. Start 163 662. Finish 230 603*
Go along Mansfield Road from Balerno, passing Upper Dean Park Farm and Marchbank.  Take the left fork just past Redmoss House, (carpark at map ref 164 638) and go straight on to cross the Threipmuir Reservoir by a bridge and go up the steep avenue. At the top turn left, then right, passing the entrance to Bavelaw Castle, which is now a private residence. After a gate/stile, the route becomes a footpath going ESE and into Green Cleuch between Black Hill and Hare Hill to reach the Logan Burn. Follow the glen round to a cottage, 'The Howe', and just west of it a path goes steeply uphill over the high pass between Carnethy Hill and Scald Law (579m) - the highest of the Pentlands. This path is the  Kirk Road to Penicuik. Continue downhill from the pass by the Grain Burn to the A702 road; turn left there and take the first road on the right and go down by Coates Farm to Penicuik.
Both Bavelaw and Loganlee are in Penicuik parish, and this was once the road to church for people living there.
By continuing E at 'The Howe' instead of climbing the Kirk Road, a narrow road leads by Loganlee and Glencorse reservoirs to join with routes 46 and 47.

#### 49  Balerno to Nine Mile Burn by the Monks Road
*10km/6miles*                    *OS Sheet 65 or 66. Start 163 662. Finish 177 577*↑
Follow route 48 to the top of the avenue at Bavelaw. Turn right then left to go S over the west shoulder of Hare Hill, then downhill slightly to cross the source of the Logan Burn in the Kitchen Moss. From there climb E to the col on the south-west side of West Kip. From that point there are three possible routes:
(a) by the Monks Road, uphill to the right over Cap Law and the Monks Rig and past the Font Stone to Nine Mile Burn.
(b) downhill to the right by a plantation and Braid Law to Nine Mile Burn.
(c) downhill to the left by Eastside Farm to Eight Mile Burn on the A702 road.
From the col on the south-west side of West Kip, a fourth route is often taken, a ridge walk going E along the spine of the Pentlands over West Kip, East Kip, Scald Law, Carnethy Hill and Turnhouse Hill to reach Flotterstone on the A702 road.

#### 50  Balerno to Carlops by the Bore Stone
*14km/9miles*                    *OS Sheet 65. Start 163 662. Finish 161 560*
Follow route 48 to Marchbank and then take the right fork just past Redmoss House to follow the road by East Rig which continues in a straight line as a path to Listonshiels.  This point can also be reached from the A70 road, 4km west of Balerno.  At Listonshiels turn S uphill to the Bore (Boar) Stone and then descend  by the North Esk Reservoir to Carlops.
From Fairliehope, 1 km south of the reservoir, a short cut is provided by a path going down to the River North Esk (footbridge) and along its east bank to Carlops.  From the south end of the reservoir another path goes over the col between Spittal Hill and Patie's Hill to Spittal Farm and Nine Mile Burn.

## 51  Mid Calder to West Linton by the Cauldstane Slap
*19km/12miles*                    *OS Sheet 65.  Start 077 676.  Finish 147 518*
From Mid Calder go through East Calder and SE by road to the A70 Lanark road and SW along this road for 1km to the path on the left beyond Little Vantage where a signpost indicates the route to West Linton. The path descends to cross the Water of Leith (footbridge) and then climbs gradually to the pass known as the Cauldstane Slap.  1km south of the pass, the path becomes a track which goes down to Baddinsgill Reservoir, from the south end of which a road continues down to West Linton.

At about 1km from the end of Baddinsgill Reservoir a signpost beside the road indicates a path going off to the left to cross the Lyne Water (footbridge) to a track going by Stonypath (where it also joins route 54) to West Linton. Roy's map calls this route the 'Road to Queensferry'. It is an old drove road, and continues S to Peebles and St Mary's Loch by routes 42 and 22.

### 52  West Calder to Dolphinton or West Linton
*15km/9½ miles    OS Sheet 72.  Start 052 578↑.  Finish 104 470 or 147 518*
From West Calder the B7008 road goes SE by Harburn and past the Roman camp at Castle Greg; turn  SW at the A70 road and go along it for ½ km.  Start at the signposted minor road on the left to Crosswoodburn from where a track goes S (keeping to the east of Mid Crosswood Farm) and then SSE uphill to a signpost on the east shoulder of Henshaw Hill.  Another right of way path joins the route at this point, coming from the A70 (Tarbrax road end) by the Dry Burn.  Descend to cross the Garval Syke, then climb to the col between Darlees Rig and White Craig and cross the high bare moor to Black Law (where there is the grave of a Covenanter fatally wounded at Rullion Green in 1666).

From there continue SE and either:
(a) go left (E) along a wide track at the foot of Black Law to cross the Medwin Water and continue along the track to North Slipperfield, thence by a local road to West Linton, or
(b) continue S over the moor to the West Water and follow its east bank to Garvald, 3km by minor road from Dolphinton.

### 53  Auchengray to West Linton
*18km/11miles*                    *OS Sheet 72.  Start 994 524.  Finish 147 518*
From the road 2km south of Auchengray go E by the farm road past East Yardhouses to the A70 Lanark road.  Cross this and continue by a path going SE through a small plantation and then by a clear track to Left Law. Take the left fork and go E over the moor between Bleak Law and Mid Hill and NE across the West Water to a track crossing the Medwin Water just north of Medwynhead. Continue  to join route 52 by the wide track to North Slipperfield and local road to West Linton.

From the fork at Left Law an alternative route goes S by Stonypath  (map ref 053 488) to the road 1½ km W of Dunsyre.  There another road goes NE by Walton, and Medwynbank, followed by a track to North Slipperfield and finally by the road to West Linton as above.

*Green Cleuch in the Pentland Hills (route 48)*

*Lowther Hill from the south end of the Enterkin Pass (route 63)*

*On Culmark Hill, Looking north to the hills east of Carsphairn (route 86)*

*Looking north-west from Beneraid to Ailsa craig across the Firth of Clyde (route 67)*

*Looking up Glen Rosa to A'Chir and Cir Mhor (route 88)*

*At the west end of Loch Katrine, looking up Glen Gyle (route 114)*

*Ben Vorlich from Glen Vorlich at the north end of the right of way from Callander (route 120)*

*Heading west along the Abhainn Shira on the way from Bridge of Orchy to Loch Etive (route 114)*

## 54  Carlops to Dolphinton
*10km/6miles*                    *OS Sheet 72. Start 160 554. Finish 110 477*
    This route follows a section of the Old Biggar Road along the line of a
Roman road. In some places the route is part of this road, but in other places
it diverges.
    It starts on the west side of the A702 road just south of Carlops and goes
SW by Linton Muir for 2½ km to join a metalled road near Stonypath (map ref
145 356). Fork left there (signposted to West Linton) and after crossing the
Lyne Water at Lynedale House, turn left then right by West Linton Golf Course.
Where the road swings right, go straight ahead (ie SW) on a path which
continues by Hardgatehead and Ingraston to rejoin the A702 road 1km from
Dolphinton.

# SECTION 5
# Clydesdale and the Lowther Hills

### 55 Lamington to Broughton
*19km/12miles*          *OS Sheet72. Start 978 308. Finish 114 358*
 Take the road which starts just south of Lamington Church and leads SE to Baitlaws. Just before reaching there, branch off left by a farm road which descends to cross Lamington Burn and then goes uphill to Cowgill Loch. Continue to Cowgill from where a road goes to Birthwood and down the Culter Water. At Snaip turn off this road, go past Nisbet Farm and when the track forks take the right-hand one to Cow Castle. From there go E through the gap between March Brae and White Hill, past a derelict cottage on the right-hand side, to reach Mitchell Hill and the old road to Broughton.

### 56 Coulter to Crawford
*20km/12 miles*          *OS Sheet 72. Start 026 338. Finish 954 208*
 From Coulter take the road up Culter Water and when it forks in 3km, take the right fork which goes past Birthwood. In about 1km and shortly after two bridges are crossed at map ref 019 304, where there is car parking, follow the path which climbs SSW over Cowgill Rig and leads down towards the ruin of Windgate House near the south-east corner of Cowgill Upper Reservoir. From the ruin go SE up the steep slope to the col between Windgate Bank and Hudderstone. From there descend SSE by the Linn Burn to the road down Grains Burn and continue along it on the west side of Camps Reservoir (limited parking) and finally go by a minor road down the Camps Water for 4km to Crawford.
 From the road junction at map ref 019 304 on the way to Windgate House an alternative route goes up the road past Cowgill Lower Reservoir to the dam on Cowgill Upper Reservoir. Continue along the east side of this reservoir by difficult going with no visible path to the ruin of Windgate House and continue as above.

### 57 Beattock Summit to Moffat
*18km/11miles*          *OS Sheet 78. Start 976 162. Finish 075 085*
 Coming from the north, the starting point of this route is reached from the roundabout (map ref 957 180) on the B7076 road and southwards along it to map ref 976 162, just before the bridge across the motorway. Coming from the south, leave the motorway at the Beattock-Moffat interchange (No.15) and take the B7076 road northwards over the Beattock Summit to reach this bridge.
 From north of the bridge go E on a metalled road for 1½km leaving it to follow an old track SE along the edge of forest for another 1½km. Fork left just before Upper Howecleuch and above there detour around sheep pens to join a forest road round the foot of Nap Hill, then drop down to cross Fopperbeck Burn at a ford. Ascend SE through forest and pass south of Errickstane Hill in an easterly direction to a fork in the track; keeping to the

forest road.  At a collapsed wooden construction (map ref 039 139) just beyond marker 84, turn SE along the cleared strip (buried gas pipeline) for 1½ km and after passing a metal tower turn south at marker 85 towards a burn at a dip in the track at map ref 047 126.

Shortly afterwards leave this cleared strip by track on the left going to a "T" junction.  There, turn right and the route (including the right of way and Roman Road) continues past a small pond on the left, then immediately leaves the track and goes SE up a clearing and through a low col to descend steeply to the A701 road.  Cross this (1½ km south of the Devil's Beef Tub) and descend by the old road to join the valley road and go by Bridgend for 3km to Moffat.  From the point where the A701 road is crossed, the line of the Roman road is due south on the high ground, as shown on the OS map.

## 58  Roberton to Douglas
*14km/9miles*                          *OS Sheet 71 or 72.  Start 946 286.  Finish 847 314*

From Roberton go by a minor road to Nap Bridge and in a further 150 metres look on the left for the line of the old drove road, now a variable path, on the north side of the Roberton Burn going NW and rising to reach the unfenced part of the road just east of Fallside.  An easier alternative to this point is to follow the broad, slightly earth-scarred buried pipeline NNW across the moor to the enclosed gas compound (make for upright stones on the skyline).

From there go W on the quiet road to Bodinglee to follow at first a farm road, then a path (indistinct in places) continuing W to the uninhabited building at Maidengill.  There, one should avoid the original way straight ahead, and instead follow a rough  access road round, down and under the M74 motorway by a tunnel, continuing to reach the B7078 road (formerly the A74).  Thence it is 1km north along this road to Parkhead Cottage. Go W from there by the south end of the wood up ahead and along the edge of a fence on a much overgrown path (just passable), then down through a farm steading to the A70 road, 800 metres north-east of Douglas.

## 59  Douglas to Wanlockhead
*23km/14½miles*                          *OS Sheet 71.  Start 837 307.  Finish 885 146*

Go up Springhill Road, passing on the east of Springhill Farm, to Pagie Hill and SE across pathless, boggy moorland between Auchensaugh Hill and Mid Rig to Crawfordjohn.  From there go SW by the B740 road for 2 km to turn left into the  minor road to Snar Farm.  Continue up the Snar Water to near Snarhead, where it is preferable to take the track which goes SE over Hunt Law before dropping down to Leadhills, 1½ km by road from Wanlockhead. Alternatively, ½ km before Leadhills take the track S and go direct to Wanlockhead over Wanlock Dod.

Places of interest at Wanlockhead are:  World's oldest lending library.  Grave of Scotland's oldest man.  Museum of Scottish lead mining.  Lead mine visit.  Beam engine.  Merrockhan water tunnel (1763).

Between Leadhills and Wanlockhead is a narrow gauge railway (working during summer months at weekends). On Roy's map of 1755 the first part of this route to Crawfordjohn is shown as a road.

## 60  Muirkirk to Wanlockhead
*32km/20miles*                    *OS Sheet 71.  Start 696 273↑.  Finish  873 129↑*

This old drove road goes S from Muirkirk past Kames and up the Garpel Water, crossing it by the bridge at map ref 698 245, to the col (410m) between Wardlaw Hill and Stony Hill. Continuing SE then E, the path, boggy in places, enters the forest on the south-east slope of Drummond's Knowe. A forest road leads on to Fingland, and from there the line of the old drove road goes E up the slopes on the south side of Spango Water. 1½ km E of Fingland the track peters out; head for a gate in the drystane dyke to the east and regain the track on the north side of Shiel Hill at a height of almost 430m.

Continue along the south side of Lamb Knowe and descend to Spango Bridge on the B740 road between Sanquhar and Crawfordjohn. From that point, 400 metres north-east of Spango Bridge, go SE by Clackleith and follow a track through the forest round the south side of Duntercleugh Rig (where the Southern Upland Way is joined) to descend to Duntercleugh and continue up the Wanlock Water to Wanlockhead.

An alternative to the forestry track from Spango Bridge towards Wanlockhead is to fork left through a field gate before the concrete bridge over the Wanlock Water and go up its east bank to rejoin the route at map ref 850 150, thence continue to Wanlockhead.

## 61  Muirkirk to Kirkconnel
*21km/13miles*                    *OS Sheet 71.  Start 696 273↑.  Finish  727 124↑*

Follow route 60 as far as Fingland, then go SW by road up the Glengap Burn for 1½ km. Leave the road just before it turns E and continue SW over the col and down the slopes of Kirkland Hill above Glenaylmer Burn to Kirkland and Kirkconnel.

## 62  Wanlockhead to Sanquhar
*13km/8miles*                    *OS Sheet 71.  Start 873 127↑.  Finish 785 098*

(a) From west of Wanlockhead the track up Black Hill can only be seen for a short distance. Keep uphill, over the ridge on the right and round the head of a rocky valley where a track across the grass marks the route to Stood Hill. From Stood Hill follow a fence W above the valley to Willowgrain Hill, and continue W along the crest of the next hill (486m) and downwards by the fence to join the Southern Upland Way at map ref 824 123 to go by Bog to Sanquhar.

(b) An alternative route follows the Southern Upland Way between Wanlockhead and Sanquhar. Take the road going down Wanlock Water for 2km, past Wanlockhead Cemetery. Cross the Wanlock Water and go up Glengaber Hill by a track which crosses the ridge north-west of the summit and goes SW down to Cogshead. From there climb SW over the col to the

south-east of Conrig Hill where route (a) is joined.
Parts of these routes should be avoided in the grouse shooting and lambing seasons. Use instead sections of route 60 and the Southern Upland Way between Meadowfoot and Cogshead *via* Duntercleuch.

### 63  Wanlockhead to Enterkinfoot by the Enterkin Pass
*11km/7miles*                    *OS Sheet 78.  Start 877 128↑.  Finish 857 043*
On the east side of Wanlockhead a signpost marks the right of way leading SE up the west side of Stake Hill.  In 1km it joins the road to the radar station and leaves the road again after 500 metres to continue due S to the Enterkin Pass between Lowther Hill and East Mount Lowther.  From the pass there is a choice of two routes to Enterkinfoot:
(a)  Descend by the west bank of the Enterkin Burn for 3km until it turns W at Glenvalentine.  From there, climb S up the track from the burn to the ridge ahead.  Then keep going S down this ridge (with spectacular views of Enterkin Glen) to join the metalled road near Inglestone.  Continue by the public road *via* Muiryhill, turning W to the A76 Nithsdale road and Enterkinfoot. To reach Durisdeermill, turn E immediately on reaching the road near Inglestone and take the track past Eastside to join the A702 Dalveen Pass road.
(b)  From the Enterkin Pass (at map ref 882 107) another path goes SW, traversing along the west side of East Mount Lowther for 1½ km and then dropping to the col (525m) between it and Threehope Height.  Descend S by a spur to cross the Auchenlone Burn and continue S over the col between Cairn Hill and Coshogle Rig and then down by Kirkbride to Enterkinfoot.
The two routes (a) and (b) can be combined as a circuit (22km/14miles).

### 64  Daer Reservoir to Durisdeer
*14km/8½ miles*                    *OS Sheet 78.  Start 967 073.  Finish 895 036*
From the A702 road take the road to the Daer Reservoir for 7km to Kirkhope Cleuch where there is good parking.  From there two routes are possible:
(a)  Proceed S for 5km past Kirkhope by a rough track and SW up Thick Cleuch, over the col and down Tansley Burn.  At map ref 924 008 (where the Tansley Burn joins Berry Grain) turn NW through a pass to the Glenleith Burn and continue NW by a track down Glenaggart to Durisdeer.
(b)  A much shorter and more direct route goes up Kirkhope Cleuch for 3km to the col between Comb Law and Hirstane Rig, then SW by the Well Path, now a tractor track, between Well Hill and Durisdeer Hill and down the Kirk Burn (easier walking is on its east side) to Durisdeer.
Part of this route was originally a Roman road, and in the Middle Ages was the road between Clydesdale and Nithsdale and the route to Galloway used by James IV on his pilgrimages to the shrine of St Ninian at Whithorn. The Lord High Treasurer's Accounts for 1497 contain an item "to the wife of Durisdeer, where the King lodged, 14s".  The King's route was by Biggar, Cold Chapel (near Abington), Crawford Muir, Durisdeer, Penpont and Dalry.
In a building behind Durisdeer Church, which is open all year, are the Queensberry Marbles.

## 65  Daer Reservoir to Thornhill
*22km/13¹/₂ miles*                 *OS Sheet 78.  Start 967 073.  Finish 879 955*
   Like route 64, this one starts from the A702 road near Daer Reservoir and goes 7km to Kirkhope Cleuch.  From there two possibilities are:
   (a)  Proceed as in route 64(a) to the  junction of the Tansley Burn and Berry Grain at map ref  924 008 where there is a choice of either continuing SW by Cample Cleuch to Burn Farm, or going W round Par Hill by a track high above Kettleton Reservoir to Burn Farm and thence by road to Thornhill.
   (b)  From the Daer Reservoir go S to Kirkhope and continue by a track up the valley to Daerhead.  Continue almost due S to the col (Daer Hass) on the west side of Earncraig Hill and descend on the south side to Burleywhag.
   At that point there is a choice of two routes:
   (i)  Go down the west side of the Capel Burn to Locherben, then W by road to Thornhill.
   (ii)  take the track past a bothy and down the east side of the Capel Burn to Mitchellslacks and from there go by road to Thornhill.
   From Mitchellslacks follow the waymarked route SW across Threip Moor, planted with trees by the Buccleuch Estates in 1997, then go NW through established trees to the north side of Hope Burn and then along the public road beyond Dollard to Closeburnmill and Thornhill. Near Dollard it is possible to take the signposted route through the picturesque Crichope Linn, but note that the path can be very slippery and has steep side slopes through this deep sandstone gully.
   A circular route is possible using route (i) above as far as Locherben, then going NW by a track and path up the Garroch Water and over the col at its head to reach the Tansley Burn and return from there to Daer Reservoir by Thick Cleuch (route 64a in reverse).

## 66  Ae Village to Beattock by the Forest of Ae
*21km/13miles*                 *OS Sheet 78.  Start 979 902↑.  Finish 077 027*
   From Ae Bridgend on the A701 Beattock to Dumfries road (bus route) a public road goes NW to Ae village. The route to Beattock is now  signposted and waymarked from 1km beyond the village. A forest road strikes off to the right (parking at a picnic area in 2km) and goes up the west bank of the Water of Ae for a further 1¹/₂ km to cross it by a bridge. Continue up the east bank, rising steadily to map ref 010 964 from where two routes are possible:
   (a)  Turn left, go NW, N and E for 2 km to reach Blue Cairn, continuing easterly and contouring NE round Hareshaw Rig to pass an old quarry on the left-hand side of the road before reaching map ref  024 994.  Here, where the forest road turns sharp right, turn left onto a green ride and go past the Shepherd's Cairn to Lochanhead. Cross the Lochan Burn just downstream of Lochanhead Cottage and turn NE along the bank. Go through a wicket gate, cross a field and join a tractor track to Kinnelhead and the public road at the bridge across the Kinnel Water. Finally, follow the 'Crooked Road' to Beattock.
   (b)  To continue directly to Beattock from map ref 010 964, carry on to leave the forest by a gate at map ref 017 974.  Follow the forest boundary eastwards by an old drove road and in 2km re-enter the forest to join a green

ride and go NE to Long Cairn, a prominent structure. Continue through the forest to join a track to Stidriggs Farm and from its road end join the public road to Beattock.

A projected walking route from Closeburnmill to Beattock by the Forest of Ae is not shown in full on the 1995 Edition of OS Sheet 78, but a brochure with map for this project is being prepared for distribution at Tourist Information Offices etc in the area.

# SECTION 6
# Galloway and Ayrshire

### 67  Ballantrae to Stranraer or New Luce.
*27km/17miles or 22km/14miles*
*OS Sheets 76 and 82.  Start 093 818↑.  Finish 087 634 or 174 647*
Leave the A77 road 1km south of Ballantrae at an SRWS signpost and go
E along a minor road towards Auchairne for 1km. Then go SE uphill past
Kilwhannel across the north-east shoulder of Smyrton Hill and over Beneraird
at a height of 424m. Continue past Lagafater Lodge and down the Main Water
of Luce to map ref 141 742. Take the right fork to go by Barnvannoch and
High Mark to a road junction (just N of the filter station) at map ref 134  696.
From there a choice is possible:
  (a) To reach Stranraer, take the road on the right going east of Penwhirn
Reservoir and continue SW over Braid Fell to reach Innermessan, 4km by the
A77 road from Stranraer.
  (b) To reach New Luce, take the road on the left still following the Main
Water of Luce SE by a quiet road to New Luce.
  An alternative from map ref 141 742 is to take the track SE and over the
Cross Water of Luce by a bridge some 700 metres south of Glenwhilly, thence
by minor road 7km to New Luce.

### 68  Girvan to Barr
*11km/8miles*               *OS Sheet 76.  Start 184 964.  Finish 276 945↑·*
  At the time of writing this route is in the process of being waymarked. At
the roundabout on the main road on the south of Girvan go due E uphill over
the railway and continue along a track, then a path by Laggan Loch over to
Barbae and Tormitchell.  From there go to Dupin and E by a faint track over
Auchensoul Hill to Barr.

### 69  Barr to Barrhill
*18km/11miles*               *OS Sheet 76.  Start 273 936↑.  Finish 245 816↑·*
  Although difficult in places due to forestry, the track is now usefully
waymarked and the route is feasible.
  From Barr go by road to Alton Albany Farm, then S uphill to White Knowes.
Follow the forest road for 1km before striking SW at a bend in the road (map
ref 273 911) to continue along a forest ride for 400 metres. A narrow path
then goes SE and follows a forest ride which ascends to a forest road and the
col 400 metres north of Loch Scalloch. Passing the loch on the right, continue
through the forest SSE by a forest road for 4km to reach White Clauchrie. 100
metres to the west of White Clauchrie proceed S for 300 metres before crossing
the burn and following a forest ride all the way to Black Clauchrie.  From
there a farm road goes WSW to Darnaconnar and Laggan to reach the A714
road at Blair Farm, 1km SE of Barrhill.

## 70  Barr to Kirriereoch and Bargrennan
*13km/8miles or 21km/13miles*
OS Sheets 76 and 77.  Start 278 940.   Finish 356 869 or 350 767
This track is not the easiest to follow, but  quite feasible when on the ground, using compass (essential), map and reference to this description.  Even so, the route may become quickly outdated given the new planting taking place.

From Barr go SE to the ruined building at map ref 283 936 and from there make for the east side of Dinmurchie Loch. Progress through recently planted trees crossing the Water of Gregg to the ruin at Darley. Now, with little or no track, ascend Cairn Hill where to the south one can pick up the outline of the forest edge (at map ref 310 904).  The old track through the Nick of Darley (not shown on the 1:50000 map) is now diffcult to pick out. This, and the burn running parallel to it, lead directly to a forest ride going E (at map ref 313 897) and is marked by two solitary posts with white tape on their tops.

The forest ride begins wide but shortly narrows.  Look out for a large cleared area to the right and pick up the forest track at a hut; then, following the forest track *via* junctions at map refs 326 896, 336 900, 345 893, 347 870 and 354 868, join the minor public road at map ref 356 869.  Kirriereoch parking and picnic area are nearby and Bargrennan is reached in 11km by public road through the forest *via* Glentrool Village.

The first part of this route is shown as a road on Armstrong's 1773 map of Ayrshire.  A note on the map reads "At the Nick of Darlae and half a mile west the Road leads on the side of a very steep Hill, it's not above two feet broad and if you stumble you must fall almost Perpendicular six or seven hundred Feet".

An alternative route to Bargrennan from the forest track junction at map ref 326 896 is to take the right-hand forest road and follow it S for about 4km to Fardin (ruin).  There go left (SE) for about 460 metres and then take another forest road which branches right (S) at map ref 335 863 to ford the Infant River Cree.  Shortly afterwards, take the right-hand fork of the forest road going SSW, and in 7km reach the A714 road about 5km NW of Bargrennan.

## 71  Pinwherry to Kirriereoch
*22½ km/14miles*        OS Sheets 76 and 77.  Start 198 869.   Finish 356 869
Take the minor road SE to Liglartrie and then go NE *via* Docherniel and Mark to the Muck Water, where the minor road ends.

There a forest road leads SE to Shalloch Well, continuing E through the forest to White Clauchrie (fork right), Ferter and Fardin (see route 72) to Kirriereoch.

## 72  Barrhill to Kirriereoch
*16km/10miles*        OS Sheets 76 and 77.  Start 238 820↑.  Finish 356 869
From Barrhill take the A714 road towards Newton Stewart for 1km to Blair Farm.  There turn left onto the minor road signposted 'Footpath by Black Clauchrie' and follow this road NE by Laggan and Darnaconnar.  At Black Clauchrie the road ends.  A track continues for 2km further to enter a forest ride which is followed for about 1km until the end of a forest road appears on

the left. Follow this track to the junction at map ref 316 870 and there take the right-hand forest track to Fardin (ruin). Continue along the forest track via junctions at map refs 335 863, 347 870 (joining route 70) and 354 868 to the minor public road at 356 869 and finally reach Kirriereoch (parking and picnic area), several hundred metres along the road.

## 73  Newton Stewart to Bargrennan by Loch Dee
*29km/18miles          OS Sheets 77 and 83.  Start 412 656.  Finish 350 767*
Go through Minnigaff and NE to Kirkland and Glenhoise by a minor road, then left by the road over the Penkiln Burn and up this burn to Auchinleck. Continue by a forest road to Drigmorn and go up the east side of the Pulnee Burn to a rough but well-defined path leading through the gap to the east of Curlywee and to White Laggan bothy. 400 metres beyond the bothy is the Southern Upland Way, running west to east. The way E is described in route 78. Turning W towards Glentrool, follow the waymarkers until 5km beyond White Laggan Bothy, where there is a choice of either:
(a) following the Southern Upland Way on the south side of Loch Trool to Bargrennan, or
(b) crossing Glenhead Burn to the road and going along the north side of Loch Trool to Glentrool Village and on to Bargrennan.

## 74  Newton Stewart to New Galloway or Dalry by the Old Edinburgh Road
*29km/18miles*
*OS Sheets 77 and 83.  Start 412 656.  Finish 634 777 or 620 813*
The line of this old road, long since disused, is marked on the OS map. It goes from Minnigaff to Kirkland and in a further 1km NE, where the modern road turns left at map ref 424 673, a section of the old road goes for 3km to meet a forestry road which continues NE by Loch of the Lowes to Black Loch.
Next comes an open section, then by forest road not quite on the line of the old road to Clatteringshaws. Beyond here the Old Edinburgh Road can be picked up again at map ref 570 772 and followed E, never more than 200 metres N of The Queen's Way (A712 road), to New Galloway. Alternatively, go NE by a minor road and then between Glenlee Hill and Maggot Hill to Dalry.

## 75  Polmaddie to Carsphairn (The Polmaddie Trail)
*7km/4½ miles          OS Sheet 77.  Start 598 880.  Finish 560 934*
At Polmaddie, just off the A713 road 2km north of Carsfad Loch, locate the access road and go between the footbridge (over the Polmaddy Burn) and the first building in the ruined village. Continue past a carpark to a track, and head NW through young forest on the west side of the Polmaddy Burn for about 4km. After cossing the burn, turn right along the track on the east side of Gairy Craig. Leave the forest at Braidenoch and go N across the slopes of Bardennoch Hill to reach Carnavel and the A713 road at the bridge over the Water of Deugh, ½ km south-east of Carsphairn.
The original line of the old pack road went from Carsfad Loch NW to Polmaddie, continuing well to the east of the Polmaddy Burn and  N across the slopes of Bardennoch Hill to reach Carnavel.

## 76  Clatteringshaws Loch to Mossdale (The Raiders Road)
*14½ km/9miles*                    *OS Sheet 77.  Start 546 752.   Finish 660 706*
Start from the north side of the bridge which carries the A712 road over the River Dee (or Black Water of Dee) where it flows out of Clatteringshaws Loch and follow a forest road on the north bank of the Dee SE for 13km to Stroan Loch. At the old railway viaduct continue along the line of the old railway (now resurfaced) to Mossdale, or take a forest road which turns N and in 400 metres a gate on the right leads to a path to Mossdale.

## 77  Glentrool Village to Merrick (and return)
*13km/8miles*                    *OS Sheet 77.  Start and finish 372 786*
Go by the minor public road up Glen Trool to the Bruce Stone, then N up the Buchan Burn to Culsharg bothy.  From there the route  goes NW uphill just on the north side of the forestry bridge and leads to the dyke which passes right over Benyellary to the west shoulder of Merrick (843m). The return from Culsharg can be made through the forest by a forest road which leads to Stroan Bridge, 1km from Glentrool Village.

An alternative descent from Merrick, not clearly defined on the ground, drops E from its summit to Loch Enoch, and thence SW past the rocky outcrop of The Grey Man of the Merrick at map ref 437 846 and along the valley of the Buchan Burn.  A faint track going S across several fords leads through the forest SW, then W, to meet forest roads and to return (as above) by Culsharg, or continue to the Bruce Stone and the Glen Trool road to Stroan Bridge.

## 78  Bargrennan to Dalry by Clatteringshaws Loch
*42km/26miles*                    *OS Sheet 77.  Start 350 767.  Finish 620 813*
This is the fourth section of the Southern Upland Way and it leaves the A714 road at Bargrennan opposite the village hall to strike E over the hill to a bridge over the Water of Minnoch.  The route then goes up Glen Trool past Caldons camp site (shop) continuing on the south side of Loch Trool to Glenhead and is joined by the alternative route from the north side of the loch. 4km beyond Glenhead is Loch Dee and White Laggan bothy. Continuing E, the Southern Upland Way crosses the Black Water of Dee, goes downstream to Clatteringshaws Loch and then crosses the hills, NNE at first to Clenrie, then E to Dalry. The official Southern Upland Way map is particularly useful for this route.

## 79  Bargrennan to Polharrow Bridge (Dalry) by Backhill of Bush
*35 km/22miles*                    *OS Sheet 77.  Start 350 767.  Finish  603 843*
From Bargrennan go by route 78 along the Southern Upland Way to reach map ref 399 788 and from there turn N to cross the Water of Trool and go up Glen Trool on the north side of Loch Trool past the Bruce Stone to Buchan.  From there take the path ENE up the hillside to the Gairland Burn and ascend beside this to Loch Valley.  Beyond this loch go NE around the east side of Loch Neldricken, then N for 1km and turn E over the ridge (494m) between Craignaw and Dungeon Hill to the Round Loch of the Dungeon.

In order to avoid the dangerous Silver Flowe bog on the south side of this loch, go round its north side.  Even so, watch carefully for sound footing across the very boggy gound there until reaching the forest.  Follow the boundary SE to map ref 474 843 where the route meets the ride at the edge of the forest leading to Backhill of Bush bothy.

From the bothy, follow a track NNE for 800 metres to map ref 483 851 and turn right by the uphill track for another 800 metres to map ref 496 850.  Then go NE directly  up a steep slope to cross a col (628m) 1½ km south of Corserine and descend steeply ESE across Hawse Burn (above the waterfall) into the forest and past a shepherd's memorial.  Then go due E by a forest ride and by tracks midway between Loch Minnoch and Loch Dungeon to join (at map ref 543 846) a track leading NE *via* Burnhead to the end of a minor public road.  Go down it for 6 km to Polharrow Bridge, 3½ km from Dalry by the A713 road .

## 80  Bargrennan to Carsphairn or Dalmellington
*35km/22miles or 42 km/26 miles*
                    *OS Sheet 77.  Start 350 767.  Finish 556 945 or 480 060*
Follow route 79 to Backhill of Bush.  Go N along a forest road for 2km and contour round Little Craigtarson to reach Riders Rig at map ref 480 883 in 3km.  From there strike NW along a forest ride, taking the fourth ride on the right which goes NE, to meet another forest road on the east side of Gala Lane leading to Loch Head (Loch Doon).  From there strike uphill by the east bank of the Loch Head Burn for about 1km, swinging ENE and heading for the pass out of  the forest to map ref 503 922.  Turn N over the top of Bow (613m) and to the next col S of Coran of Portmark (623m), then head ENE down a steep slope to reach the disused mines beside the Garryhorn Burn.  From there go E along the track past Garryhorn to reach the A731 road near to the Green Well of Scotland, 1km north of Carsphairn.

An alternative way from Backhill of Bush follows route 79 to the col (628m) 1½ km south of Corserine.  Then go N over Corserine (814m), Carlin's Cairn, and Meaul (695m) to Bow and the col south of Coran of Portmark to descend from there to Carsphairn as above.

To go to Dalmellington from the head of Loch Doon at map ref 482 925, cross the Gala Lane to take the secondary road past Starr, turning N along the west side of Loch Doon.  800 metres beyond the end of the loch go left at Caw Glen Burn to Bellsbank and Dalmellington.

## 81  Bargrennan to Dalmellington by Tunskeen
*43km/27miles*                    *OS Sheet 77.  Start 350 767.  Finish 480 060*
From Bargrennan either go by road to Glen Trool or follow route 79 to reach there.  Then go by the road up Glen Trool for 2km to the Buchan Burn and up this burn to Culsharg bothy, turning right 200 metres beyond it onto a forest track and go up the NW bank of the Buchan Burn for 2km, leaving the forest at map ref 430 836.  Continue NE to the south-west corner of Loch Enoch, go along its west side and then head NNW on the lower slopes of Kirriereoch Hill (no path, rough and boggy) and cross Castle on Oyne to Tunskeen bothy.

Continue N, keeping W of the forest fence until a track is reached at map ref 424 916 below the ruins of Slaethornrig. Follow this track above the west side of Loch Riecawr, and just beyond this loch join a forest road where two alternatives are:
(a) Go E to Loch Doon and along its west side to Dalmellington.
(b) Go NW to the south end of Loch Bradan and then W to Stinchar Bridge, and 2km north of there join route 84 to Dalmellington.

## 82  Clatteringshaws Loch to Dalmellington
*38½ km/24miles*          *OS Sheet 77. Start 567 771. Finish 480 060*
From the A712 Newton Stewart road, 8km west of New Galloway, a forest road strikes NW to Upper Craigenbay. In 1km further the Southern Upland Way is joined and followed S for 1km to Clatteringshaws Loch, then 4km W to the point where the Way crosses the Black Water of Dee at map ref 495 794. At that point do not cross the river, but go NW then N along a forest track to reach Backhill of Bush in 6km and join route 80 to Dalmellington.

## 83  Barr to Carsphairn
*37km/23miles*          *OS Sheets 76 and 77. Start 276 941. Finish 556 945*
From Barr take the road E up the Water of Gregg for about 1½ km, forking left along a forest road past a public carpark and up the side of a wood to High Changue. Continue through the forest to Balloch Hill, where the road turns N downhill. Join and follow the cycle route to the public road at Pinvalley and go N by this road to North Balloch.
From there go E and along a forest road, which after about 1½ km goes up by the Whiterow Burn to the north side of Dunamoddie and over Eldrick Hill (329m) before turning SE to the River Stinchar. Follow the river SE along a waymarked trail to the Stinchar Bridge. From it a metalled road goes E to map ref 417 960, then a forest road leads to Ballochbeatties and the north side of Loch Riecawr to Loch Doon. Finally, go from Loch Head at the head of the loch to Carsphairn as in route 80.

## 84  Barr to Dalmellington
*31km/19miles*          *OS Sheets 76 and 77. Start 276 941. Finish 480 060*
Follow route 83 until the River Stinchar is reached and where it bends SE strike E for 1km to the Straiton road. Then go N and 400 metres past Talaminnoch turn off E by a forest road through Tairlaw Plantation to Knockdon on the Water of Girvan. Here an SRWS signpost points the way initially up the west side of the burn until a dry-stane dyke is reached and the burn crossed. From there the route goes over the moor to the south and east of Widows Loch and Black Loch. A faint track leads to Little Shalloch (ruin) from where a track is followed to the ruin of Nether Berbeth at map ref 463 040. A farm road then leads past Dalcairnie Farm to the B741 road at the bridge over the River Doon, 2km from Dalmellington.

## 85  Barr to Straiton and Patna
*21km/13miles*
>        *OS Sheets 76 and 77.   Start 276 941.   Finish 380 050 or 414 106*
This route goes mostly through developed forests and needs a detailed description.

Follow route 83 as far as North Balloch. From there continue N by road for 1km to the Dalquhairn Burn and head NE up its north side for 1½km to enter the forest. 500 metres further upstream, at map ref 347 978, make a diversion 450 metres E then 400 metres N before joining a forest road. Turn right and continue for 1km, at which point the route crosses a forest road to head in a NE direction, leaving the forest at map ref 366 999. Crossing the Palmullan Burn at map ref 372 008, follow the burn downstream to Knockskae and Dalmorton, and go by road down the west side of the Water of Girvan to Straiton.

Proceed to a point ½km up the B741 road to Dalmellington where a minor road leads NE uphill for 1km to a plantation. Enter it and follow the track through the forest to the ruins of Dhu Loch Cottage, seen to the left of the route. Continue past the cottage for 200 metres, crossing a fence and a small burn which is followed upstream for 300 metres before bearing left to follow a forest ride in a northerly direction. Passing the end of a forest road on the right, continue downhill to a bridge over a burn at a point 200 metres east of Loch Spallander (map ref 399 082). Bear uphill and go through a gap in a dry-stane dyke to head E and then N, following a forest ride (keeping another dry-stane dyke on the right) leading to a forest road. Turning right, keep on this road (ignoring another road which branches to the right) and go NE through forest to a point just west of Patna.

## 86  St John's Town of Dalry to Sanquhar
*43km/27miles*       *OS Sheets 77 and 78.   Start 626 814.   Finish 774 097*
This route follows a long section of the Southern Upland Way across the hills and moorland between the River Ken and Nithsdale. In Dalry go up the main street to the left fork beyond the B7000 road, then go NE by Ardoch Hill to Butterhole Bridge and over Culmark Hill to the B729 road to Stroanfreggan. Go E there for 250 metres, then turn left NE up Manquhill Hill to Benbrack (580m) on the watershed.

On the east slope the Southern Upland Way is at first partly through forest, where the official map of the Way is essential for route finding, until a tarred road is joined at Polskeoch. This road is followed for 3 km as far as Polgown and then left to follow the Southern Upland Way NE over Cloud Hill and down the Whing Burn to Sanquhar.

## 87  New Cumnock to St John's Town of Dalry by Glen Afton
*42km/26miles*       *OS Sheets 71and 77.   Start 616 133.   Finish 626 814*
Follow the road S up Glen Afton for 9km to Afton Reservoir and then continue above the plantation on its west bank to the south end. From there keep S up the Afton Water and go over the col on the west side of Alhang, then down the Holm Burn, crossing it to the path on the slope of Mid Hill of

Glenhead and down the glen to Dalquhairn.

From there go SW down the Water of Ken by the road to Strahanna, then strike due S up the hillside by a forest track to Meikle Auchrae and S to join the Southern Upland Way 1km before reaching Stroanpatrick. Continue S by Culmark Hill, Butterhole Bridge and Ardoch to Dalry.

This route is shown as a road on Armstrong's 1773 map of Ayrshire.

## 87X  Eaglesham to Darvel

*13 km/8miles*              *OS Sheets 64 and 71.  Start 574 519.  Finish 574 411*

From Eaglesham take the road SE to Ardoch Burn and continue SW up it by Over Enoch to Carrot where the public road ends. From there a track goes S over Crook Hill (339m) to High Overmuir and down S by the east edge of the forest to join the minor road at Longgreen, 4km from Darvel.

# SECTION 7
# Arran

In this section only a few of the walking routes in Arran are described. Some of these are rights of way, but in general on Arran there is little difficulty in enjoying the freedom of the hills. Where there is room for doubt, a Hillphones system is in operation to enable walkers and climbers to check the access situation during the stalking season. There is a good bus service along the main road round Arran, and this is a great help for reaching the starts of the routes or returning to base at the end of the day. Local maps produced by Hugh McKerrell are recommended

## 88  Brodick to Sannox by Glen Rosa
*15km/9¹/₂ miles*          *OS Sheet 69. Start 012 360. Finish 016 454*
Leave Brodick northwards and take The String road (B880) for about 100 metres then turn right up the minor road to Glen Rosa. Beyond its end near a riverside campsite continue along the right of way by a track to the footbridge across the Garbh Allt and then by the footpath heading due N up the west side of the Glenrosa Water through the grandest of Arran's scenery, with the splendid peak of Cir Mhor straight ahead. The path has been much improved and it leads with a final steady climb to The Saddle, the pass between Cir Mhor and North Goatfell.
   The descent to the head of Glen Sannox is steep and rocky at first, but has been stabilised by some path works. Just below the steep section, the new path is initially on the right side of the stream, but crosses to the left side and about 200 metres further it leads to the old path. Continue along it on the left bank of the Sannox Burn for 2¹/₂ km before crossing  back to the right bank just before reaching the old barytes mine. Finally, go along a track and minor road past  the mine and a graveyard to reach the A841 road.

## 89  Brodick to Lochranza by Glen Rosa
*18km/11miles*          *OS Sheet 69. Start 012 360. Finish 933 505*
   From Brodick follow route 88 up Glen Rosa to the junction of paths at the foot of Fionn Choire at map ref 978 414.  Follow the left-hand path up this corrie, heading NNW then NW below the great granite spire of the Rosa Pinnacle to reach the col (560m) on the ridge between Cir Mhor and A'Chir. On the north-west side of this col descend quite steeply at first down a bouldery slope, then make a long descending traverse NNW across the grassy corrie on the west side of Caisteal Abhail to reach the pass at Loch na Davie. From there descend the path down Gleann Easan Biorach to Lochranza.

## 89X  Brodick to Pirnmill by Glen Rosa and Glen Iorsa
*24km/15miles*          *OS Sheet 69. Start 012 360. Finish 873 442*
   This route is regarded by many as the classic island crossing, but it is a great deal more arduous than either of the two preceding routes, being longer as well as pathless and very rough for half its distance and involving more

*The decent to Spittal of Glenshee from An Lairig on the right of way from Strath Ardle (route 159)*

*Looking up Glen Tilt from the hillside above Marble Lodge (route 177)*

*Ruthven Barracks at the north end of the Minigaig and Gaick passes (routes 178 and 179)*

*Sluggan Bridge across the River Dulnain (routes 203 and 205)*

climbing. Follow route 88 as far as the footbridge over the Garbh Allt in lower Glen Rosa and climb west up a rough and frequently muddy path on the north side of this burn. Continue N beside the Garbh Allt into Coire a' Bhradain and at its head reach the Bealach an Fhir-bhogha (*bowman's pass*). Descend N into a boulder-strewn corrie and go down to Glen Iorsa along the south side of the Allt Garbh-choire Dhuibh.

Cross the Iorsa Water just south of the point where this burn joins it and climb SW up very rough ground across Cnoc Breac Gamhainn to reach the south end of Loch Tanna. Then head NW round the north end of Dubh Loch and continue in the same direction to the Bealach an Fharaidh. Do not descend into Glas Choirein as it can be very boggy, but traverse N over Beinn Bhreac and follow the ridge NW then W to Meall Don. Descend SW to find the start of an old peat road at about map ref 893 447, and follow it down to the Allt Gobhlach and so to the tearoom at Pirnmill.

## 90  Lochranza to Dougarie (near Machrie) by Glen Iorsa
*19km/12miles*　　　　　*OS Sheet 69. Start 933 505. Finish 882 370*
This is a long route which is quite hard going as it is pathless and liable to be boggy for much of the way. Leave the A841 road at the signpost (map ref 944 498) near Ballarie at the south-east end of Lochranza where the road crosses the Easan Biorach. Follow the right of way by a well-defined path on the west bank of the burn, climbing gradually to the watershed where lies Loch na Davie, unique in Arran in that it has burns flowing from it both north and south. Then there is a long descent of Glen Iorsa, steep at first and largely pathless, but relieved by the fine views of the great range of hills on the east side of the glen.

Keep to the west bank of the Iorsa Water but well away from it, as this is a very wet glen, getting more boggy the further down one goes. About 6km from Loch na Davie, having crossed the Allt Tigh an Shiorraim, a faint path coming down from Loch Tanna may be discerned. Continue to keep well above the river along the lower slopes of Sail Chalmadale until Loch Iorsa is reached. From the boat house at the west end of the loch a good track passes through a gate in the deer fence and further on small signs and waymarker posts indicate the footpath over a number of stiles and walls to the road at map ref 882 370, passing between Dougarie farm and lodge. Machrie is 3km further south along the coast road.

## 90X  Catacol to Dougarie (near Machrie) by Loch Tanna and Glen Iorsa
*16km/10miles*　　　　　*OS Sheet 69. Start 910 490. Finish 882 370*
This alternative to route 90 starts 4km from Lochranza along the A841 road round the north-west coast of Arran. Leave the road on the north side of the bridge over the Catacol Burn (Abhainn Mor) at a signpost indicating 'Gleann Diomhan Nature Reserve & Loch Tanna 4 Miles'. The well-worn grassy path follows the east (right) bank of one of Scotland's finest mountain streams all the way up Glen Catacol to Loch Tanna, passing below the noted waterfall on the Allt nan Calman. Adders may be encountered in this glen and trout seen in the loch.

Continue along the west shore of Loch Tanna and the west bank of the Allt Tigh an Shiorraim, but keep well above the burn as the descent steepens, contouring round the lower slopes of Sail Chalmadale until the small boat house on Loch Iorsa comes into sight. Then descend to the track past the loch and reach Dougarie as described above.

## 90Y  Catacol to Lochranza by Gleann Diomhan
*12km/7¹/₂ miles*                    *OS Sheet 69.  Start 910 490.  Finish 933 505*
This is a further variation of the two preceding routes giving a short walk which may be extended to a complete circuit by walking along the road between Lochranza and Catacol.

From the bridge over the Catacol Burn follow the path up the north-east side of the burn and where the path forks in 2km keep left up Gleann Diomhan. In the Nature Reserve two species of service tree, *Sorbus pseudofennicus* and *Sorbus Arranensis*, the latter unique to Arran, are protected. The route continues to the boggy bealach between Beinn Bhreac and the eastern outliers of Beinn Tarsuinn.  Contour E below Beinn Bhreac to reach the head of Glen Iorsa and go N to Loch na Davie, thence N by the path down Gleann Easan Biorach to Lochranza.

## 90Z  Sannox to Lochranza by The Fallen Rocks
*13km/8miles*                    *OS Sheet 69.  Start 016 455.  Finish 933 505*
This is a very fine walk round the north-east corner of Arran where the rocky hillside drops steeply into the Firth of Clyde. Start about 100 metres north-west of the narrow road up Glen Sannox and cross the Sannox Burn by stepping stones. Then go along the shore to the mouth of the North Sannox Burn where it is usually easy to cross to the picnic place on the north side. This point can also be reached by road from the A841.

From a signpost indicating 'The Fallen Rocks' a good path goes N along the shore, passing the Measured Mile beacons. This is one of the best places in Arran to see basking sharks. Leave the forest and reach the Fallen Rocks, remains of an 18th-century landslide.  Beyond there the path is narrower, but easily followed past Millstone Point to the lonely white cottage at Laggan, near the sites of abandoned coal and salt workings which can still be traced 1km further along the shore. A grassy path zigzags up through the bracken above the cottage and then heads NW high above and parallel to the shore until the ruins of Cock Farm are seen about 1km ahead. Although it is possible to reach Lochranza round the north end of the island, the steep path leading W over the col to the south of Torr Meadhonach is more straightforward and gives better views.  From the col descend WSW for 2km to reach a narrow road, turn right along it for 800 metres and then turn left along the side of the golf course into Lochranza.

## 91  Monamore (near Lamlash) to Kilmory and Lagg
*16km/10miles*                    *OS Sheet 69.  Start 015 299.  Finish 961 215*
An old right of way goes from the Dyemill on The Ross road near Monamore Bridge to Kilmory and Lagg in the south-west corner of Arran. The

line of this route has been extensively overplanted by forests and is no longer a practical proposition for walkers, and an alternative way has come into use which passes through forest for virtually its whole length. Start from the Forest Enterprise carpark  and follow the main forest road which is waymarked as a cycle route. It goes SE at first, then S and there are some unexpectedly fine views where it passes above Whiting Bay. Then the road swings SW and a short diversion enables one to look at the Glenashdale Falls.  This point is accessible directly from Whiting Bay.

The road turns NW for 1½ km, then SW past remote Auchareoch, recently rebuilt after fire, to reach the A84 at Kilmory, 1½ km east of Lagg. To minimise walking along the main road, turn right along a minor road about 500 metres before reaching it to go W as far as Kilmory Church and turn left to the creamery at Laigh Kilmory, ½ km from Lagg and its choice of eating places.

A variation of the route described can be made about ½ km before reaching Auchareoch at a Forestry Commission signpost. Turn right and go along another road to Aucheleffan, where a track to the standing stones is signposted. Continue SW over the shoulder of Meall Buidhe and past the craft centre at Cloined to Kilmory Church, where the previous route is joined. This variation is not waymarked.

The approximate line of the old right of way from Monamore Glen can be followed for 3km SW to leave the forest and reach Urie Loch, an area rich in bird life. It is possible to continue a further 1km across the rising moor to Tighvein (458m), the highest point south of The Ross road and a fine viewpoint. However, the onward route from there towards Kilmory is not recommended.

### 91X  Lamlash to Brodick by Dun Fionn
*8km/5miles*                    *OS Sheet 69.  Start 032 316.  Finish  021 359*
This is perhaps the gem of the shorter walks in Arran. It has it all - pleasant farmland, an ancient fortified summit with seaward views, a dramatic skyline formed by the northern mountains and the best view of the Holy Island. It can easily be done in half a day.

Leave Lamlash along the shore road towards Clauchlands Point, turn uphill at the sign to Oakbank Farm and go up the steep brae, taking the right fork to an old house called Prospect Hill. The right of way goes just west of the house through woods, across a burn and a fence, then N along the edge of a field to a farm track. Turn E at the signpost past two houses and just beyond the second one, before Clauchlands Farm, cross a stile and climb diagonally NE up a field to a gate and then towards the prominent knoll of Dun Fionn. The summit is the site of an ancient hill fort and commands a superb view.  Descend W for 200 metres to join a path and follow it N through forest for a short distance, then  along a lane past Corriegills Farm and by a narrow road to reach the eastern outskirts of Brodick.

# SECTION 8
# Argyll

## 92  Holy Loch to Ardtaraig (Loch Striven)
*17km/10½ miles      OS Sheets 63 and 56.  Start 133 814.  Finish 060 829↑*
 The start of this walk is on the B836 road about 2km west of the head of the Holy Loch at the foot of Glen Kin.  The way up this glen described in the previous edition of this guidebook is no longer possible, the track south of Stronsaul having been obliterated by clear-felling of the forest.  The best route now is along the road high on the west side of Glen Kin to map ref 121 782 where there is a picnic shelter beside the road.  Opposite this, follow a path SW uphill through the forest to emerge at a stile onto the steep grassy hillside.  Climb beside the forest to its upper edge and continue SW along a fence to the flat Bealach na Sreine, where three fences meet.

 Descend W down quite steep grassy slopes to cross the burn in the Inverchaolain Glen, and go along a path high above the burn on its west side to a small lochan, from where a recently made road leads down to the narrow public road beside Loch Striven.  Go N along this road by the lochside for 2km  to the SRWS signpost which indicates the right of way to Ardtaraig.  The last 4½ km of this walk follow this right of way, at first beside the loch and then higher up on the hillside above the loch through attractive oak and birch woods, where pleasant stretches of grassy path alternate with some very wet and boggy sections.  Waymarkers show the route at several points.

## 93  The Younger Botanic Garden (Loch Eck) to Glenbranter
*15km/9½ miles            OS Sheet 56.  Start 141 855.  Finish 113 980*
 This is hardly a hill track, as the route follows a private road along the west side of Loch Eck without any climbing, however it does give a very pleasant walk along the side of this fine fiord-like loch.  It can be combined with a visit to the Younger Botanic Garden and a walk up and down Puck's Glen whose entrance is about 1km south of the Botanic Garden carpark along the A815 road.  For the Loch Eck walk, go round the north side of the garden to Benmore Home Farm and continue N along the road quite close to the lochside.  The Paper Cave, which is passed after about 4km, is in the forest about 100 metres above the loch, and can be more easily reached  from the upper forest road.  According to tradition, the deeds and documents of the Campbell family were hidden in the cave during troubled times at the end of the 17th century  when Cowal was plundered by Highlanders from Atholl.  The lochside road leads to Glenbranter village, and it is possible to walk a further 5km along a minor public road to Strachur on the shore of Loch Fyne.

## 94  Ardentinny to Carrick Castle
*9km/5½miles            OS Sheet 56.  Start 188 875.  Finish 194 945*
 This short walk goes along the west shore of Loch Long just south of its junction with Loch Goil.  Start from Ardentinny and go round the shoreline of Finart Bay by a private road and path to Stronvochlan, where there is a carpark

at the end of the public road. It is possible to start the walk from there at map ref 191 885. Follow the forest road, uphill NW at first, then E and NE above Loch Long, gradually dropping to the lochside at Knap. 1km further the road climbs again under the electricity transmission lines to reach the tall pylon on the west side of Loch Long. From there go N through the forest by a waymarked path. After about ½ km the path descends through natural oakwoods to Loch Goil. Go along the grassy fringe below the woods past Ardnahein to reach the road end 1km from Carrick Castle. From there it is a further 9km to Lochgoilhead along a narrow and fairly quiet road.

### 95  Lochgoilhead to Invernoaden or Strachur by the Curra Lochain
*11km/7miles*          *OS Sheet 56. Start 188 999. Finish 118 977 or 099 011*
This walk goes across the rough hilly peninsula west of Loch Goil, crossing the pass between Beinn Bheula and Beinn Lochain, the two highest peaks in this area. The route described in the previous edition of this guidebook is now very difficult if not impossible to follow on the north side of the Lettermay Burn due to windblown trees, but a perfectly good alternative is possible. Start just south of Lettermay and walk up the forest road heading W. In 1km take the right-hand road down to the Lettermay Burn, do not cross it but continue SW along a narrow path on its right bank. 1km further emerge from the forest and head W up steeper grassy slopes on the south side of the waterfall to reach flatter ground at the east end of Curra Lochain.

Cross the burn and continue W along a path on the north side of the lochan and over the grassy Bealach an Lochain. A few hundred metres beyond a small fank go left through a clearing in the forest towards the Leavanin Burn and follow a faint path high on its north side. Then go down easy grassy slopes towards the burn, cross it at map ref 130 004 and reach the forest road which encircles Beinn Lagan. This road may either be followed S to Invernoaden or round the north side of Beinn Lagan to Strachur.

### 96  Lochgoilhead to Invernoaden by Lochain nan Cnaimh
*11km/7miles*          *OS Sheet 56. Start 188 999. Finish 123 975*
This walk has the same starting and finishing points as route 95, but is less frequented as can be seen in its highest part where signs of the path which once existed are now almost gone. Go W along the forest road beyond Lettermay for 1km, then take the left-hand road heading SW and follow its continuation along a path through a gradually ascending fire-break. At its end climb steeply SE up the path beside the stream flowing from Lochain nan Cnaimh. Go round the west end of the lochan and climb SW up rough grassy slopes to the col between Beinn Bheula and Cnoc na Tricriche. There is virtually no sign of a path, but a few decaying marker posts indicate the line to follow.

From the col go SW down the grassy upper slopes of Coire Ealt, preferably on the south side of the main burn in the corrie to reach the upper edge of the Loch Eck Forest, much of it now felled. Turn right along the forest road to cross the Coire Ealt burn and continue NW gradually downhill to the A815 road a short distance from Invernoaden.

It is possible to combine routes 95 and 96 in an energetic circular walk.

## 97  Ardgartan (Loch Long) to Lochgoilhead
*10 to 19km/6 to 12miles        OS Sheet 56.  Start 270 037.  Finish 198 015*
There are three possible routes from Ardgartan to Lochgoilhead, two of them fairly direct over the cols to the north and south of The Brack, and the third much longer, going almost round the Ardgoil peninsula.

The Forest Enterprise office at the foot of Glen Croe is a convenient starting place.

(a) Go NW up the forest road on the south side of the Croe Water for 3½ km, climbing gradually to a height of about 230m. A waymarker shows the start of the path  which climbs S to the col between The Brack and Ben Donich.  From the col go SW downhill on the north side of the Allt Coire Odhair and after entering the forest cross this burn and continue along a gradually descending path to meet  another path in a wide fire-break. Go down it and soon reach a well made path which leads down to a forest road which in turn leads to Lochgoilhead.

(b) Go S along the private road past Ardgartan for 2km and keep right above Coilessan. A short distance further turn right up the Coilessan Glen and go to the bend at the top of the forest road, then continue W by a path to the col between The Brack and Cnoc Coinnich.  Descend grassy slopes to enter the forest and go down a wide clearing to join the previous route.

(c) Start along route (b) and at the Coilessan Glen keep going SSW along the main forest road for a further 7km to reach Corran Lochan near the tip of the Ardgoil peninsula. Turn N and follow a path, very boggy but waymarked, which climbs slightly to cross a col at 300m. Continue along the path, which is fairly rough in places, until it descends steeply to reach the road in the Ardgoil Forest above Stuckbeg.  Finally, go N along this road for almost 4km to reach Lochgoilhead.

## 98  Butterbridge (Glen Kinglas) to Ardlui (Loch Lomond)
*12km/7¹/₂ miles        OS Sheet 56.  Start 236 096.  Finish 317 154*
For most of its length this route follows a well made track, but there is a short pathless section where it crosses the north ridge of Ben Vorlich just above Ardlui. The starting and finishing points of the route are both accessible by public transport services, the south end being on the bus route between Arrochar and Inveraray, and the north end on the West Highland Railway as well as the bus route between Tarbet and Crianlarich.

From Butterbridge in Glen Kinglas follow the track NE up the glen past Abyssinia cottage and through a section of forest to reach the head of Srath Dubh-uisge.  The track ends at a small aqueduct on the south-east side of this wide glen. Go NE along the aqueduct for a short distance and continue in the same direction for about 1km along a grassy path which crosses a succession of little dams and weirs which collect water for Loch Sloy.  At the last dam (map ref 300 156) bear E up the grassy hillside to the 390m col just south of Stob an Fhithich and descend a wide grassy gully on the east side of this col towards Ardlui.  Lower down, a path appears and can be followed past Garristuck cottage to reach the A82 road about 100 metres south of Ardlui station.

**98X   Circuit of the Arrochar Alps through Coiregrogain and Glen Loin**
*15km/9¹/₂ miles*                                      *OS Sheet 56.   Start and finish 294 049*
   This interesting circular walk goes through the heart of the Arrochar Alps,
passing between the five best known peaks of this group including The Cobbler
and Beinn Ime.  Start from the carpark at the head of Loch Long, cross the A83
road and go up the much-trodden route to The Cobbler along the remains of
an old narrow gauge rail track.  At 320m a horizontal track is reached and
followed  SW to a dam on the Allt a' Bhalachain. Continue up the path on the
north-east side of this burn to its source at the col between The Cobbler and
Beinn Narnain.  Go N along a path to reach a fence crossing the Bealach a'
Mhaim, and continue NE along this fence to descend grassy slopes at the
head of Coiregrogain. Lower down, once the first trees are reached, bear left
across the burn to reach the end of a track and go down it to join a wider road
at a dam.
   At that point the shortest way goes right along the road through the forest
round the lower slopes of A'Chrois to return to the head of Loch Long.  A
better route goes to the left down the north side of Coiregrogain, and across
the stream flowing from Loch Sloy.  ½ km beyond the bridge go right to cross
the Inveruglas Water and follow a recently made footpath SE through the forest
to the clearing under the electricity transmission lines in Glen Loin. Continue
S along the path, which becomes a track and leads down the east side of the
glen to Stronafyne and the A83 road at the head of Loch Long.

**99  Loch Fyne to Inverarnan (Glen Falloch)**
*17km/11miles*                      *OS Sheet 56.  Start 194 125.  Finish 317 185*
   This is another route whose two end points are on bus routes.  Start from
the A83 road at the head of Loch Fyne and walk along the private road  to the
bridge 1km beyond Glenfyne Lodge.  Cross to the east side of the glen and
continue up the road to the reservoir on the Allt na Lairige.  Go along the
south side of the reservoir and continue by pathless and boggy ground over
the Lairig Arnan to the end of another road on the north side of the Allt Arnan.
Go down this road to Glen Falloch Farm just over 1km north of Inverarnan,
the famous drovers' inn of two centuries ago.  It is possible to reach Inverarnan
more directly down the hillside beside the Allt Arnan.
   An alternative and slightly longer route (20km/13miles) goes right up Glen
Fyne to the end of the path 3km beyond Inverchorachan.  Leave the glen just
beyond that point and go E along the Allt Coir' an Longairt for 3km to reach
the hydro-electric road in  Gleann nan Caorann.  Finally, go down this road to
Glen Falloch Farm.
   Another very much longer route (32km/20miles) starts from the A83 road
at the foot of Glen Shira, 2km north-east of Inveraray (map ref 112 103).  Go
up the private road in Glen Shira  on the south-east side of the River Shira to
reach Lochan Shira.  Cross the dam and continue along the road on the north
side of the reservoir and across a col to reach the head of Glen Fyne.  Descend
E along the right bank of the headwaters of the River Fyne to reach the preceding
route at the Allt Coir'an Longairt and continue to Inverarnan as described
above.

## 100  Dalmally to Inverarnan (Glen Falloch)
*21km/13miles*                    *OS Sheet 50.  Start 193 275.  Finish 317 185*
     This route follows part of a very important old drove road from Dalmally
to Inverarnan and onwards to The Trossachs and the trysts of central
Scotland.  The walk may be started from the A85 road in Strath Orchy 3km
east of Dalmally.  From there go along the private road to Succoth Lodge, and
follow the track SE along the north side of the Eas a' Ghaill to the line of electricity transmission pylons.  Continue along the track under the pylons
through the native woodland of the Ben Lui Nature Reserve to a gate at its
edge.  Go up the Allt a' Chaorainn and cross the pass (470m) between Beinn
a' Chleibh and Meall nan Tighearn, then follow the Allt a' Mhinn downstream, with the electricity pylons in sight on the left, to reach the end of a
hydro-electric road.  Follow this road ESE down the south side of Gleann nan
Caorann to reach the A82 at Glen Falloch Farm just over 1km north of
Inverarnan.  The Glasgow to Oban bus service passes both ends of this route.

## 101  Furnace (Loch Fyne) to Durran (Loch Awe)
*11km/7miles*                    *OS Sheet 55.  Start 029 032↑.  Finish 958 080↑*
     Start from the A83 road at Auchindrain, about 3km north of Furnace, and
follow a minor road SW for 1km to the bridge over the Leacann Water.  Go
steeply up the zigzag track NW into the forest and continue W out of the forest along a path to Loch Leacann, then NW past Loch Airigh na Craige to re-
enter the forest.  After 1km cross the Allt nan Sac by a footbridge to join a
forest road and follow it, first SW for ½km, then NW on the north-east side
of the Abhainn a' Bhealaich as far as map ref 963 075 where a path diverges
left from the forest road.  Follow this path, which is not very well defined, out
of the forest and into a field to reach a cottage along the outside edge of the
forest.  Finally, go down a track to the B840 road at Durran.

## 102  Furnace (Loch Fyne) to Ford (Loch Awe)
*20km/12½miles*                    *OS Sheet 55.  Start 024 019.  Finish 889 038↑*
     Start from the A83 road 2km north of Furnace and cross the 18th-century
stone bridge to follow a private road past Brenchoillie, where the minor road
from Auchindrain is joined.  Go WSW along a road into the forest and pass
under a power line where the route forks.  The way ahead continues by a forest road, or alternatively the original route which is more interesting can still
be followed by going NW along the  right-hand track for about 400 metres
uphill, then turning WSW to cross the headstreams of the Abhainn Dubhan,
after which the track is overgrown.  Then a defined grassy stretch, boggy in
places,  leads to the forest road mentioned above.  After leaving the forest,
continue along a rough track to the partly restored bothy at Carron.
     From there go NW uphill, steeply at first, along a rough track which is
indistinct in places and crosses  open country past several lochans on the
undulating moorland.  About 1½km from Loch Awe cross an estate road and
continue NW downhill to reach the B840 road near the ruined Kilneuair
Church.  Keep left at a junction just before reaching the church.

### 103  Furnace (Loch Fyne) to Kilmichael Glassary
*20km/12¹/₂ miles*          *OS Sheet 55.  Start 024 019.  Finish 859 935*
  Go by route 102 to the bothy at Carron, beyond which the route is affected by forestry operations in the Knockalava area.  The original line of the right of way goes slightly north of the route described below and is difficult to locate.  From the bothy continue SW through an iron gate into the forest, at first along a grassy break with no path, then becoming more defined.  After 1¹/₂ km turn right (marker post at map ref 931 986) by a stone dyke and almost immediately join a forest road.  It is best to follow this road for 4km until it leads out of the forest by a gate into open country.  Continue to Lechuary and the minor public road which leads to Kilmichael Glassary.
  Routes 102 and 103 are shown on Roy's map of 1755.  In droving times Kilmichael Glassary was a tryst for drovers coming from Islay, Jura and southwest Argyll, and route 103 was an important drove road.

### 104  Dalavich (Loch Awe) to Kilmore (Loch Feochan)
*18km/11¹/₂ miles*          *OS Sheets 49 and 55.  Start 970 139.  Finish 877 254*
  Start from Barnaline Lodge about 1¹/₂ km north of Dalavich and walk along the forest road on the south-west side of the River Avich past the falls to cross the river by a footbridge and reach the public road on the north side of the river.  This part of the route is the historic String of Lorne; it continues round the east end of Loch Avich to Lochavich House and then at an SRWS signpost goes NNW up the track past Loch na Sreinge (loch of the string) just beyond which is Carn Chailein where Macailein Mor was slain in 1294.  Just beyond the cairn take the path on the left which continues NW above the Allt Bragleenmore, gradually descending to the glen.  From the farm of the same name go W for 2km along the north side of Loch Scammadale, then N up a track by the Eas Ruadh to enter the forest, where the route is well cleared and signposted and leads NW to Balinoe, 1km south of Kilmore on the A816 road.

### 105  Kilchrenan (Loch Awe) to Kilmore (Loch Feochan)
*20km/12¹/₂ miles*          *OS Sheets 49 and 50.  Start 037 230↑.  Finish 877 254*
  Kilchrenan can be reached by bus from Oban.  This route follows the line of the old drove road and right of way.  The first section going W from Kilchrenan crosses open ground on the north side of the Allt na h-Airigh to enter the forest and go along a ride to meet a forest road on the north side of An Dun.  Continue N to reach the Bealach Mor and descend from there to join the private hydro-road on the south side of Loch Nant.  The section just described, of the right of way going through the forest, is quite wet, and also requires some navigational skill.  An option is to go along the hydro-road from Achnacraob 1km north of Kilchrenan, which leads without difficulty to the junction with the above forest road.
  From the south-east corner of Loch Nant, follow the hydro-road going W to the head of the loch, cross the Abhainn Cam Linne and continue on its north side to Sior Loch and the ruin of Midmuir.  Just beyond there the track goes through a col between two rocky knolls, and a stony path branches off

left to lead in 2km down to the narrow public road in Glen Feochan. Kilmore is 6km further on along this road.

Both routes 104 and 105 end at the village of Kilmore, which is 5km as the crow flies south of Oban. The most pleasant way of walking from Kilmore to Oban is to follow the minor road north to Loch Nell, and go from there to Oban by Glen Cruitten. This adds 8km/5miles to the lengths of these two walks.

# SECTION 9
# Loch Lomond to Loch Tay

### 106 Queenzieburn to Kippen
*25km/15½miles*        *OS Sheets 57 and 64. Start 693 773. Finish 652 948*
Go N from Queenzieburn by road uphill to Corrie. Beyond there a well-used track continues up to the Birkenburn Reservoir. Cross the dam and continue N alongside a fence for about 200 metres until it meets another fence at right angles. Go W along this for almost 300 metres to a third fence going N, and follow this down to the edge of the mature forest at map ref 674 814, where a stile gives access to the forest road which is followed down to Burnhouse. From there take the forest road NW along the south side of the Carron Valley Reservoir to the dam at its west end.

Go E on the B818 road for 200 metres, then NE by a minor public road through the forest for 1km. At map ref 684 865 turn N along a track to the ruined house at Cringate and continue NW up the Endrick Water keeping to high ground, with no real track, to Burnfoot, which is also a ruin. The Burnfoot Burn may be difficult to cross if it is in spate. Continue by a rough vehicle track past the Spout of Ballochleam (waterfall) and down to Ballochleam farm. Go NE along the minor public road for 1km until, just beyond Auldhall, turn left along a track over the Boquhan Burn to reach Dasher, from where it is 1½km to Kippen.

### 107 Drymen to Aberfoyle
*16km/10miles*        *OS Sheet 57. Start 474 885. Finish 520 010*
Go N from Drymen by the old Gartmore road, climbing gradually to Bat a' Charchel (229m), then in another 2km (just before Drymen Road Cottage) turn left into the Queen Elizabeth Forest Park. Coloured signs mark the way from there through the Loch Ard Forest, which is a maze of roads. Significant landmarks to aim for are the junctions at map refs 486 964, 496 979 and 496 984. From the last of these the forest road goes NE to Aberfoyle. An alternative starting point is Auchentroig - see route 108.

### 108 Drymen to Kinlochard
*21km/13miles or18km/11miles  OS Sheet 57. Start 474 885. Finish 455 023*
From Drymen follow route 107 to the Queen Elizabeth Forest Park, or take the Aberfoyle bus or go by car to Auchentroig Old Schoolhouse (map ref 534 926) on the main A81 road and from there go W by the road past Hoish to join route 107 at map ref 506 936 (where there is parking). The way onwards is marked by coloured signs. Follow route 107 to map ref 496 984 and then go WNW, crossing the Duchray Water to reach Couligartan on the south shore of Loch Ard. Finally, go W round the head of the loch to Kinlochard.

## 109  Aberfoyle to Rowardennan

*19km/12miles*          *OS Sheets 56 and 57.   Start 520 010.   Finish 360 986*
Two ways are possible for this route, which crosses the south ridge of Ben
Lomond 3km south of its summit:
(a) Cross the River Forth towards Kirkton and in 200 metres turn right to
go past Lochan Spling and Duchray Castle and at map ref 466 992 join route
108 for 2km.  Shortly after passing under an aqueduct, turn sharp left at map
ref 453 004 on to another track passing back under the same aqueduct.  Turn
due S after 100m to cross the Duchray Water and take the next turn right up
a new forest road.  This heads in a westerly direction and past a quarry forks
left to continue and cross the Bruach Caorainn Burn, then immediately
rejoins the interrupted 'blue route' (bridge undergoing replacement, map ref
423 013, at the time of writing).  Continue west uphill to the broad south
ridge of Ben Lomond and reach the well-made hill path for the final 2km
down through forest to Rowardennan.
(b) For a slightly shorter route, go W by road from Aberfoyle for 2km to
Milton, turn left and after crossing the River Forth take the second forest road
on the right which goes WSW in an almost straight line to map ref 453 004
near Couligartan, where route (a) is joined.
The walking distance can be further shortened by starting from Kinlochard
and going S round the head of Loch Ard to join route (b) near Couligartan.
Coloured signs (blue for Rowardennan) make it easy to follow these routes.

## 110  Rowardennan to Inversnaid and Inverarnan

*12km/7¹/₂miles and 23km/14¹/₂miles*
                    *OS Sheet 56.   Start 360 986.   Finish 337 089↑ and 318 185*
This route follows part of the West Highland Way along the east side of
Loch Lomond. Scenically it is one of the best parts of the Way and is very
popular. As a result the path has been subject to severe erosion and a great
deal of work has been done in the last fifteen years to contain this damage.
Rowardennan can be reached by road via Balmaha, or by ferry from Inverbeg
(April to September). A very pleasant day in summer can be had by taking this
ferry across the loch, walking to Inverarnan and getting the bus back to
Inversnaid.  From Rowardennan a private road goes N past Ptarmigan Lodge.
Continue along the forest road for 4 km beyond the lodge to its end just
beyond Rowchoish bothy and onwards by the footpath past Cailness to
Inversnaid Hotel. From there it may be possible to cross Loch Lomond by private ferry to Inveruglas, and there is a Post Bus service to Aberfoyle.  The
route to Inverarnan continues N past Rob Roy's Cave and onwards by the
path past Doune and Ardleish to Beinglas Farm. There cross the River Falloch
to reach the A82 road 300 metres north of Inverarnan.

## 111  Aberfoyle to Callander

*12km/7¹/₂miles*          *OS Sheet 57.   Start 541 006.   Finish 627 080*
This walk through the Menteith Hills starts from the A81 road 2km east of
Aberfoyle at a Forest Enterprise carpark just beyond the east end of Aberfoyle
golf course. Go NE uphill through the forest by a road, then a path, for 2¹/₂ km

to the north-east edge of the forest and continue for 1km along a path across open moorland. Re-enter the forest along the path through the pass which divides the Menteith Hills in two and reach a small lochan, from where a track goes down to East Lodge on the minor road on the south side of Loch Venachar. From there it is 4km along this road to Callander

## 112 Callander to The Trossachs
*18km/11miles* OS Sheet 57. Start 627 080. Finish 495 072

The first part of this route is along the minor public road from Callander westwards on the south side of Loch Venachar, usually a quiet and pleasant walk. 2km beyond West Dullater, before reaching the grounds of Invertrossachs House, go uphill to Culnagreine and the path leading W. Skirting the north end of Loch Drunkie, go W by forest roads to the Black Water and the east end of Loch Achray and follow the path along the south side of this loch.

At the Loch Achray Hotel take the forest road W and keep straight ahead to the sluices at the outflow of Loch Katrine. Cross the Achray Water and return by road to the A821 at a point midway between Loch Achray and Loch Katrine. The end of the road at Loch Katrine is the starting point of route 114 to Inverarnan, or less energetically, a cruise on the loch.

Alternatively, 2km beyond Loch Drunkie go N across the Black Water by the bridge at map ref 533 064 and then E by road to Brig o' Turk, where the south end of route 115 is joined.

## 113 Kinlochard to The Trossachs by Ben Venue.
*10km/6miles* OS Sheet 57. Start 459 023. Finish 503 063

From Ledard, on the north side of Loch Ard, go up the path beside the Ledard Burn, at first on the west side along the edge of the forest, then on the east side. As the head of the glen is reached, go NE across the col between Beinn Bhreac and Creag a' Bhealaich and continue along the level path just below the ridge leading to Ben Venue to reach another col, marked by a cairn. From there climb a steep rocky path up to the north-west top of Ben Venue (729m). Continue along a path which leads to the south-east top. From there descend S to the point where a path enters the Achray Forest. In the forest this path has been much improved in recent years and it leads down Gleann Riabhach to a road which in turn leads to the Loch Achray Hotel.

If you do not want to climb Ben Venue, leave the route described above at a cairn on the col between it and Creag a' Bhealaich. From there go SE down a rather discontinuous path into the head of Gleann Riabhach to reach the edge of the forest where the route described above is joined.

## 114 Loch Katrine (Stronachlachar or The Trossachs) to Inverarnan (Glen Falloch)
*13km/8miles. OS Sheets 56 and 57. Start 400 100 or 495 072. Finish 318 185*

From Stronachlachar, which may be reached by Post Bus from Aberfoyle, go NW along the private road on the south shore of Loch Katrine to its west end. From there follow the rough track up Glen Gyle below a line of electricity pylons for 3km and continue beyond the end of the track for a further 2km on the north-east side of Glengyle Water (indistinct path) to the col at the head of the glen. Descend NW down a wide boggy corrie to cross the Ben Glas Burn and reach the path on its north side. Follow this path down to Beinglas farm and cross the River Falloch to reach the A82 road 300 metres north of Inverarnan and 3km north of Ardlui.

From The Trossachs this route may be started by taking the Loch Katrine steamer *Sir Walter Scott* (during summer months only) to Stronachlachar and continuing as above. Alternatively, walk along the private road from the east end of Loch Katrine on the north shore of the loch to its west end and continue as in (a), in which case the total distance is 25km/15miles.

This route (in reverse) was, together with route 100 from Dalmally to Inverarnan, one of the most important drove roads in Argyll. The hotel at Inverarnan, now a popular climbers' hostelry, was two centuries ago an equally well used drovers' inn.

### 115  The Trossachs (Brig o' Turk) to Balquhidder or Strathyre

*16km/10miles     OS Sheet 57.  Start 537 066.  Finish 534 208↑ or 561 172*
From Brig o' Turk go N along a minor road for ³/₄km and turn right, uphill, on the branch which goes N on the east side of the Glen Finglas Reservoir. Continue up Gleann nam Meann on a rough hill road to map ref 517 148 where the road turns W. From there go NE at first for about 300 metres on a very faint grassy path (cairn on the right) to a gate in a fence. Continue along a much more obvious path descending N to Gleann Dubh and and then E to Ballimore. Finally, go down the road in Glen Buckie to Balquhidder.

To reach Strathyre, go E from Ballimore to Immeroin, climb SE up grassy slopes (very faint path) over the south shoulder of Beinn an t-Sithein (gate in deer fence) and finally go down a waymarked path through the forest to Strathyre.

### 116  Inverlochlarig to Inverarnan

*15km/9¹/₂ miles     OS Sheets 56 and 57.  Start 446 184.  Finish 318 185*
This is the old coffin route from Glen Falloch to Balquhidder, as the name of the pass Bealach nan Corp (*pass of the corpses*) indicates. One can start by walking an additional 10km/6miles from Balquhidder along the narrow public road on the north side of Loch Voil and Loch Doine to the carpark at its end, ³/₄km east of Inverlochlarig farm, which is on the site of the house where Rob Roy died.

Walk up the glen past the farm on a good track for 5km. Beyond its end continue for 2km beside the headwaters of the River Larig and make a rising traverse on the south side of the river to the Bealach nan Corp at map ref 360 160. This col is broad and boggy and may be confusing in mist.

Bear W to pass through a fence at the foot of Sidhean a' Chatha, then go NW on a slightly descending traverse across the grassy south-west flank of Parlan Hill to reach the col at the head of Glen Gyle where there is a small lochan and the old drove road, route 114, is joined. Descend NW down a wide boggy corrie to cross the Ben Glas Burn and reach the path on its north side. Follow this down to Beinglas farm and the A82 road in Glen Falloch 300 metres north of Inverarnan.

It is equally possible to follow the River Larig to its source at the col between Parlan Hill and Beinn Chabhair, cross this col and descend to Lochan Beinn Chabhair and the start of the path down to Beinglas farm.

## 117 Balquhidder to Crianlarich
*20km/12¹/₂ miles*

OS Sheets 50, 51,56 and 57. Start 534 208↑. Finish 414 258

Follow the public road W from Balquhidder to Inverlochlarig farm, with some beautiful sections along the side of Loch Voil. Alternatively the walk may be started at the carpark at the end of the public road ³/₄ km east of Inverlochlarig, thereby reducing the distance by 10km. From the farm go N along a road up the Inverlochlarig Glen and continue over the bealach between Stob Garbh and Stob Binnein. Go down the Benmore Glen on the east side of the Benmore Burn to join another bulldozed road below the west slopes of Ben More and follow this down to the A85 a short distance east of Benmore Farm and 3km east of Crianlarich.

## 118 Balquhidder to Killin by Glen Dochart
*16km/10miles*        OS Sheet 51. Start 534 208↑. Finish 571 325

From Balquhidder Church go N up the road through the forest, then by a path beyond it on the east side of the Kirkton Glen to reach the huge boulder called Rob Roy's Putting Stone. Continue below the frowning crag Leum an Eireannaich (*the Irishman's leap*) to Lochan an Eireannaich at the bealach. Descend N down the east side of the Ledcharrie Burn to the A85 road at Ledcharrie farm, where at the time of writing walkers may have to negotiate a morass of cattle slurry. To reach Killin, go E along the A85 for about 200 metres, then cross the River Dochart and continue down its north side by the minor road to Killin.

The route from Balquhidder to Glen Dochart is shown as a road on Roy's map of 1755 and named Lairig Earne.

## 119 Ardchullarie (Loch Lubnaig) to Lochearnhead
*12km/7¹/₂ miles*        OS Sheets 51 and 57. Start 584 136↑. Finish 589 238

Ardchullarie More is on the east side of Loch Lubnaig, 10km north of Callander on the A84 road, and 5km south of Strathyre. From a roadside carpark go uphill on the private road leading to the house for only 50 metres and keep left along a path which climbs steeply NE to enter the forest. Higher up join a forest road which goes N up the glen. Beyond the forest a path continues over the watershed, from where it is 7km down Glen Ample below the west slopes of Stuc a' Chroin to Glenample farm. As you approach the farm take a path on the left which leads down to a footbridge over the Burn of Ample and follow the right of way on the west side of the burn through pleasant woodland. About ¹/₂ km further, join the private road leading down to the Falls of Edinample, 2km by road from Lochearnhead.

## 120   Callander to Ardvorlich (Loch Earn)

*18km/11¹/₂miles        OS Sheets 51 and 57.   Start 633 077.   Finish 633 232↑*
This is a fine route, much used at both its south and north ends as approaches to Ben Vorlich. From Callander take the narrow public road signposted to the Bracklinn Falls to its end at Braeleny farm. It is possible to drive to within a short distance of the farm, a distance of 3¹/₂ km. Continue N along the track to Arivurichardich and climb the obvious path rising across the west slope of Meall Odhar and over Meall na h-Iolaire into Gleann an Dubh Choirein. Descend NE by a faint path to a footbridge just below the junction of streams in this glen near the ruined bothy of Dubh Choirein.

From there go N up the deep glen between Ben Vorlich and Meall na Fearna, following traces of a path. Be careful in misty weather as you approach the head of the glen not to go up either of the burns that flow down from Meall na Fearna, but keep heading NNW to cross the bealach at about 590m. This part of the route is very impressive, as the east face of Ben Vorlich rises steeply for 400m directly above the pass. Descend towards Glen Vorlich along traces of a path marked by wooden posts. Lower down the path improves and eventually a track leads down the west side of the burn to Ardvorlich. From there it is 6km by road to Lochearnhead.

The amount of climbing can be reduced, and the distance increased by about 4km, by going ENE from Arivurichardich along a track to the bridge over the Allt an Dubh Choirein, and then following the path up the north-east side of this stream to Dubh Choirein.

## 121   Callander to Comrie by Glen Artney

*24km/15miles              OS Sheet 57.   Start 633 077.   Finish  768 220*
Go by route 120 to the bridge at map ref 642 130 near Arivurichardich. Then continue ENE below Meall Odhar and Tom Odhar along a pleasant grassy track to the crossing of the Allt an Dubh Choirein, and in another 2km reach the end of the public road in Glen Artney, 300 metres from the bridge over the Water of Ruchill. From there the road goes down the south side of Glen Artney to Comrie.  A better route for walkers instead of going along the public road is not to cross the bridge over the Water of Ruchill, but to cross a stile and go NE to a bridge over the Allt Srath a' Ghlinne and follow a path, then a track, on the north side of the Water of Ruchill. Approaching Blairmore, where the track goes uphill, keep  straight on along a path through woods to the continuation of the track which becomes a minor public road at Dalrannoch, 2¹/₂ km from Comrie.

"Lone Glen Artney's hazel shade" figures in Sir Walter Scott's *Lady of the Lake*. This route is shown as a road on Stobie's 1783 map of Perthshire.

## 122   Comrie to Ardeonaig (Loch Tay)

*20km/12¹/₂ miles             OS Sheet 51.   Start 770 221.   Finish  670 358↑*
From the centre of Comrie take the quiet public road up Glen Lednock, which is finely wooded for the first 2km.  Go past Invergeldie and 1km further cross the bridge over the River Lednock at map ref 732 279 to continue by the tarred road on the south side of  Loch Lednock Reservoir. Go round the head

ol the reservoir across the river and climb NE up grassy slopes for almost ½ km to reach the indistinct old track which climbs NW up the hillside. Careful route-finding is necessary as there are many sheep tracks over the SW shoulder of Creag Uchdag, and the col that you are aiming for between Ruadh Mheall and Creag Uchdag is rather featureless. Beyond it go NNW down the grassy glen, with barely any trace of a path, to the site of old shielings at the head of the Finglen Burn. Below there a path appears and leads down the right bank of the burn to Ardeonaig.

### 123  Comrie to Ardtalnaig (Loch Tay)
*24km/15miles*                    *OS Sheet 51. Start 770 221. Finish 702 393*↑
Follow route 122 for 6km up Glen Lednock as far as Coishavachan and continue N along a track on the west side of the Invergeldie Burn. The track crosses to the east side of the burn and heads NE towards Ben Chonzie, but before long, at map ref 755 291, take a left turn and follow the track back to the Invergeldie Burn and up it to its end. Continue NNW up to the bealach (633m) by a boggy and indistinct path which loses itself in the peaty terrain. There is, however, no difficulty in finding the way in clear weather. Descend NW across the grassy hillside (no path) to the footbridge and SRWS signpost just east of Dunan near the head of Glen Almond. This section is very featureless and in bad visibility a map and compass are essential, particularly if doing this route in reverse and climbing from the footbridge towards the bealach. From Dunan go N by a rough road over the watershed and down Gleann a' Chilleine to Ardtalnaig.

### 124  Newton Bridge or Amulree to Ardtalnaig (Loch Tay)
*25km/16miles*    *OS Sheet 52. Start 887 315*↑ *or 899 364. Finish 702 393*↑
This walk goes for most of its length along the upper part of Glen Almond, following a private road. Newton Bridge is on the A822 road in the Sma' Glen, 13km north-east of Crieff and 5 km south of Amulree. From there go W up Glen Almond by the track on the north bank of the River Almond for about 19km to Dunan. Continue N across the watershed and along the rough road down Gleann a' Chilleine to Ardtalnaig.
An alternative start to this walk, which increases the distance by about 2km, is from Amulree. Go along the minor road in Glen Quoich for 4km to Croftmill and then take the track SW to Lochan a' Mhuilinn. From there continue along the path in Glen Lochan through a fine narrow cleft in the hills to join the route described above at Auchnafree in Glen Almond, 10km from Amulree.

### 125  Crieff to Aberfeldy by General Wade's Military Road
*37km/23miles*                    *OS Sheet 52. Start 868 216. Finish 856 491*
This route is the southern half of the Crieff to Dalnacardoch road 'for wheel carriages' built by General Wade and his Hanoverian soldiers in the 1730s. Much of the Crieff to Aberfeldy section can still be walked off the modern roads and for most of the way it is an enjoyable route.
Traditionally, the route starts from the centre of Crieff and heads up

Ferntower Road, along the upper edge of the golf course and round the base of The Knock to the entrance to Monzie Castle. Continue uphill to join the A822 road at map ref 884 243. About 600 metres further along the main road the track of the Wade Road diverges and goes directly NE across the moor to a point close to the Foulford Inn  at map ref 898 267.

Opposite the inn, there starts the first really distinct section of the old road, going  NNE over the shoulder  of the hill towards the Sma' Glen, dropping down to the modern road 2km further at map ref  905 294. A kilometre further on there is the option of leaving the A822 briefly to view Clach Ossian, which was moved aside by the Hanoverian engineers.

The major off-road section of the route starts 1km further north beyond Newton Bridge. There, at map ref 890 318 a few metres west of the tarmac, the divergence of the old road from the new one is easily spotted at a simple grass-topped bridge. Cross this picturesque old Wade bridge and go for 2km along the old road, parallel to the new one. 800 metres further on the old road passes above Corrymuckloch and goes direct to the old King's House at Amulree.

From Amulree, Wade's Road continues N, cutting the corner of the A826 road by climbing over the hillside, across Glen Fender and into Glen Cochill. After crossing and recrossing the A826 road, the Old Military Road keeps straight up the west bank of the Cochill Burn for over 3km, passing the hidden and delightful little Wade bridge opposite Scotston. The straight section continuing across the moorland after passing Scotston is on rather boggy ground and eventually is lost in forestry plantations about 800 metres south of Loch na Craige where the modern road is rejoined. Old and new roads cross again just before Loch na Craige and the Wade Road passes the loch 100 metres to its east.

On the descent towards Aberfeldy the Wade Road goes arrow-straight down through trees towards Gatehouse. The two roads coincide there, but 1km further on they finally part at map ref 870 485 and the old road goes straight to the heart of Aberfeldy down the Old Crieff Road directly to The Square.

Campbell Steven's book *Enjoying Perthshire* contains further information about this and other walks.

## 126  Harrietfield (Glenalmond) to Kenmore
*32km/20miles*                 OS Sheet 52.  Start *982 297*.  Finish *775 452*

Harrietfield on the B8063 road on the north of the River Almond may be reached by car (very limited space for parking) or by walking from Methven. If walking, go along the minor road from Methven to Glenalmond College and take the lane marked 'Back Avenue' to a footbridge over the River Almond to Harrietfield, 6km from Methven. From there go W along the B8063 road for 1km to a hairpin bend where the walk really begins.  Go NW up a private road bypassing Logiealmond Lodge to Craiglea quarry.  Follow the main track through the quarry and over the knoll Craig Lea, then down to the Shelligan Burn. Join another track which goes NW for several kilometres over a col between Meall Reamhar and Meall nan Caorach and down to Girron and the A822 road 1km south of Amulree.

At Amulree a right of way signpost 'Footpath to Kenmore' stands where a private road heads W from Amulree bridge. Follow this road up Glen Quaich along the north bank of the River Braan and Loch Freuchie and on by Tirchardie to join the road over the Lairig Mile Marcachd to Kenmore. Lairig Mile Marcachd - *the pass of the mile of riding* - is so named because of the level part on the summit.

The second part of this route is a very old road which is mentioned in the Chronicle of Fortingall and is shown on Stobie's 1783 map of Perthshire, as well as on Roy's map of 1755.

### 127  Little Glenshee (Glen Almond) to Strathbraan
*8km/5miles*                    OS Sheet 52.   Start 987 341.   Finish 938 386

This walk leads from Glen Almond to Strathbraan by a short and direct route along Glen Shee, not to be confused with the better known Glen Shee between Blairgowrie and Braemar. The south end of the walk at Little Glenshee farm can be reached by driving along one of two minor roads, one from Bankfoot and the other from Glen Almond. The two roads converge ½ km before Little Glenshee and it is possible to park at map ref 988 340 on the southern approach road.

A right of way signpost points the way NW past the farm and up Glen Shee. The route along a rough track is obvious all the way over the pass at just over 300m near Rosecraig and down to Ballachraggan in Strathbraan. The line of rocky knolls and crags which crosses the moor near Little Glenshee is part of the Highland Boundary Fault.

Having reached Ballachraggan, one possibility for continuing is to walk 5km along the A822 road to Amulree and return to Glen Almond along the southern half of route 126 by the Shelligan Burn and Craiglea quarry to Harrietfield.

# SECTION 10
# The Ochils, Lomonds and Sidlaws

## 128 Tillicoultry to Blackford or Gleneagles
*15km/9miles*        *OS Sheet 58. Start 914 975↑. Finish 896 086↑*
Start from the Mill Glen carpark at the top of Upper Mill Street in Tillicoultry and go up the path high on the east side of Mill Glen. An alternative which is more scenic is to follow the path up the glen itself, crossing and recrossing the stream which cascades in many waterfalls down this narrow defile, and at the point where this path begins to descend above the junction of the Gannel and Daiglen burns, climb steeply up the grassy hillside to join the upper path. Continue NE along this path on a long rising traverse above the Gannel Burn to the pass to the north-west of King's Seat Hill. Then turn NW over the pass (570m), skirting west of Skythorn Hill (path indistinct) and down the Broich Burn, high above its east bank, until opposite Backhills. From that point there are two possible routes, depending on one's destination:
(a) Going to Blackford, cross the Broich Burn below Backhills and go NW (no path) round the head of Upper Glendevon Reservoir over boggy ground. Cross the River Devon and go NW up Glen Bee to join a good track at the watershed and go down the Glen of Kinpauch (or over Kinpauch Hill) to Kinpauch and the A9 road. Cross this very busy dual carriageway with great care to reach Blackford.
(b) Going to Gleneagles, go downhill to the Upper Glendevon Reservoir dam and along the road past Lower Glendevon Reservoir. Just before the A823 road in Glen Devon is reached, take a track on the left which is an old road going at first alongside the modern one and then down the west side of Glen Eagles to the A9 about 2 km from Blackford and 1 km from Gleneagles Station.

## 129 Dollar to Auchterarder
*19km/12miles*        *OS Sheet 58. Start 964 984. Finish 956 127*
From the clock in the centre of Dollar go up the Burnside, the Mill Green and Dollar Glen to Castle Campbell. From the carpark continue N along a path on the east side of the Burn of Care between forest plantations to Maiden's Well. Continue past Glenquey Reservoir and cross the River Devon near Burnfoot to reach the youth hostel. Go up Borland Glen by a path on its west side and cross the pass (the Cadgers' Yett) west of Green Law to descend to the Coul Burn. Go down the burn by a path which becomes a minor public road at Coulshill. This road goes down Cloan Glen to a bridge across the A9 road at the east end of Auchterarder.

## 130 Glenfarg to Bridge of Earn
*10km/6mls*        *OS Sheet 58. Start 135 105. Finish 132 183*
This is part of the old road to Perth shown on Roy's map of 1755 and referred to by Scott in the first chapter of *The Fair Maid of Perth*, where he says that the summit of it is "one of the most beautiful points of view in Britain".

Take the B996 road north from Glenfarg for 800 metres, forking left at the signpost to Wicks of Baiglie almost due north. In another 1km turn left to Lochelbank and continue NNW by the 'Wallace Road' to Scott's favoured viewpoint on Dron Hill. Go steeply downhill by a track to West Dron and then N, either along the public road or more directly by a field track. Finally, skirting the boundary wall of Kilgraston School, go E to Kintillo and thence to Bridge of Earn.

## 131 Lomond Hills - Falkland to Kinnesswood

*14½ km/9miles          OS Sheets 58 and 59.   Start 253 074.   Finish 175 030*
From Falkland go S steeply up through woods towards East Lomond, or from a point 2km south-east of Falkland at map ref 272 062 on the A912 go uphill by the marked side road to the relay station and carpark on Purin Hill. By either route reach the top of East Lomond (424m).

Descend W to Craigmead carpark at map ref 227 063 and continue WNW along a good track over Balharvie Moss to the short steep climb up West Lomond (522m). Descend SW to Glen Vale (also called the Covenanters' Glen) where there are interesting caves, one of which is known as John Knox's Pulpit. Continue down the path westwards in Glen Vale to reach a minor road between Strathmiglo and Kinnesswood 1km north of Glenlomond Hospital.

## 132 Dundee to Glamis

*16km/10miles          OS Sheet 54.   Start 377 354.   Finish 385 464*
The walker leaving Dundee for the Sidlaws may choose to drive right to the base of the hills at Balluderon (map ref 375 383) or to walk out from Templeton Woods or Clatto Country Park along the network of quiet minor roads between the city and the hills. From Balluderon, a farm road leads NW, soon deteriorating into a rough stony track. Shortly after a green metal gate (map ref 371 389), double back up the zigzag leading directly towards the hill and, after a further 300 metres of steady ascent on a rough vehicular track, fork right, taking the narrow footpath which leads to the watershed and a gate on the fence which goes west to east from Auchterhouse Hill towards Craigowl. From this point a magnificent panorama opens out with distant views over Strathmore to the Grampians. Descend to Wester Denoon and from there follow the public road by Holemill and Slaughs to Glamis.

## 133 Longforgan to Newtyle

*19km/12miles          OS Sheet 53.   Start 318 301.   Finish 296 413*
This walk is mainly on minor public roads and tracks, some of them rights of way, across the undulating countryside of the Sidlaws, with good open views north to Strathmore and south across the Tay. From Longforgan go N to Dron, turning NW to map ref 288 332 at the corner of a wood. Continue NW across field and moorland for about 1½ km. Enter mature woods and go as far as a junction of forest roads at map ref 272 347 and turn NE for 250m to emerge into open country. Follow a narrow grassy path N then NE, where the line over Balshando Hill is very faint on the ground, but it is shown accurately

on the Landranger map, and leads to the A923 road at map ref 279 357. Follow a minor road to Lundie, whence a well maintained right of way heads NW then NE towards Thriepley and the Round Loch. There take the private road (right of way) along the east side of the loch to Sunnyhall where a track goes N to a cottage. Take the left-hand track entering the wood and climb it through the wood to a gate. Thereafter the route is largely trackless across fields between Newtyle Hill on the left and Burnside Quarry, below which the B954 road is reached 1km from Newtyle.

# SECTION 11
# Tay, Tummel, Glen Lyon and Rannoch

### 134 Pitlochry to Grandtully
*8km/5miles*                    *OS Sheet 52. Start 939 574. Finish 913 532*
Start from the entrance to the Pitlochry Festival Theatre. Take the road SW uphill, cross the A9 and go up by Middleton of Fonab and onwards by a zigzag track through the forest, over the ridge and down to the Tullypowrie Burn. Follow the burn downhill by a path past the east end of Strathtay Golf Course and on to the public road. Finally go SW along the road for 250 metres and cross the bridge over the River Tay to reach Grandtully.

### 135 Blair Atholl to Loch Tummel
*10km/6miles*                    *OS Sheet 43. Start 871 650. Finish 819 601↑*
Cross the River Garry by a footbridge at Blair Atholl and go 3km up the river by a footpath along the narrow strip between the river and the new A9 road. Cross the A9 with great care as this is a very busy road and go due S along a track to Balnansteuartach at the foot of the Allt Bhaic. Go S up a path on the west side this burn then SW uphill to the west side of Loch Bhac. Enter the forest and go S over the hill to leave by a gate at map ref 815 609 and continue down to the Loch Tummel Hotel. Although this route, along with 136, is waymarked through the forest, compass bearings are advisable from time to time.

This route is shown as a road on Stobie's map of Perthshire in 1783, and on a map of 1725 (in the British Library) as part of the road between Inversnaid Barracks and Ruthven Barracks at Kingussie. The route from Inversnaid was by Stronachlachar, the head of Loch Katrine, the north side of Loch Voil, Balquhidder, Lochearnhead, NE to Loch Tay and Kenmore, the west end of Loch Tummel, Blair Atholl, and thence N by the Minigaig Pass.

An alternative parallel route ending at the east end of Loch Tummel can be taken from Blair Atholl. After crossing the River Garry, cross the busy A9 road and go S ascending by a zigzag path through open woodland to reach Tomanraid. Just beyond there, at map ref 864 629, turn left to descend past Fincastle Farm and down Glen Fincastle to the B8019 road near the east end of Loch Tummel.

### 136 Calvine to Loch Tummel
*8km/5miles*                    *OS Sheet 43. Start 804 658^. Finish 819 601↑*
From Calvine cross the River Garry and go E to Old Struan church and across the Errochty Water for 700 metres to the SRWS signpost at map ref 816 654. Proceed S over a field to a gate and uphill through a birchwood to a forestry gate and ladder stile at map ref 810 646. Follow the forest track SSE to leave the plantation at map ref 815 635 over a ladder stile. (Do not follow the

bulldozed track which stays within the forest). Climb S over the shoulder of the hill to a ladder stile at map ref 816 625 and enter the older forest west of Loch Bhac. Then go due S, joining route 135, to leave the forest again by a gate at map ref 815 608 and continue down to the Loch Tummel Hotel.

### 137  Fortingall to Kinloch Rannoch
*17km/11miles*                              *OS Sheet 51.  Start 736 470.  Finish 662 587*
This old route gives a fine way across the hills between Glen Lyon and the beautiful strath of lochs Rannoch and Tummel. From the west end of Fortingall village take the access road leading to Glenlyon House for 200 metres and turn right past some cottages to go ENE at first, then NNE by a track up the hillside to the east of the Allt Odhar. Higher up the track bears NW to cross the col between Meall nan Eun and Meall Crumach, from where there is a fine view of Schiehallion across Gleann Mor. Continue NW over a spur of Meall nan Eun and descend past Glenmore Bothy and across the Allt Mor to Uamh Tom a' Mhor-fhir (cave and old sheilings), where the Gleann Mor divides in two. Go up a path in the north-west branch of the glen to the start of a track which leads N over the col west of Schiehallion and down the Tempar Burn to the road 3km east of Kinloch Rannoch.

Note:  This route is not a right of way, and those exercising access rights should, as advised by the Access Code, contact the Estate (Tel: 01882 632 314) during the prime stalking period from mid-September to the end of October.  The area to the west of Schiehallion, Coire Ghlas, is particularly important from the local deer management point of view.

### 138  Innerwick (Glen Lyon) to Carie (Loch Rannoch)
*11km/7miles*                              *OS Sheet 51.  Start 587 476↑.  Finish 617 572↑*
From the church at Innerwick in Glen Lyon, 1 km east of Bridge of Balgie, follow the track NNW up the east side of the stream, then in 1 km turn NNE to the Lairig Ghallabhaich (478m), also known as the Kirk Road. Continue down along the Allt Droilichean and into the forest until the stream turns NE. At that point there is a cross-roads and the route turns NE down the Allt na Bogair to Carie on Loch Rannoch, 5km from Kinloch Rannoch. An alternative way from the cross-roads is to go straight ahead past a small lochan to reach Dall (Rannoch School) at the foot of the Dall Burn.

The route from Innerwick to Dall is shown as a road on Stobie's 1783 map of Perthshire. It is part of an old drove road and those prepared to add 19km to the walk can start along this old route from Killin. From there take the road up Glen Lochay for 5km to Duncroisk, then go NE up the Allt Dhuin Croisg by a track on the west side of the burn past old shielings. Continue up the Allt Dhuin Croisg to the long flat summit of the Lairig Breisleich. Descend NNE beside the Allt Breisleich and cross the Allt Bail a' Mhuilinn to reach the road leading down to Bridge of Balgie.

**139  Innerwick (Glen Lyon) to Camghouran (Loch Rannoch)**
*13km/8miles*          *OS Sheet 51.  Start 587 476↑.  Finish 549 564*
For its first kilometre from Innerwick this route is the same as 138. Then, instead of turning up the Allt Ghallabhaich, cross this stream and go NW up a track along the Lairig a' Mhuic (*pass of swine*). From the end of the track climb W over the col between Meall nam Maigheach and Meall nan Sac and descend NW to reach the Dall Burn. Continue by the track down this burn for 1km, then NW to the Allt Camghouran and down it to Loch Rannoch. From the point where the road is reached at Camghouran it is 14km west to Rannoch Station or 12km east to Kinloch Rannoch.

## 140  Killin to Bridge of Orchy or Tyndrum by Loch Lyon
*40km/25miles*
        *OS Sheets 50 and 51.  Start 570 340.  Finish 297 396 or 328 306*
From Killin go by the public road up Glen Lochay to Kenknock, then by the private Hydro Electric road NW over the pass to the dam at the east end of Loch Lyon. (The dam can also be reached by public road up Glen Lyon from Aberfeldy, and there is a Post Bus service from Aberfeldy to Lubreoch at the dam).

From this point onwards the route follows a right of way which many years ago was the route used by the MacGregors of Glen Lyon carrying their dead to the clan burial ground at the Church of Glenorchy. Go along the north side of Loch Lyon for 4½ km by a bulldozed track to the inlet at the foot of Gleann Meran, go round this inlet and continue SW along the lochside to the head of the loch. Continue W over the pass between Beinn Mhanach and Beinn nam Fuaran, reaching the start of a track at the watershed, and go down to the ruined house at Ais-an t-Sidhean, where the Gaelic poet Duncan Ban MacIntyre once lived. Continue along the track beside the Allt Kinglass down the Auch Gleann and under the long curving viaduct of the West Highland Railway.

Just before reaching Auch, turn NW and follow the track, which is part of the West Highland Way, beside the railway for 5km to Bridge of Orchy. Alternatively, turn S and follow the West Highland Way (which at this point is also a right of way) for 5km to Tyndrum.

An alternative route to avoid the last part of the difficult N shore of Loch Lyon beyond Gleann Meran is to head up Gleann Cailliche to the col between Beinn a'Chuirn and Beinn Achaladair and from there go down to Ais-an-t-Sidhein.

## 140X  Killin to Crianlarich by Glen Lochay
*28km/17½ miles*          *OS Sheets 50 and 51.  Start 570 340.  Finish 384 254*
This route goes up the whole length of Glen Lochay through the heart of the Forest of Mamlorn and then crosses to Strath Fillan over a pass which once had many shielings, but is now almost pathless and seldom visited.

From Killin walk up the quiet public road in Glen Lochay to Kenknock and continue along the almost treeless upper glen by a rough private road past Badour to Batavaime. A track goes SW for 5km further up the west bank of the headwaters of the River Lochay, eventually petering out near Lochan Chailein, but beyond it there is no path for some distance and the going over the pass is fairly boggy. Descend on the west side of the Inverhaggernie Burn to a track which leads under the West Highland Railway and over the River Fillan to reach the A82 road 2km north-west of Crianlarich.

### 141   Bridge of Orchy (Loch Tulla) to Bridge of Gaur (Loch Rannoch)
*25km/15½ miles*        *OS Sheets 50 and 51. Start 312 437. Finish 501 567*
This was once an important drove road but today it gives the walker a fairly hard outing although there are long sections of easy walking at both ends. A shorter middle section across peat bogs can be quite difficult and give some idea of the many problems which the builders of the West Highland Railway had more than a hundred years ago.

From Bridge of Orchy the old drove road coincides with the new A82 road for 2km and for the next 2km it is close to the railway. Starting from the A82 road, 4km north of Bridge of Orchy at the north-east corner of Loch Tulla follow the farm road NE to Achallader Farm where there is a car park. Go along the track on the south bank of the Water of Tulla crossing after 2km by bridge at Barravourich (ruin) and continuing a further 5km to the end of the track at Gorton bothy. From here it is advisable to head towards the old bridge over the Water of Tulla and keeping to the rough and pathless north bank continue for 2½ km, then go under the railway at the point where it crosses the river close to the Madagan Moineach, a mossy place which was once a drove stance.

Beyond the underpass, waymarker posts lead to a vertical stile over the forest fence from where the route of the old drove road (by way of Meall Doire Meallaich) has long been overplanted. An easier way through the forest now is at first to follow the overhead electricity pylon line NE. This soon brings one to the northward-flowing Allt Criche and in 1km onwards cross this burn, which could be troublesome. Continue on a path below the pylon line for a short distance to join a forest road (where at map ref 412 502 nearby is a small windmill providing power for the electrified fence). Leaving the pylon line follow this road NE along which the only junction of note is at map ref 437 525. There the route goes to the right, and by ford across the Duibhe Bheag continues 5km more through forest, passing the ruin near Lochan Dubh Grundd nan Darachan, before emerging onto open ground. Go down the west side of Gleann Chomraidh and by road to reach Bridge of Gaur which is on the Post Bus route between Pitlochry and Rannoch Station.

# SECTION 12
# Glen Coe and Appin

### 142  Tyndrum to Kingshouse Hotel and  Kinlochleven
*44km/27¹/₂ miles        OS Sheets 41 and 50.  Start 328 306.  Finish 188 619*
There have been four stages in the history of the road across the Black Mount and through Glen Coe:
(a) the original drove road, for centuries the main route from north-western Scotland to the Lowlands;
(b) the Old Military Road, constructed about 1750, largely on the line of the original drove road, with occasional deviations;
(c) the 19th-century road, also largely on the original line but deviating in considerable stretches from the military road so as to provide easier gradients;
(d) the present A82 road.

Very little of road (c) is now in use by vehicles, but it provides a fine route for walkers and is the line of the West Highland Way, which coincides with the whole of this route.

From Tyndrum go up the west bank of the Crom Allt for 1km, then cross the West Highland Railway and continue close to it, first on one side and then the other, to Bridge of Orchy. There cross the River Orchy and go NW uphill through forest over the Mam Carraigh and down to Inveroran Hotel and Forest Lodge. Then go N by the 19th-century road which gives excellent walking along the foot of the great range of the Black Mount peaks and corries to Ba Bridge and Kingshouse Hotel. (30km/19miles)

Leaving Kingshouse, go along its western access road to within 300 metres of the A82 and then follow the Old Military Road parallel to it along the foot of Beinn a' Chrulaiste to Altnafeadh. Just to the west of there start climbing NNW up the Devil's Staircase, a fine section of the Old Military Road with easy gradients and a series of well engineered zigzags, to reach the highest point. On the north slope the path makes a long easy descent across the hillside to join the access road to the Blackwater Reservoir, and the route finishes down this road to Kinlochleven. The continuation of the West Highland Way to Fort William is described as route 223.

### 143  Rannoch Station to Kingshouse Hotel
*19km/12miles        OS Sheets 41 and 42.  Start 423 579.↑  Finish 260 546*
From Rannoch Station go W round the head of Loch Laidon and follow the signposted track through the wood, then climb gradually and contour across the hillside until above the ruined cottage of Tigh na Cruaiche, about 6km from Rannoch Station.

From there continue due W at the same level for 3¹/₂ km to the start of a track which is followed across several streams to reach Black Corries Lodge at the foot of Meall nan Ruadhag. Follow the diversion of the right of way round the lodge buildings. Finally go along the private road for 5km to Kingshouse Hotel. Electricity poles mark the line from Rannoch to Black Corries. The middle section of this route is very boggy when wet, so it is best to do it in dry weather when the ground underfoot is reasonably firm.

## 144  Bridge of Orchy to Bridge of Awe
*38km/24miles*                    *OS Sheet 50. Start 297 396. Finish 032 297*
      Take the West Highland Way (route 142) for 5km past Inveroran Hotel to Victoria Bridge. There is a carpark at the end of the public road just before Victoria Bridge. From Forest Lodge go W by the track along the north bank of the Abhainn Shira past the little climbers' hut at the foot of the Allt Toaig. Just beyond there do not take the road through the forest to Clashgour Farm, but follow the right of way along the bank of the river, with a short diversion through the forest if the ground near the river is very wet. 4km west of Victoria Bridge cross to the south bank by a suspension bridge and continue W to Loch Dochard.
      From there go SW over to Glen Kinglass and descend this long and desolate glen, with a good track from Glen Kinglass Lodge onwards to Ardmaddy on Loch Etive, 25km from Inveroran and 28km from Bridge of Orchy. From Ardmaddy the track continues along the lochside for 5km to Glennoe, whence a forest road leads to Bridge of Awe. Taynuilt is about 4km away along the A85 road.
      An alternative finish to the route from Acharn, about halfway down Glen Kinglass, is to climb over the Lairig Dhoireann (610m) and go down Glen Strae to Dalmally. This way is about 5km shorter than going to Bridge of Awe. See route 145.

## 145  Dalmally or Bridge of Awe to Glen Etive
*30km/19miles or 25km/15¹/₂ miles*
                    *OS Sheet 50. Start 168 272 or 032 298. Finish 137 469*
      This route takes one through some mountainous country between Loch Awe and Glen Kinglass and from there along the shore of Loch Etive below the steep slabby face of Ben Starav to Glen Etive, where the next two routes to be described are joined. From Glen Etive there are three or four possible ways for the continuation to Glen Coe, and these are described as part of route 147.
      The Dalmally start goes along the B8077 road through Stronmilchan to the bridge over the River Strae and up the track on the west side of Glen Strae for about 2km. Leave the track and go N uphill by a path on the west side of the burn flowing from the Lairig Dhoireann. Cross this pass and go downhill, N at first for about 1km then W to Acharn in Glen Kinglass. Cross the river and continue along the private road in the  glen to Ardmaddy on Loch Etive. Go along the east shore of the loch to its head. The crossings of the Allt Ghiusachan and Allt Coire na Larach may be difficult in spate conditions. Continue to Coiletir and cross the bridge over the River Etive just beyond there to reach the narrow public road in Glen Etive 2km below Invercharnan.
      A shorter and easier alternative can be made by starting at Bridge of Awe

and following the private road through the forest on the south-east side of Loch Etive for 5km, then along the lochside past Glennoe and Inverliver to Ardmaddy, where the longer route from Dalmally is joined.

## 146 Bonawe (Loch Etive) to Glen Etive
*21km/13miles*                    *OS Sheet 50.   Start 011 333↑.   Finish 137 469*
This walk is a shorter and easier version of route 145. It goes along the west shore of Loch Etive for most of its length and involves virtually no climbing. Like route 145, it can be used as the first part of a much longer walk to Glen Coe.

From Bonawe (reached by bus from Oban or Connel) go along the west side of Loch Etive by a forest road past Craig and Cadderlie. 2km beyond Cadderlie the road leaves the lochside to reach the bridge over the Allt Easach between Dail and Barrs. Descend towards Barrs and go along the birch fringe of the Loch Etive by a rough path which is often very wet. An alternative way is to go along the forest road to its end 1½km beyond the bridge over the Allt Easach and continue along a recently made very rough track which traverses well above the lochside and ends below the Etive Slabs, from where a path drops down to the head of the loch. There the public road is reached and followed up Glen Etive for 4km to within 2km of Invercharnan, where routes 145 and 147 are joined.

## 147 Bridge of Orchy to Glen Etive
*21km/13miles*          *OS Sheets 41 and 50.   Start 297 396.   Finish 137 469*
This is a fine route across the lowest pass in the great chain of mountains stretching from Ben Starav to the Black Mount. Most of the way is on tracks and paths, but there is a pathless section of about 6km over the pass which does not present any difficulties in good conditions. However, when the weather or visibility is bad, this route should only be attempted by experienced hillwalkers.

From Bridge of Orchy follow the West Highland Way (route 142) past Inveroran Hotel to Victoria Bridge, and turn W along the track to the climbers' hut at the foot of the Allt Toaig. Just after crossing that burn keep to the right along the track through the forest to Clashgour farm. Continue NW by the path on the west side of the Allt Ghabhar to the bealach called Mam nan Sac (588m). From there go NW on a slightly descending traverse across the south face of Stob a' Bhruaich Leith to the Allt Dochard and go up this burn to the pass at its source (630m). Descend WNW along the headwaters of the Allt Ceitlein and stay on its north side to find a path which leads down to Glenceitlein. Go SW along a track for 1½km, then turn right to cross the bridge over the River Etive and reach the road in Glen Etive 2km below Invercharnan.

The three routes just described all end in Glen Etive at map ref 137 469, a long way from the nearest hostelry. There is a Post Bus service from Glen Etive to Glen Coe just after mid-day. Failing this, there are four possible ways

to reach the A82 road between Kingshouse Hotel and Glencoe village:
    (a)  Walk up the road in Glen Etive to Kingshouse Hotel (17km/11miles);
    (b)  Walk up the road to Dalness and follow the path leading NE through the Lairig Gartain to reach the  A82 road near Altnafeadh (13km/8miles);
    (c ) Walk up the road to Dalness and follow the path leading N then NNE through the Lairig Eilde to the A82 road  in Glen Coe (12km/7½ miles);
    (d) This is the finest end to this long cross-country walk, similar in character to the section from Bridge of Orchy to  Glen Etive and like it recommended only for experienced hillwalkers if the weather is unfavourable. Go up the road in Glen Etive for 3km to map ref 148 492 and climb steeply NW up the edge of the forest to a height of 300m on the south ridge of Beinn Maol Chaluim. From there make a slightly descending traverse NNW across the south-west flank of this hill to reach the Allt Charnan and go up it. Careful route-finding in bad visibility is needed to leave the burn at map ref 133 516 and climb steeply N to the Bealach Fhionnghaill (570m). Descend N into the Fionn Ghleann and go down it to the A82 road just across the River Coe from the Clachaig Hotel (11km/7miles).

### 148 Loch Creran to Ballachulish
*16km/10miles*        *OS Sheets 41 and 50.  Start 007 460.  Finish 080 578↑*
    From the A828 road bridge at the head of Loch Creran (reached by the Oban to Fort William bus) go NE up the Glen Creran road. About 6km up the glen, and after entering the forest, go uphill along the forest road above Salachail. It turns N and goes to within 1km of the pass (410m). Continue along a path through the forest to the pass and on its north side descend steeply NNE down to Gleann an Fhiodh. Cross the River Laroch and follow a good path down its west bank to Ballachulish.

# SECTION 13
# Mull

### 149  Salen to Lochbuie by Loch Ba and Loch Scridain
*28km/17½ miles       OS Sheets 48 and 49.  Start 572 431.  Finish 608 249↑*
 This route goes from coast to coast through the heart of the mountainous centre of Mull, which is dominated by Ben More. From Salen follow the Loch na Keal road for 6km to a very sharp corner after the bridge over the River Ba. Turn left through the open gateway of a private road and immediately turn right along the right of way, which is signposted. Follow this along the south side of Loch Ba for 3km, then climb up Glen Clachaig by the path to the col (332m) 2½ km due east of Ben More. From the col make a rising traverse for 1km S over the south-east ridge of A'Chioch and descend to Ardvergnish.

 Go round the head of Loch Scridain to Rossal Farm and climb SSE beside the Allt Atharaidh, then NE to reach Lochan Tana at the col between Beinn nam Feannag and Beinn na Croise. Go E round the head of Glen Byre to the flat col between Cruach nan Con and Beinn nan Gobhar, and from there descend ESE to Lochbuie.

### 150  Lochbuie to Salen by Glen Forsa
*24km/15miles       OS Sheets 48 and 49.  Start 615 256.  Finish 572 431*
 From Lochbuie go NE up the path on the east side of Gleann a' Chaiginn Mhoir and the east bank of Loch Airdeglais. Beyond there cross the stream to the west side of Loch an Ellen and climb up to the A849 road. Follow the old road NE for 4km almost to the ruined house of Torness, then go N over the low pass to Glen Forsa and down this glen by a forest road to join the A849 road 2km east of Salen.

### 151  Dervaig to Salen
*19km/12miles       OS Sheet 47.  Start 432 520.  Finish 572 431*
 From Dervaig go E along the Tobermory road for 2km to Achnadrish (8km from Tobermory). There follow a minor road and track leading SE above the south-west shore of Loch Frisa into a forest. Leave the forest and continue along a path which climbs away from the loch round the south-west side of Cnoc nan Dubh Leitire and goes beside the edge of the forest to reach Tenga in Glen Aros. Finally, go along the minor road down this glen to join the A848 about 2km north-west of Salen.

# SECTION 14
# The Southeast Grampians

## 152 Dunkeld to Kirkmichael by Lochan Oisinneach Mor
*24km/15miles        OS Sheet 52 or 53.  Start 025 433↑.  Finish 079 600↑*
Start ½km north of Dunkeld where a signpost beside the A923 road indicates the route northwards past a car park to Cally Loch and Birkenburn. In 3km, on reaching the south end of Mill Dam, fork right and follow the track on its east side for 1km, then forking right again go NE below Deuchary Hill to Santa Crux Well, an inconspicuous spring beyond Grewshill.

Continue to the junction at map ref 042 500 turning right to go N by the Buckny Burn and through a large plantation east of Lochan Oisinneach Mor to reach Lochan Oisinneach. Continue N past Creag Gharbh, then NE across moor to the south-west corner of Kindrogan Wood. From there go E along its south side into maturing pine woods by a path which descends to a track reaching the road leading to Kirkmichael at a deserted church.

Alternatively, from Dowally (7km N of Dunkeld) go E uphill to Raor Lodge, the NE to Loch Ordie and N by the west side of Lochan Oisinneach Mor to join the above route at Lochan Oisinnieach. The route can also be joined from Ballinluig *via* Tulliemet.

If doing the routes in reverse, be careful when leaving Kirkmichael to take the road to Croft of Cultalonie and not the one to Cultalonie.

## 153 Dunkeld to Kirkmichael by Loch Benachally
*24km/15miles        OS Sheet 52 or 53.  Start 027 426.  Finish 079 600*
Follow the A923 Blairgowrie road for 5km to Butterstone, then go NNE by Riechip to the south-east end of Loch Benachally. Continue N over the moor and across the head of the Baden Burn to the west corner of Blackcraig Forest. From there descend to Loch Charles, then go down a zigzag track towards Woodhill and when you meet a path to the left follow it to remain on the west side of the River Ardle. Go N past Dalnabreack, Pitcarmick, Dalvey and Cultalonie to reach Kirkmichael. Between Dalnabreack and Dalvey keep uphill above the hill dyke to avoid the policies of Pitcarmick.

If your objective is Ballintuim, 6km south of Kirkmichael, continue down the zigzag track mentioned above, cross a burn and enter the policies of Woodhill at a gate, then go down a private drive to a bridge over the River Ardle and reach the A924 road at the north end of Ballintuim.

## 154 Blairgowrie to Kirkmichael
*22km/14miles        OS Sheet 53.  Start 150 448.  Finish 079 600*
From Kinloch, 3km west of Blairgowrie along the A923 road, go N to Middleton Farm. ½km further on, at map ref 146 483, bear NW by a new track which crosses a burn and rejoins the older path near the 296m trig point close to the highest point of Cochrage Muir. Continue NW along the path and enter Blackcraig Forest by the gate at map ref 127 497. Continue NW to

*The summit of the Lairig Ghru, looking towards Cairn Toul (route 181)*

*The path through Rothiemurchus Forest at the north end of the Lairig Ghru (route 181)*

*Strath Ossian on the way from Corrour to Tulloch (route 218)*

*Ben Nevis and Aonach Beag from the watershed at the head of Glen Nevis (route 219)*

Croft of Blackcraig, which can also be reached by a forest road going W from Bridge of Cally.

Descend NW to Blackcraig and Balmachreuchie, where the route passes through a householder's garden to continue along the west side of Strathardle to Woodhill. On reaching the cattle grid at the edge of the Woodhill policies, take the left fork and continue along the path on the west side of the River Ardle (as described for route 153) to Kirkmichael.

## 155 Ballinluig to Kirkmichael

*16km/10miles*      *OS Sheet 52 or 53. Start 977 526. Finish 079 600*

From Ballinluig go uphill by a minor road heading E towards Tulliemet. In 2km at map ref 998 526 turn N along the private road leading to Tulliemet House. Go past there, heading NE onto the open hillside and continue NNE along the track to within ½km of Loch Broom at map ref 014 573. At that point bear NE to reach the south corner of the forest deer fence (map ref 021 579) and go ENE along its boundary to north of Sgorr Gorm (502m). Descend NE across The Back Burn to join a track 300 metres east of Mains of Glenderby and continue E through forest and down past chalets to reach Kirkmichael

## 156 Aldclune (Killiecrankie) to Kirkmichael by Glen Girnaig

*26km/16miles*      *OS Sheet 43. Start 902 636. Finish 080 601*

Start at Aldclune on the B8079 road near the site of the Battle of Killiecrankie. From there walk up a minor road under the A9 towards Orchilmore, but before reaching there turn left up a track on the west side of Glen Girnaig. In 2½km the track crosses the Allt Shinagag by a ford, and 200 metres upstream there is a rickety footbridge. (A safer crossing may be made lower down the burn at map ref 927 653 at a flow metering bridge) Go ½km further to the end of the track at Loinmarstaig, then along a path E towards Reinakyllich. Just before reaching there, strike E across a low col to reach the track which goes SE from Shinagag and forms part of route 157, which is followed to its end, see below.

Alternatively, a much shorter walk can be had by going from Reinakyllich to Shinagag and from there westwards along the track past Loch Moraig (where the public road is reached) and down to Old Bridge of Tilt and Blair Atholl.

## 157 Blair Atholl to Kirkmichael by Glen Girnaig

*29km/18miles*      *OS Sheet 43. Start 876 656. Finish 080 601*

Go N from Blair Atholl to Old Bridge of Tilt and Middlebridge, (signpost to Strathardle), then E to the north end of Loch Moraig, where the public road ends. Continue ENE along a track below the foot of Carn Liath and SE to Shinagag. From there follow a recently made track SE for almost 3km, joining route 156, and cross a flat col to the Allt na Leacainn Moire. Cross this burn and go along its left bank for about 1km, then climb SE over the level spur ¾km north of Balgholan Craig and descend by a path past the ruins of Stronhavie to A924 road at Dalnavaid in Glen Brerachan. Follow the road E

for 3km, then cross the River Ardle to reach the road to Kindrogan. Continue on the west side of the river, passing Dalreoch and Tullochcurran, to Kirkmichael.
This route is shown on Roy's map of 1755.

## 158  Kirkmichael to Blair Atholl by Gleann Fearnach and Glen Tilt
50km/31miles                    OS Sheet 43.  Start 080 601↑.  Finish 876 656
From Kirkmichael take the private road on the west side of the River Ardle past Tullochcurran and Loch Cottage  to Dalreoch. Cross the river to Enochdhu and continue NW along the A924 road for 2km, then turn right and go N by Glenfernate Lodge up Gleann Fearnach for 7km to Daldhu. From there two routes are possible:
(a) The shorter route goes up the Glen Loch Burn by a track to Loch Loch, along the east side of the loch and then N down the An Lochain Burn to Glen Tilt. If the Tilt is too deep to ford to reach the path on its west bank, follow the east bank for 3km down to a bridge. Another 3km down Glen Tilt is Forest Lodge, from where a road runs down the glen for 13km to Blair Atholl.
(b) A slightly longer route from Daldhu is to go N along the private road to Fealar Lodge and then descend from the lodge to Glen Tilt, reaching it near the Falls of Tarf. The walk through Glen Tilt is described as part of route 177.

## 159  Kirkmichael to Spittal of Glenshee
13km/8miles                    OS Sheet 43.  Start 080 601↑.  Finish 110 699↑
Take route 158 to Enochdhu, then go NE by a private road through the Dirnanean estate, where the route is well signposted along a gravel road up the hillside (stiles over two deer fences) towards Elrig. Further on is an open shelter and the track becomes grassy and continues waymarked over An Lairig. Finally, go NE down the Coire Lairige on an easily discernable path to Spittal of Glenshee.
This route is shown as a road on Roy's map of 1755.

## 159X  Spittal of Glenshee to Inverey
24km/15miles                    OS Sheet 43.  Start 110 699.  Finish 089 893
This is a fine direct pass which with route 159 enables the long-distance walker to link the routes in the Kirkmichael area described earlier in this section with the long passes through the Cairngorms. From Spittal of Glenshee take the track starting on the east side of the stone arch bridge taking the old A93 road over  the Glen Lochsie Burn and follow it NW then N up Gleann Taitneach on the east side of the burn. Beyond the end of the track continue up the narrowing glen to Loch nan Eun, a high and lonely place surrounded by the rounded hills of the Mounth.
Go round the east side of the loch, which is at the watershed,  and descend NE then N along the Allt Beinn Iutharn. Lower down there is a path on its west bank leading to the ruins of Altanour Lodge. From there a good track , crossing and recrossing the Ey Burn and meandering across grassy haughs, leads down to the lower glen. Before reaching Inverey cross to the east side of the burn to go down past Mar Estate Lodge.

160  Kirkmichael to Glen Shee
*8km/5miles*            *OS Sheet 43. Start 081 601↑. Finish 141 632↑*
The original route, starting at a signpost beside the hotel in Kirkmichael, is up a sunken, muddy track for 400 metres and then continues NE across open fields following faint paths that are waymarked to Ashintully Castle and past there towards two small lochs. Beyond these descend E to cross the Ennoch Burn and climb over the south ridge of Lamh Dearg to reach Lair in Glen Shee. From Lair a road goes E to Folda in Glen Isla at the west end of route 162.

### 161  Alyth to Glen Shee and Kirkmichael
*30km/19miles*            *OS Sheets 43 and 53. Start 246 485. Finish 081 601↑*
Take the minor road leading NW out of Alyth which climbs over the lower western slopes of Hill of Alyth to Whiteside. Continue NNW by the road past Gauldswell to Tullymurdoch, and there go N by the track to Craighead. Continue N to the top of the Hill of Three Cairns, and then descend W to the Alyth Burn. Go up the burn on the west side of the forest and from the corner of the forest at map ref 180 568 strike NW straight over the moor towards Blacklunans in Glen Shee. The route is rather featureless, so follow the Drumturn Burn until it turns south, and then head NW over a col and descend to Blacklunans, aiming for the telephone box (exchange) to avoid straying into the private grounds of Drumfork.

One way from Blacklunans to Kirkmichael which avoids too much road walking is to go N up the minor road on the east side of the Shee Water to Cray, cross to the A93 road at Lair and then do route 160 in reverse to Kirkmichael.   An alternative and slightly shorter way is to go from Blacklunans along the A93 road to Dalrulzion and then along the B950 road to Kirkmichael.

### 162  Glen Isla (Folda) to Glen Clova
*25km/15½miles*            *OS Sheets 43 and 44. Start 189 642. Finish 357 697↑*
From Folda in Glen Isla go N for 800 metres by road until 100 metres short of the bridge, then NE up a forest road for 400 metres and left up the hill track and over the ridge to the north-east of Auchintaple Loch. Descend into trackless moor, heading E for the glack (meaning col or pass) between Bada Crionard and Craigie Law. Go through the glack and past a new fence and SE on the forestry road ahead which descends steeply to the Finlet Burn. This is crossed by a concrete bridge from where the road leads S past the junction in Glen Finlet at map ref 231 654 to Glenmarkie Lodge.

From Glenmarkie Lodge go first E, then SE, and then NE through the Moss of Glanny. Go NE through Drumshade Plantation (gates at both ends) and over Hill of Strone to Cormuir on the Glen Prosen road. Go down the glen for 2km to Glenprosen Village, and then NE by the east side of the Burn of Inchmill and over Drumwhern to the B955 road in Glen Clova near Eggie, 5km SE of Clova Inn.

There is a straightforward connection between this route and route 163:

From Cormuir in Glen Prosen follow the road NW to Glenprosen Lodge and continue for a further 5¹/₂ km by the track along the Prosen Water past Runtaleave and Old Craig Lodge to the ruined deerwatcher's house at Kilbo, where route 163 is joined.

## 163  Glen Isla to Glen Doll and Glen Clova
*21km/13miles*                          *OS Sheet 44. Start 215 605.  Finish 283 761*↑
Kirkton of Glenisla is reached by road from Alyth or, if walking, over the east side of the Hill of Alyth, then by Dykehead and Kilry, and N over Broom Hill. From the village go E along the B951 road for 1¹/₂ km to East Mill and turn N to Freuchies (carpark). From this point two routes are possible:

(a) Continue along the private road to Glenmarkie Lodge and from there go NW then N along a forest road up Glen Finlet. At map ref 231 654 there is a road junction, but keep right heading N beside the Finlet Burn. The road leads to the north end of the forest and emerges onto open moorland at a stile and SRWS signpost just below the bealach called the Glack of Balquhader leading to Glen Prosen.

(b) The alternative to this route is to go NW from the carpark at Freuchies by a forest road which leads N past Loch Shandra and Tulloch and through the forest to the glack between Craigie Law and Bada Crionard. From there route 162 is followed to reach the junction at map ref 231 654 where (a) above is joined and followed N.

After crossing the Glack of Balquhader, go steeply down to the ruined deerwatcher's house at Kilbo in Glen Prosen, crossing the burn by a narrow log bridge. From there take the path N through larch woods onto the open hillside at Cairn Dye and along a barely discernible path on the Shank of Drumwhallo. The plateau is reached at about 850m and a SRWS signpost at map ref 253 737 indicates a turn of direction to ENE for about 700 metres to the edge of the plateau just north-west of the col between Mayar and Driesh. Very careful navigation is needed in mist. Descend the path on the east side of the Shank of Drumfollow into Corrie Kilbo and Glendoll Forest, and continue along a track over the White Water to Glendoll Youth Hostel and the carpark at the end of the public road in Glen Clova.

## 164  Clova to Tarfside (Glen Esk)
*24km/15miles*                          *OS Sheet 44. Start 327 731*↑.  *Finish 492 797*
From Clova go NE steeply uphill for 3¹/₂ km on the path which goes S of Loch Brandy to the top of Green Hill (870m). The best route across the high ground to the east is over the tops of White Hill and Muckle Cairn then north-east to Cairn Lick. There a track is reached which leads down the Shank of Inchgrundle to Inchgrundle at the head of Loch Lee. Go along the north side of the loch to the end of the public road in Glen Esk. The little village of Tarfside is 5km further down the glen.

**165  Noranside (Tannadice) to Tarfside (Glen Esk)**
*24km/15miles*                    *OS Sheet 44.  Start 468 610.  Finish 492 797*
   From Noranside, 3km north of Tannadice, go E along the Edzell road to
Fern and Balquharn.  There take the road NNW to Afflochie and the track up
the east side of Cruick Water for 2km.  Proceed NNW on a track up the south
ridge of Hill of Garbet round to the south-west shoulder of Hill of Mondurran
and then descend NE to Waterhead on the Water of Saughs.  Go down Glen
Lethnot for 3km to Tillybardine and follow the signposted track north through
the Clash of Wirren to Tarfside by East Knock and Cowie Hill.

# SECTION 15
# The Mounth Roads

The long range of hills between Deeside and the Glens of Angus, extending for some 80km, has been known from early times as the Mounth, and this name has come to be applied to the old rights of way which cross the hills. The following list of Mounth passes prepared in the 17th century by Sir James Balfour of Denmilne (1600-1651) is printed in the Spalding Club Collections on the Shires of Aberdeen and Banff, published in 1843:

1. Causey or Cowie Mounth. This is the old road from Aberdeen to the south, mentioned in writings from the 14th century onwards. It leaves the South Deeside road 1km from the (old) Bridge of Dee and is still in use by motor vehicles as far as Causeyport. The Local Authority has embarked on a scheme to open the onward route to Muchalls for pedestrians, cyclists and horse riders.
2. Elsick Mounth  (route 166).
3. Cryne Corse Mounth  (route 167).
4. Stock Mounth  (route 168).
5. Builg Mounth  (route 169).
6. Cairn o' Mount  (public road).
7. Forest of Birse Mounth  (route 170).
8. Mounth Gammel or Firmounth (route 171)
9. Mount Keen  (route 172).
10. Capel Mounth  (route 173).
11. Cairnwell  (public road).

Balfour does not mention the Tolmount (route 175), nor the Monega Pass (route 176). The Mounth Roads are more fully described in the Scottish Mountaineering Club's guide *The Cairngorms* (1992) by Adam Watson, and also in G.M.Fraser's *The Old Deeside Road* (1921).

### 166 Drumoak to Stonehaven by the Elsick Mounth
*19km/12miles*                    *OS Sheet 45. Start 792 988. Finish 838 890*
At Drumoak, 18km west of Aberdeen, turn SE to cross the Dee at Park Bridge, then go S by minor public roads past Durris House, Denside and West Brachmont to the Y-junction at map ref 807 945. From there a forest road goes S for some 400 metres until another forest road leads E, then S and finally SE to emerge from the forest north-east of Bawdy Craig.

This is not the original route, which enters the forest about 100 metres beyond the last mentioned forest road and goes S through Strathgyle Wood to reach the forest boundary south-west of Bawdy Craig. This way is not easy to follow because of recent forestry operations.

The route then goes S over a spur to Easter Auquhollie and from there SE past Nether Auquhollie to join the Slug Road (A957) at Mowtie, 5km from Stonehaven. Above Mowtie is the site of the Roman camp at Raedykes.

This route by Auquhollie is the only route from Stonehaven to Deeside shown on Garden's map of Kincardine in 1776. One branch by Denside went to the old ford on the River Dee at Tilbouries, 1km south of Drum. It is also shown on Roy's map of 1755. Balfour (see note above) describes the Elsick Mounth as going from Stonehaven to Drum.

## 167  Banchory to Glenbervie by the Cryne Corse Mounth
*22km/14miles*                    *OS Sheet 45. Start 701 950.  Finish 766 807*
There is a good deal of road walking at the northern and southern ends of this route, with a section through the Fetteresso Forest in the middle. From Banchory cross the Bridge of Feugh, take the road upstream and at the first fork go left for 5km to join the Slug Road (A957) at Blairydryne. Proceed along it to the sharp bend beyond Spyhill Farm and from there go S up the minor road towards the TV station. Some 250 metres before reaching it turn SE off this road to shortly meet a line of electricity pylons which follow the Cryne Corse Mounth for the most part to the main track along the Cowie Water.
Follow this SW for a short distance before turning left across a bridge over the Cowie Water by a forest road (signposted as a mountain bicycle track) which leads uphill passing a large gravel pit on the left. Keep straight on at the immediately following junction and aim SE for the road on the west side of Hill of Quithel  (map ref 774 856). This descends to the road to Stonehaven. Turn right there to the former schoolhouse at map ref 757 837 and then go left by Goosecruives to Glenbervie.

## 168  Strachan to Glenbervie by the Stock Mounth
*19km/12miles*                    *OS Sheet 45. Start 675 923.  Finish 766 807*
Take the B974 road S across the Water of Feugh for 400 metres to turn first left to Moss-side and about 600 metres beyond there take a farm track going S and climbing across the west side of Blarourie to a gate at map ref 700 897. This gives entry to a forest road which goes SE between Shillofad and North Dennetys. The route then descends and crosses the Burn of Sheeoch, skirts the west side of Monluth Hill and meets the main forest road on the north side of the Cowie Burn at map ref 733 868. Crossing the bridge over the burn, the walker may follow the main forest road SW then S to go round the west side of Leachie Hill and descend past the site of Maxie Well to Chapelton Croft (map ref 736 832). From there a farm track is followed past Chapelton Farm to the Stonehaven road and across it to Glenbervie.

## 169  Strachan to Auchenblae by the Builg Mounth
*20km/12½ miles*                    *OS Sheet 45. Start 675 923.  Finish 728 787*
This is an ancient right of way from Strachan in Feughside to Paldy Fair near Glenfarquhar Lodge, 3km north of Auchenblae.
Take the B974 road from Strachan as far as the Bridge of Bogendreip. Just before the bridge over the Water of Dye take the signposted track leading parallel to the river. After about 400 metres, transfer to a forest road some 200 metres higher up the hillside and continue S through the forest for about 3½km. On leaving the forest the track is quite clear, curving round the base of

Hare Hill to join a forest road below Little Kerloch. Leave it at about map ref 683 868 by a path heading SE along a forest ride towards the Builg Burn. Continue over rough ground to the col between Tipperweir and Kerloch where an old track leads into the forest. This is followed SE, then W for a short distance then SE along the West Burn of Builg.

Alternatively, where the old track in the forest turns W, a ride with a wall on its left-hand side, possibly the old track, may be followed E to join another track at East Burn of Builg, which is followed S. From the junction of the two burns continue the descent SE to Corsebauld and Chapelton Farm, from where a farm road going SW leads to the Stonehaven road, Mains of Glenfarquhar and Auchenblae.

Garden's map of 1776 marks this route as 'Builg Road, a Foot Path.'

### 170   Aboyne to Tarfside (Glen Esk) by the Fungle Road
*20km/12¹/₂ miles*          *OS Sheet 44.  Start 525 977↑.  Finish 492 797↑*

From the bridge over the River Dee go S up The Fungle by a steep road between Birsemore Hill and Craigendinnie to a cottage, The Guard. From there a track continues through woodland and across the Allt Dinnie to join a track which goes S over the col south-west of Carnferg to Birse Castle. Leave this track before reaching the castle and turn S at a SRWS signpost to follow a path to another SRWS signpost at map ref 521 900.

From there the route continues SSW up a path on the west side of the stream to the col between Mudlee Bracks and Tampie. 800 metres beyond the col the path is joined by the Fir Mount (route 171) and descends by Shinfur and the Water of Tarf to Tarfside village in Glen Esk.

The road to Edzell follows the left bank of the River North Esk, but for walkers wishing to make this very long extension to the Fungle Road, a better route is to cross the North Esk at Tarfside and go down its right bank by Keenie and Dalhastnie to Dalbog, thence by a minor road to Gannochy Bridge. Then turn down the path on the river bank from the bridge to reach Edzell. This riverside walk from Tarfside to Edzell adds 20km/12¹/₂ miles to the Fungle Road.

Balfour calls this route the Forest of Birse Mounth, 'from Cairn Corse to Birse on Deeside'. Cairncross is at Tarfside. The route is shown on Roy's map.

### 171   Dinnet to Tarfside (Glen Esk) by the Firmounth
*21km/13miles*          *OS Sheet 44.  Start 459 987.  Finish 492 797↑*

From Dinnet the route is across the River Dee and SE by Burnside and Belrorie to the old bridge over the Water of Tanar at Braeloine. This point can also be reached from Aboyne by Bridge o' Ess. On the road near Belrorie a stone erected in the last century by Sir William Brooks of Glentanar describes this crossing incorrectly as the route used by Edward I in 1296.

From Braeloine Bridge, go upstream to Knockie Bridge, then up past Knockie Viewpoint. In about 2km cross the Burn of Skinna and climb the ridge between it and the Water of Allachy to Craigmahandle (574m). After a slight drop the path rises again to St. Colm's Well, and goes just W of the summit of  Gannoch (731m) and S over Tampie (723m). 1¹/₂ km further south the path joins the Fungle Road on its descent to Tarfside.

**172 Ballater to Tarfside (Glen Esk) by Mounth Keen**
*26km/16miles*                    *OS Sheet 44. Start 372 956. Finish 492 797*
    Cross the River Dee and go SW along the B976 for 1km to Bridge of
Muick. Strike uphill to the left by a narrow road to Balintober, and continue
by a track which climbs S then SE round the side of Craig Vallich to a col on
its south side. Descend a short distance NE along the track and then go E by
an indistinct path across the headwaters of the Pollagach Burn to a gate in the
fence at 600m on the ridge opposite. Beyond it the track descends, first SE
then S to a footbridge over the Water of Tanar. (This point can also be reached
from Dinnet to Glen Tanar House and from there on foot.) The track climbs S
up the north ridge of Mount Keen (939m) and reaches 750m on its west side.
An alternative path goes over the summit.
    Continue S and in 1km the track begins to drop steeply by the Ladder
Burn to the cottage of Glenmark, beyond which is the well commemorating
Queen Victoria's crossing by this route in 1861. The track continues down the
east bank of the Water of Mark to the end of the public road at Invermark,
5km fromTarfside.

**173 Ballater to Clova (The Capel Mounth)**
*29km/18miles*                    *OS Sheet 44. Start 372 956. Finish 327 731*
    From Ballater cross the River Dee and go by road up Glen Muick for
14km to the Spittal of Glenmuick, the site of an old hospice for travellers
and now a much-used carpark. Go SW along the track for 400 metres and
take the left-hand track diagonally uphill across the west side of Black Hill
and continue SSW over undulating moorland west of Watery Hill to Gallow
Hillock. From there the path climbs slightly over the shoulder of Capel
Mounth and then descends steeply in zigzags down the ridge between
Moulzie Burn and Capel Burn and through a plantation to reach Glen Clova.
The carpark at the end of the public road is 1km further down the glen, and
from there Glen Doll Youth Hostel is ½ km up Glen Doll, and Clova Inn is
5km down Glen Clova.
    This old route is marked as 'Mounth Capell' on a map dated about 1360.

**174 Crathie to Clova**
*34km/21miles*                    *OS Sheet 44. Start 264 950. Finish 327 731*
    Although this is not strictly speaking a Mounth Road, it is included in this
section as a variation of the Capel Mounth.
    Starting at Crathie, go along the B976 road to Easter Balmoral and the
distillery. Turn S at map ref 272 938 and go SE along a road to a deer fence
and gate at map ref 276 933. Continue SE then S along a good track round the
east slope of Tom Bad a' Mhonaidh to the col south of Meall Gorm. Just beyond
the col take the right-hand track which leads directly to Allt-na-giubhsaich,
and cross the glen to Spittal of Glenmuick. At this point the Capel Mounth
route is joined and may be followed to Clova as described above.
    An alternative way from Spittal of Glenmuick goes SW along a track just
above Loch Muick for 3km and then climbs by steep zigzags to the level
plateau above. Continue along the track on the edge of this plateau to the

little hut at the col between Broad Cairn and Sandy Hillock. From there take the path S to the ruins of Bachnagairn at the head of Glen Clova. Go down the glen by a track, joining route 173 to reach the end of the public road near Braedownie, and Clova Inn 5km further down the glen.

### 175 Auchallater (Braemar) to Glen Clova by the Tolmount
*25km/15¹/₂ miles        OS Sheets 43 and 44. Start 156 883↑. Finish 327 731*

Auchallater is 3km south of Braemar along the A93 road. From there go SE up Glen Callater by a good track to Loch Callater. Continue along the path on the north-east side of the loch and up the Allt an Loch with a steep climb up the headwall of Glen Callater to reach the col at 880m between Tolmount and Knaps of Fafernie. The path turns SE across the featureless plateau, climbs slightly to 900m just below the top of Crow Craigies and continues along the undulating crest of a broad ridge towards Craig Lunkard. Before reaching that point descend steeply S into the head of Glen Doll, but do not go right down to the White Water. The path passes a small shelter and continues SE for almost 2km (at this point it is called Jock's Road) before it drops down to the floor of the glen and enters the forest. Glen Doll Youth Hostel is 3km further on, and ¹/₂ km beyond it routes 173 and 174 are joined 5km from Clova Inn.

This is one of the most serious walks described in this book. It crosses a high, exposed and featureless plateau which in winter is frequently swept by storms. At that time of year the path over the plateau is likely to be covered by snow and completely invisible for several months, and accurate route-finding in bad weather will require considerable skill.

This right of way was the subject of an action in the Court of Session in 1886-87, and in the House of Lords in 1888, when it was proved that it had been for long the practice of drovers to take sheep from Braemar over the Tolmount to the market at Cullow, near Kirriemuir.

### 176  Glen Clunie to Glen Isla by the Monega Road
*14km/9miles                OS Sheet 43. Start 147 800.  Finish 192 697↑*

This is the highest of the Mounth Roads, reaching just over 1000m near the summit of Glas Maol. The route begins from the A93 road in Glen Clunie 12km south of Braemar, at a carpark near a footbridge over the Cairnwell Burn. Cross this burn and the smaller Allt a' Gharbh-choire to go SE up Sron na Gaoithe, where there is virtually no path up the steep and in places rocky nose of this ridge. Continue SE along a path on the broad crest to reach the plateau 1km north of Glas Maol where the path joins a vehicle track.

Follow this track S towards the summit of Glas Maol for about ¹/₂ km, then bear SSE above the very steep slopes at the head of the Caenlochan Glen, traversing 50m below and 400 metres east of the top of Glas Maol. The track bears SE along the edge of the cliffs above the Caenlochan Glen over the slight rise of Little Glas Maol, then S (bypassing the summit of Monega Hill) and down to Glen Isla 1km above Tulchan Lodge. The end of the public road in the glen at Auchavan is 3km further. From there it is 10km down the glen to Kirkton of Glenisla.

The remarks about the serious nature of the Tolmount route, particularly in winter, apply equally well to the Monega Road.

# SECTION 16
# The Cairngorms

This section, which extends to the west and east well beyond the true boundary of the Cairngorms, includes some of the longest and most serious of mountain walks in Scotland. Not only do the routes go through country which, with the exception of a few isolated lodges, is entirely uninhabited, but they also penetrate into the heart of some of the highest mountains in Scotland, mountains which are well known for their vast scale and arctic climate. Such is the nature of this climate that storms of winter severity can blow at any time of the year, and walkers essaying the long-distance routes between Deeside, Strathspey and Atholl should be fully equipped and prepared for serious mountain expeditions and not just cross-country walks. However, the rewards of such expeditions are great, for the walker will experience the whole range of mountain scenery and solitude among the great plateaux-hills and glens and the ancient pine forests of Rothiemurchus, Derry and Dee.

## 177  Blair Atholl to Linn of Dee by Glen Tilt
*35km/22miles*                    *OS Sheet 43  Start 876 656.  Finish 062 897↑*

This is one of the great historical rights of way in Scotland, and it is likely that the legal battle to establish its status in 1849 did more than any other event to raise the awareness of rights of way in the public eye. The traditional route of the right of way goes from Blair Atholl to Old Bridge of Tilt and from there by the road to Fenderbridge and a short distance further uphill. At map ref 884 672 turn left and follow a track through fields and woodland on the hillside above the river. The track descends past Croftmore to the river beyond Gilberts Bridge, and the way continues up the road past Marble Lodge, across the river and 4km further to Forest Lodge. Continue along the road, which 5km beyond Forest Lodge bears uphill to the left on its way to Tarf bothy.

The route to Braemar continues unmistakably up Glen Tilt by a path which in 2km crosses the Tarf Water by the Bedford Memorial Bridge, erected in 1886 as a memorial to a young Englishman drowned while trying to ford the Tarf. The Falls of Tarf are partly seen from the bridge. The path continues NE up the narrow glen of the Allt Garbh Buidhe and reaches the watershed at about 490m.

Continuing N from there, the landscape is very different, for the deep, straight and narrow trench of Glen Tilt changes to the more expansive rounded hills and open glens that hold the Bynack and Geldie burns on their way to join the River Dee. Go N along the wide glen of the Allt an t-Seilich past the ruins of Bynack Lodge to reach the Geldie Burn, where there is no bridge and the crossing may be difficult if the burn is in spate. Beyond there a rough track leads alongside the Geldie Burn to White Bridge, where the River Dee is crossed, and onwards beside the river to Linn of Dee, where the public road is reached. Braemar is 10km further on.

**170 Blair Atholl or Calvine to Ruthven Barracks or Tromie Bridge (Kingussie) by the Minigaig Pass**
*42km/26miles*
   OS Sheets 35,42 and 43.  *Start 876 656.  Finish 764 996↑ or 790 995↑*
   From Blair Atholl go up the east side of the River Tilt to the old bridge, cross it to Old Blair and then go NW by the road up the Banvie Burn. In another 2km turn N up the Allt na Moine Baine for 1km, then cross this burn and go NW over to the Allt an t-Seapail and then, still NW, over to the Allt Sheicheachan, where the track ends at a bothy. Continue NNW along a path round the hillside, descend into Glen Bruar and go up to Bruar Lodge, where the track from Calvine is joined. This track, which starts from the A9 road 7km west of Blair Atholl, can be used as an alternative start to the Minigaig Pass.
   From Bruar Lodge, continue up the east bank of the Bruar Water for another 5km and when the glen divides climb due N up the steep hill straight ahead to reach the crest of Uchd a' Chlarsair. Descend slightly, still heading N, and climb a gradual slope to the Minigaig Pass (833m). The descent across the west slopes of Leathad an Taobhain continues N, then lower down the path bears NW down the north bank of the Allt Bhran to reach the private road in Glen Tromie. At this point route 179 is joined.
   The way down Glen Tromie for the next 2½km goes along the road, and then there are three possible finishes
   (a)  To follow the original soldiers' route to Ruthven Barracks, cross the River Tromie by a footbridge at map ref 753 923 and climb just E of N up heathery slopes past Carn Pheigith and over the east shoulder of Sron na Gaoithe. Just beyond the top of this rounded hill a faint path may be found at map ref 760 946. Follow it N slightly downhill to about map ref 760 959 where a better path is reached. Follow it NNE along the flat crest of the heathery moor to a junction of paths at map ref 770 974 and from there go N down a good path to Ruthven Barracks. Kingussie is 1½ km further across the River Spey.
   (b)  The second way is down Glen Tromie as far as Glentromie Lodge. Cross the River Tromie by a bridge and go over a stile on the right just beyond it to follow a waymarked path NW uphill through the birchwoods. At the upper edge of the trees cross the fence by a stile and continue NW for 400 metres to the crest of the moor where route (a) above is joined.
   (c)  The third finish goes right down the private road in Glen Tromie to Tromie Bridge, 2½ km along the B970 from Ruthven Barracks.
   The Minigaig is the only road to the north shown on Greene's map of 1689 and Moll's map of 1725. It was superseded by the military road over the Drumochter Pass constructed by Wade in 1728-30, although after that date the Minigaig still appeared on maps as a 'summer road to Ruthven'.
   If doing this route from Ruthven Barracks southwards, the start is at a field gate about 50 metres south-west of the carpark at the barracks. Go along the edge of a field, turn right along the edge of the next field and aim S along a track up a small wooded glen to a ruined cottage, beyond which a stile gives access to the open hillside. Follow the path S almost to the crest of the moor and look out for the point (marked by a small cairn) where the right of way turns SSW while the more obvious path continues SE to Glentromie Lodge.

## 179  Dalnacardoch to Ruthven Barracks or Tromie Bridge by the Gaick Pass
*32km/20miles*
>     *OS Sheets 35 and 42.   Start 723 704↑.   Finish 764 996↑ or 790 995↑*

Dalnacardoch is 11km north-west of Calvine on the A9 road. Be careful if crossing the very busy dual carriageway at the start of this right of way. A private road goes N from the roadside through a plantation past a radio mast and continues N beside the Edendon Water for 8km to Sronphadruig Lodge. ¹/₂ km beyond the lodge leave the track to cross the Edendon Water and follow a good path N along the west side of Loch an Duin across the foot of the very steep slopes of An Dun, which plunge for 300m from its summit into the loch.

At the north end of the loch cross the Allt Loch an Duin, usually easy at some sandy banks, and go NE for a short distance to reach the start of a track. This track, known as Domingo's Road, continues down the east side of the glen past Loch Bhrodainn to the Allt Gharbh Ghaig, which may be difficult to cross in wet weather. Continue past Gaick Lodge and Loch an t-Seilich to join route 178 at the bridge across the Allt Bhran. The final part of this route down Glen Tromie to Ruthven Barracks or Tromie Bridge goes by any one of the three possibilities described above for route178.

## 180  Drumguish or Feshiebridge (Strathspey) to Linn of Dee by Glen Feshie and Glen Geldie
*38km/24miles*
>     *OS Sheets 35 and 43.   Start 789 998↑ or 851 043↑.   Finish 061 897↑*

This is one of the three great, long Cairngorm rights of way. It does not go through the heart of these mountains, but rather round their south-western perimeter. The start of the route goes through the forested lower reaches of Glen Feshie culminating in the fine stands of Scots pine at Ruigh-aiteachain, beyond which there is a very fine section through the narrow glen enclosed by steep crags. Then the way goes for many kilometres over more open country across the watershed between the Feshie and the Geldie and eastwards to join the River Dee.

Drumguish at the foot of Glen Tromie is one possible starting point in Strathspey. It is 5km from Kingussie along the B970 road past Ruthven Barracks. From there follow the right of way east, at first along a road through the forest to the Allt Chromhraig. This stream may be difficult or impossible to cross if in spate, but is easy in dry weather. Continue E along a grassy track over open ground to re-enter the forest and reach the private road up Glen Feshie, ¹/₂ km north of Stronetoper.

This point may equally well be reached from Feshiebridge, 2¹/₂ km from Kincraig, by going up the west bank of the River Feshie by paths and tracks past Ballintean and along the public road in Glen Feshie for 2km to Tolvah.

Continue up Glen Feshie by the private road to Carnachuin and cross to the east bank of the river by a footbridge. Follow the track (in places a path) along the right bank of the River Feshie through fine old pine woods and below the steep crags and screes of Creag na Gaibhre. About 11km from Carnachuin, the River Eidart is reached. Go upstream for several hundred metres to cross this potentially dangerous river by a bridge at map ref 914 886 and a short distance beyond it resume an easterly course to cross the watershed to the north bank of the Geldie Burn. About 5km beyond the Eidart, the road from Geldie Lodge (ruin) is joined and the route is then down the Geldie, in a further 5km joining the path from Glen Tilt, route 177. Continue NE to White Bridge and the River Dee, which is followed to the Linn of Dee. Braemar is 10km/6½ miles further down the valley.

## 181  Linn of Dee to Coylumbridge  by the Lairig Ghru
*32km/20miles*      *OS Sheets 36 and 43. Start 061 897↑. Finish 915 107↑*

This great pass is the most frequented route across the Cairngorms, going through much grander scenery than the Glen Feshie or Lairig an Laoigh routes. It is a long strenuous walk, requiring 10 to 12 hours, on a well trodden, but in places very rough path marked by cairns on its higher reaches. The walking distance quoted above is longer if one starts from Braemar or Inverey and walks all the way to Aviemore, in which case the total is about 45km/28miles

From Linn of Dee two routes are possible, either west to White Bridge and onwards by the path on the east side of the Dee to the entrance to the Lairig Ghru below The Devil's Point, or up Glen Lui and Glen Luibeg to reach the same point. The latter route gives better scenery and easier going, and is better for those reasons. The start is ½ km east of Linn of Dee at the foot of Glen Lui. Go along the road to Derry Lodge and from there W along the path on the north bank of the Luibeg Burn, crossing this burn where it comes down from Ben Macdui by a footbridge just upstream. Continue W over a broad col into Glen Dee opposite The Devil's Point and Corrour Bothy on the other side of the Dee. The route then goes N up Glen Dee; on the left are Cairn Toul, the great cliffs of An Garbh Choire, and then Braeriach, and on the right are the seemingly endless slopes of Ben Macdui. The path passes the Pools of Dee, one of the sources of the River Dee, and reaches the rough boulder strewn summit of the pass (833m).

The descent to Strathspey is at first on the west side of the Allt Druidh, but below the site of the now demolished Sinclair Memorial Hut (map ref 959 037) the path crosses to the east side of the stream and leads down to the first scattered pines of Rothiemurchus Forest.

If aiming for Glenmore, the best route is to follow the path branching to the right from a point just below the site of the demolished hut. It leads N on a gradual ascent to the Creag a' Chalamain gap and then goes NE to cross the Allt Mor by the bridge near the reindeer enclosure and joins the Coire Cas road 2½ km south-east of Loch Morlich.

Continuing along the path towards the first trees of Rothiemurchus Forest, another branch path goes right to Rothiemurchus Lodge from where a private road leads down to the west end of Loch Morlich. This is the shortest finish to reach a public road.

The traditional Lairig Ghru path goes down through the forest on the north-east side of the Allt Druidh to a junction of paths at map ref 938 075 where a right turn leads NE to the west end of Loch Morlich, and a left turn leads in 1km to the Cairngorm Club footbridge, erected in 1912, and in a further 3km to Coylumbridge, 2½ km from Aviemore.

In the reverse direction, there is a signpost at Coylumbridge and another one 800 metres further on where the Lairig Ghru and Gleann Einich paths diverge. At the junction of paths at map ref 938 075 turn right. After passing the Pools of Dee, follow the left bank of the River Dee, and just after the Corrour Bothy footbridge take the left-hand path which goes slightly uphill and over a col to Glen Luibeg and Derry Lodge. W.J.Watson in *Place Names of Celtic Scotland* considers ghru to be a corruption of druidh, the name of the stream flowing N from the pass.

## 182   Linn of Dee to Nethy Bridge by the Lairig an Laoigh
*38km/24miles        OS Sheets 36 and 43.   Start 061 897↑.   Finish 001 206↑*

As far as Derry Lodge the way is the same as route 181 for the Lairig Ghru. Just beyond the lodge cross the footbridge and continue up Glen Derry, at first on the west side of the Derry Burn through a beautiful remnant of the Old Caledonian forest, then on the east side. At the foot of Coire Etchachan the path to Ben Macdui strikes off to the left. For Nethybridge keep straight on up to the pass (745m) and descend by the Dubh Lochan to the Fords of Avon, where the ford may be quite deep and dangerous in spate conditions.

Keeping N, the path in another 2km passes Lochan a' Bhainne and reaches the headwaters of the Water of Caiplich, which flows down to Tomintoul. Care must be taken to follow the path when it goes uphill over the east shoulder of Bynack More at a height of 774m. From there the route goes NW across the wide slopes of Coire Odhar and over the highest point of the route at 790m on the north ridge of Bynack More. It is imperative not to stray eastwards from the path in this area. Then descend 350m along the path to the River Nethy, crossed by the footbridge at Bynack Stable, and follow a track WNW past Loch a' Gharbh-Choire. Just beyond there the track forks, the left-hand branch leading SW through Ryvoan Pass. The other track to the right goes N past Ryvoan Bothy to Forest Lodge, where there are several roads and tracks in Abernethy Forest, but by keeping N there is no difficulty in reaching Nethy Bridge by Dell Lodge.

The way through Ryvoan Pass past An Lochan Uaine, which lives up to its name as the green lochan,  to the end of the public road at Glenmore Lodge gives a much shorter end to this long walk, and 2km beyond the lodge Loch Morlich is reached, from where there is a bus service to Aviemore.

## 182X Feshiebridge to Nethy Bridge through the Forests of Inshriach, Rothiemurchus, Glenmore and Abernethy
*32km/20miles        OS Sheet 36.   Start 851 043.   Finish 001 206↑*

This is an excellent low-level walk through the forests of the Cairngorms, ideal for a day when cloud covers the high mountains. From Feshiebridge go up the B970 road towards Coylumbridge for 200 metres and turn right along the road up Glen Feshie. In 100 metres further turn left and follow a forest road NE to cross-roads, then E to emerge from the forest, at present being felled, at map ref 879 057. Continue E along a track for ¹/₂ km past Inshriach bothy and beyond it by a path heading N to Loch an Eilein. Go along the south-east side of the loch for 1¹/₂ km and turn right along the track which leads F for ?km to the Cairngorm Club Footbridge. Cross it and turn right along a path up the Allt Druidh to the junction at map ref 938 075. There go NE by the path which joins the road leading from Rothiemurchus Lodge to the bridge across the River Luineag at the west end of Loch Morlich.

About 300 metres before reaching the bridge turn right along the forest road on the south side of Loch Morlich to reach the road to Coire Cas at map ref 980 091. Go S along this road for ½ km and take a path on the left across the Allt Mor (not named on the Landranger map) to reach the end of a forest road. Follow this NE then N to join the road through Ryvoan Pass. Turn right and go past An Lochan Uaine, then ½ km further keep left to Ryvoan Bothy. Continue along the track, at first across open moorland and then into the pinewood of Abernethy to Forest Lodge and Nethy Bridge, following the last part of route 182.

### 183 Coylumbridge to Achlean (Glen Feshie) by Gleann Einich
*20km/12½ miles*          *OS Sheet 36.  Start 915 107↑.  Finish 852 977*
This route crosses the hills between Loch Einich and Glen Feshie, and it involves the ascent of a steep little corrie. It is only suitable for those with some hillwalking experience, particularly in winter and spring when the hills are snow-covered. On a dry summer day, however, it should present no problems. It is advisable to do this route from north to south, as described, as the descent of the corrie at the head of Loch Einich may be more difficult than the ascent.

From Coylumbridge go S along the Lairig Ghru path, but keep right in 800 metres to pass below Whitewell (where this route may be started) and continue along the track up Gleann Einich. It is equally possible to start from the end of the public road at Loch an Eilein. The crossing of the Beanaidh Beag 5km up Gleann Einich may be difficult in spate, particularly in spring when snow in the high corries of Braeriach is melting. At the outflow of Loch Einich go round the west side of the loch along a path beside the loch below the crags of Sgor Gaoith.

The path makes a rising traverse above the south end of Loch Einich and ends at a little stream flowing down from the plateau. Climb up to the south of this stream, aiming for the rocky base of a spur at map ref 905 976, go round to the south side of this spur and climb its crest to the plateau. Walk up gentle grassy slopes WSW to Carn Ban Mor (1052m) and continue SW from the summit for 400 metres to join a path leading NW down towards Glen Feshie. The path goes along the spur towards Carn Ban Beag and then down the slopes on the north side of the Allt Fhearnagan to Achlean at the end of the public road on the east side of Glen Feshie.

### 184  Nethy Bridge to Tomintoul
*20km/12½ miles*          *OS Sheet 36.  Start 001 206↑.  Finish 166 190*
Go from Nethy Bridge along the Tomintoul road for 5km and then take the right-hand fork which goes to Dorback Lodge. Go to the left behind the lodge and along the track to Letteraitten and then continue E by an old road to the Burn of Brown, which must be crossed at a shallow ford. From there a

path leads down the east side of the burn to meet a forestry road which goes E uphill and past Stronachavie, then downhill to join the A939 road at Bridge of Avon, 2km north-west of Tomintoul.

For a longer and more interesting route to Dorback Lodge which avoids the road walking of the previous route, leave Nethy Bridge past Dell Lodge and take the road on the west side of the River Nethy almost to Forest Lodge. Just before reaching the lodge cross to the east bank of the river and go by a forest road, first SE for 800m, then S for nearly 2km. There turn E round the southern slope of Carn a' Chnuic, passing on the north of Loch a' Chnuic and head E for a narrow pass, the Eag Mhor. From there go down the slope to Upper Dell and cross the Dorback Burn at a ford. Take a shortcut to join the track between Dorback Lodge and Letteraitten and continue to Tomintoul as described above (27km/17miles).

### 185  Invercauld (Braemar) to Tomintoul
*32km/20miles        OS Sheets 36 and 43.  Start 187 913↑.  Finish 166 190*
The start of this route across the eastern flank of the Cairngorms is just east of Invercauld Bridge on the A93 road, 5km east of Braemar. 200 metres east of the bridge go along the minor road to Keiloch and continue NW towards Invercauld House. After approximately 1km, at an SRWS signpost, take the steep track on the right uphill heading N by the west side of Meall Gorm and the east of Creag a' Chait to the Bealach Dearg at map ref 180 981. There either take the foopath down the Allt na Claise Moire to the River Gairn or continue along the track which climbs 1km NE towards Culardoch before descending to the Gairn. Cross the bridge and go along the north side of the Gairn, then N along the east side of Loch Builg and down Glen Builg to Inchrory. From there it is 11km along the private road down Glen Avon to Tomintoul.

As an alternative, go to Keiloch as above, but there turn right (instead of left), and go NE to Felagie, and N for another 2km by Balnoe to Balmore. (This may be shortened by starting from Inver on the A93 and going by Knockan to Balnoe). Turn E at Balmore across the Fearder Burn and follow the path to Ratlich. Continue on an old track E then N, keeping to the west of Carn Moine an Tighearn, then NW across the eastern flank of Culardoch, and descend in another 5km by Tom a' Chuir to the River Gairn and Loch Builg to join the route described above.

### 185X  Linn of Dee to Tomintoul by the Lairig an Laoigh and Glen Avon.
*45km/28miles        OS Sheets 36 and 43.  Start 061 897↑.  Finish 166 190*
This is a combination of routes 182 and 185. It starts from Linn of Dee and follows route 182 to Derry Lodge and north across the Lairig an Laoigh to the crossing of the River Avon. There follows a very long walk down Glen Avon, first along a path, then a rough road to Inchrory. Finally, the last 11km of route 185 lead to Tomintoul.

# Northeast Scotland

### 186  Crathie to Tomintoul
*35km/22miles          OS Sheets 36 and 37.  Start 264 950.  Finish 166 190*
For most of its length this route follows an old drove road between Deeside and Tomintoul. From Crathie to Glen Gairn it is also coincides with the line of the Old Military Road constructed in 1750-54.

From Crathie follow the A93 road towards Braemar for 400 metres, then go N by the B976 for about 1km until just beyond Bush Crathie. There take a track going off to the left and go N, passing just to the west of Blairglass and then NW down to the River Gairn. Descend the Gairn for 2km and then cross it to Easter Sleach. (This point may also be reached by a shorter walk from Braenaloin on the B976 road). From Easter Sleach go N by a track just west of Tom Odhar, then due N to Carn Meadhonach where a track is reached which leads past Carn Mor to Ordgarff and Cock Bridge. Then go W up the north bank of the River Don for 3km to Dunanfiew, and from there N over the ridge between Carn Ealasaid and Tolm Buirich, and down to Blairnamarrow on the Lecht road, 6km south-east of Tomintoul.

An alternative after passing Blairglass is to go up the River Gairn to Loch Builg and continue by route 185 to Inchrory and Tomintoul.

### 187  Ballater to Cock Bridge (Donside)
*19km/12mls          OS Sheet 37.  Start 370 958.  Finish 257 092*
Leave Ballater by the road to Braemar and at Bridge of Gairn turn to the right up the road on the east bank of the River Gairn to Lary. Continue by a path up Glen Fenzie to the Glas Choille road, the Old Military Road which crosses to Donside. 1½ km beyond the summit of this road, strike left along the Old Military Road across the Burn of Tornahaish, down to the River Don and up its south bank to Cock Bridge.

For an alternative, go up the left bank of the River Gairn from Lary to the bridge on the A939 road and continue for another 2km to Tullochmacarrick. 'The Ca' Road' goes N from there to the Allt Coire nam Freumh; its continuation north is now lost where it climbs over the ridge between Carn a' Bhacain (751m) and The Ca' (678m) to join the Old Military Road 400 metres southeast of Delavine at map ref 285 068.

Routes 186 and 187 are shown as an old road from Corgarff to Crathie on a rough map in the British Museum drawn by George Campbell, Cadet Gunner, about 1748.

The next two routes are extensions of 187 northwards and westwards which enable long cross-country routes to be made, the longest of these leading to Aviemore and Nethy Bridge.

## 188  Cock Bridge (Donside) to Tomintoul by Inchrory

*21km/13miles*          *OS Sheets 36 and 37.  Start 257 092.   Finish 169 186*
Go W by the rough road up the south side of the River Don past
Delnadamph Lodge and over the pass near the source of the Don to Inchrory,
then N by the private road down Glen Avon to Tomintoul.

## 189  Cock Bridge (Donside) to Nethy Bridge or Aviemore

*51km/32miles*          *OS Sheets 36 and 37.  Start 257 092.  Finish 001 206↑.*
Follow route 188 up the River Don and over the pass to Inchrory. Then
go W by a rough road and path for a long way up the River Avon past
Faindouran bothy. Reach the Lairig an Laoigh path (route 182) at the Fords of
Avon and turn N to follow this route past Ryvoan bothy and Forest Lodge to
Nethy Bridge. It is equally possible to reach Glenmore Lodge and Aviemore
by turning left at the track junction just south-west of Ryvoan, and if you
catch the bus or get a lift from Loch Morlich to  Aviemore, the walking distance from Cock Bridge is 40km/25miles.

## 190  Ballater to Boultenstone (Donside)

*20km/12½ miles*          *OS Sheet 37.  Start 370 958.   Finish 411 109*
Morven (871m) dominates the countryside between Ballater and the
River Don, and there are many tracks and paths across this area which give
good walks. The following routes starting from Ballater  and heading north
and north-east are just two of several that cross the lower slopes of Morven
and go high enough to give splendid views of Deeside, Donside and the more
distant mountains, among which Lochnagar reigns supreme.
One way from Ballater over to Donside follows route 187 from Bridge of
Gairn up the east side of the River Gairn to Lary, then goes N up the road
towards Morven Lodge. Leave this road in 2km at map ref 341 022 to go NE
for ½ km by a track and thence up the Morven Burn to the col on the north-
west  side of Morven. Continue ENE down the Braes of Fintock to reach a
track which leads along the east side of the Deskry Water to Boultenstone
Hotel and the A97 road between Donside and Dinnet.
Another route follows the preceding one to the point 2½ km beyond Lary
at map ref 344 027 where the track turns E across the south slopes of Morven.
Follow this for about 5km, mostly at about the 500m contour, and drop down
the east side of Morven to Milton of Whitehouse, from where it is 2km further
to Logie Coldstone on the A97 road.

## 191  Tarland to Glenkindie (Donside)

*13km/8miles*          *OS Sheet 37.  Start 482 046.   Finish 437 138*
One route which is presently used by walkers goes north from Tarland by
minor roads past Douneside and Ranna, then NNE to Pressendye Hill (619m).
Descend NW along the ridge leading to The Socach and Craiglea Hill and
continue downhill in the same direction by a path to Haughton and Milltown
of Towie. Cross the River Don and reach Glenkindie 2km further along a
minor road.

An alternative route with less climbing goes NW from Tarland along the minor road past East Davoch to Lazy Well. Continue along the track which leads over the col between Baderonach Hill and Gallows Hill and descend to the public road. Turn right and go to Towie and 1km beyond there reach Glenkindie across the River Don.

### 192 Alford to Rhynie across the Correen Hills
*16km/10miles* OS Sheet 37. Start 576 160. Finish 499 271
From Alford go N by the public road to Montgarrie and Tullynessle, then NW by Dubston and the old quarry road to Correen Quarry, now abandoned. From there continue over the Correen Hills between Badingair Hill and Mire of Midgates to Cairn More and the road to Rhynie.

### 193 Glenkindie (Donside) to Cabrach
*16km/10miles* OS Sheet 37. Start 428 142. Finish 388 270
Leave the A97 road in Donside1km west of Glenkindie and go N up the Kindie Burn by Glencuie and Rinmore to Largue, where the road ends. Then go NNW by a track which ends ¹/₂ km south of the col between Dun Mount and Mount Meddin. Go N across this col over very rough ground - peat bog and heather - to find the end of the track on the north side of the watershed. Accurate navigation is necessary. This track leads down the north-flowing Kindy Burn past Bracklach to Powneed, from where a farm road goes to Cabrach.

### 194 Strathdon to Cabrach
*18km/11¹/₂ miles* OS Sheet 37. Start 370 123. Finish 388 270
Leave the A944 road 2km east of Strathdon village, then go N by road to Glen Buchat and NW up the glen for 1¹/₂ km to the access road to Upperton. Continue N by the track on the east side of White Hill and over the col (466m) east of Creag na Gamhna. Cross the Burn of Westlewie at Roch Ford, go over Broomknowe of Garbet and continue N across the east side of Keirn, where several other recent tracks cross the old one, to reach the end of the narrow public road near Aldivalloch. Finally, go 3km along this road to Cabrach on the A941 road between Rhynie and Dufftown.

### 195 Bellabeg (Donside) to Knockandhu or Tomintoul by The Ladder Road
*20km/12¹/₂ miles or 26km/16miles*
OS Sheets 36 and 37. Start 354 131. Finish 213 237 or 166 190
Start from Bellabeg , ¹/₂ km from Strathdon village, and go along the road up the north-east side of the Water of Nochty to Auchernach and W through the forest to Aldachuie. 1km further the edge of the forest is reached and the burn crossed to Duffdefiance. The route continues NW uphill by a path, joining a track over Finlate Hill, and finally along the line of the old path, of which there is now little evidence, to the summit of the Ladder Road (735m) at the col just north-east of Dun Muir. Descending on the north-west side, a good path leads down into the wide bowl of the Braes of Glenlivet at Ladderfoot.

Continue to Corry and Chapeltown, from where it is 4¹/₂ km to Knockandhu on the B9008 road.   Alternatively go via Clashnoir, Lettoch and the path through the forest plantation to the B9008 road, about 4km from Tomintoul.

## 196  Tomintoul to Cabrach by The Steplar
*27km/17mls*          *OS Sheets 36 and 37.  Start 166 190.  Finish 388 270*
This is an old right of way and drove road.  From Tomintoul take the B9008 Dufftown road for about 3¹/₂ km.  Go up the access road to Inchnacape and take the track which goes NE through forest, then downhill to Lettoch and the public road.  Cross it and, almost straight ahead, follow a field boundary and a forest ride to a fly-tip above Chapeltown.  Here turn left, then right between double fences to the public road junction (telephone and post box) and continue to Achnascraw.  Turn N then NE to Burnside of Thain, from where a path continues NE over heather moor to the River Livet and joins the track to Suie, now deserted.  Before Suie this track fords the Kymah Burn, but there is a footbridge near Knochkan, a deserted red-roofed cottage upstream.

About 300m beyond Suie bear right, leaving the better road which carries on up Glen Suie, and  follow an eroded bulldozed track round Carn na Bruar and down to ford the Black Water at map ref 330 267.  The rough track continues up to the Dead Wife's Hillock (543m), where there is a pedestrian gate in the deer fence, and then descends to a gate at the top of a large field.  From there a clear track runs down to Aldivalloch, (scene of the song Roy's Wife of Aldivalloch), which is also deserted but from where there is a good road to Cabrach.

Routes 195 and 196 are described in more detail in the Scottish Mountaineering Club guidebook The Cairngorms by Adam Watson.

## 197  Tomintoul to Dufftown by Glen Fiddich
*36km/22¹/₂ miles   OS Sheets 28, 36 and 37.  Start  166 190.  Finish 323 399*
Follow route 196 to Suie and continue NE up Glen Suie by a track to the head of the glen where one branch goes off up Corryhabbie Hill. Continue by the other branch down Glen Fiddich to cross a bridge near Glenfiddich Lodge, and go past the lodge down the left bank of the river to Bridgehaugh. If you want to avoid walking 5km along the A941 road, go NNW from Bridgehaugh to Smithstown and reach Dufftown along paths and farm roads round the east side of Goodman's Knowe.

## 198  Tomintoul to Knockando and Elgin
*54km/34miles          OS Sheets 28 and 36.  Start 166 190.  Finish 220 622*
The southern part of this route from Tomintoul to Knockando is probably best done, and is more pleasurable, along the Speyside Way, which is well waymarked.   Its line is shown on the most recent editions of the OS Landranger maps and it is worth pointing out that this section of the Way climbs to approx 548metres twice (Cairn Daimh and the Hill of Deskie) giving unparalleled views over upper Banffshire on the way to Knockando. Several well known whisky distilleries are passed which may add interest to the walk.

Leave Tomintoul at the north end of the village and go N to cross the Conglass Water by a footbridge and reach Croughly. From there go NNE across an expanse of peat bog known as the Feith Musach where a map and compass may be needed in bad weather, then pass just to the east of Cairn Ellick and bear NW to Carn Daimh. Continue due N on the west side of Carn Liath and descend to Blairfindy Lodge and the Glenlivet Distillery. Cross the River Livet and go N by Deskie and a path over the Hill of Deskie to descend to Auldich Farm and the A95 road above the River Avon. Go along the A95 and B9137 roads to Cragganmore, cross the River Spey by the old railway bridge and continue along the left bank of the river to Knockando.

To continue to Elgin, from the distillery turn N by road and pick up the road below Knockando Kirk (east of Upper Knockando) to go past Mannoch Cottage. Continue N along the edge of Elchies Forest on the east side of Carn na Cailliche just west of Pikey Hill and keep going due N along a narrow road to reach Shougle. Finally, go from there to Elgin 8½km along a minor road.

### 199  Grantown-on-Spey to Tomintoul by the Hills of Cromdale
*24km/15miles*                    *OS Sheet 36.  Start 033 278.  Finish 166 190*
From The Square in the centre of Grantown go S along Forest Road to the River Spey. Turn left and follow the private road along the left bank of the river for 5km to the Cromdale bridge. Cross it to reach the village of Cromdale. Continue SE by a track up the Haughs of Cromdale along the side of Claggersnich Wood, then climb steeply SE to cross the Hills of Cromdale about 2km north of Creagan a' Chaise. Descend SE to Milton and continue S by a minor road on the west side of the River Avon for 2km to a footbridge at map ref 146 231. Cross this, go up to the B9136 road and N along it for about 100 metres to the minor road past Tomachlaggan to join the Speyside Way at Croughly. Continue along the road for 1km and then go down to the right to cross the Conglass Water by a footbridge and reach the A939 road just north of Tomintoul.

# SECTION 18
# Moray and the Monadhliath

**200  Grantown-on-Spey to Forres**
*35km/22miles*         *OS Sheets 27 and 36.  Start 035 284.  Finish 034 582*
    This is a long walk, following minor roads, land rover tracks and, for one stretch, no visible route.  In the southern section over Dava Moor there is a delightful feeling of spaciousness. The northern section is more wooded and agricultural.  It is possible to traverse separate parts of the route individually.
    The first 3½km is along the A939 road from Grantown to Cottartown. From there go along the minor road past Lynmore and Lagg until ½km from Auchnagallin at map ref 047 338, then turn N there along a track passing Huntly's Cave and the ruin of Badahad.  On reaching the Allt Bog na Fiodhaig, where the track goes off westwards, continue on a difficult trackless section down the left bank of the Ourack Burn for less than 1½km to join a recognisable track in a conifer plantation, where fallen trees impede progress. The track improves, crosses the River Divie at map ref 047 423 and continues N down to Shenvault and Feakirk.  A less used track is then followed N, and after a heavily overgrown section crosses an insecure bridge to reach Lurg. Farm roads cross two more streams to reach the road to Johnstripe.
    From there a track rises over a ridge on the east side of Hill of Glaschyle and descends to the lowland country of Greens and Tomnamoon.  Continue along a minor road to Craigroy and 1km beyond there leave the obvious route at map ref 038 523 and head N to cross the Altyre Burn by a bridge. Beyond there follow a forest track steeply up into Altyre Wood high above the burn to Scurrypool Bridge at map ref 043 536.  Although much of the old railway is still walkable, the temptation to follow its more direct line should be resisted as a vital bridge has been washed away.  Good tracks lead on past Wardend House to the minor road passing the distillery at Manachie to reach Forres.

**201  Dulnain Bridge or Grantown-on-Spey to Dava by Lochindorb**
*18km/11miles*
                *OS Sheets 27 and 36.  Start 977 250 or 033 278.  Finish 966 341*
    This walk, much shorter than the preceding one, crosses the south-west corner of Dava Moor.  The most convenient starting point is 2km west of Dulnain Bridge on the A938 road. From there go N along the minor road past Achnahannet and continue up the track which ends at the ruined cottage of Easter Rynechkra (there is no continuing path despite what some OS maps show). The line of the route runs north of NNW for little over 1km to a prominent cairn at map ref 978 314, where traces of the old track can be seen in places where the heather is not too deep.
    Descend NNW, keeping well above the east side of Loch an t-Sidhein until descending to its outflow. In passing map ref 977 317 note a rough stone slab upright in the ground, suggesting an ancient grave and reminding the traveller of the dangers of these lonely heights.  A short distance NW of the

loch the start of a grassy track is reached and this leads down to the south end
of Lochindorb. Finally, go NE along the minor road on the south-east side of
the loch to reach Dava on the A939 road. An alternative start can be made
from Grantown-on-Spey. From the centre of the town go NW up a minor
road to Dreggie and continue by a private road which climbs NW across the
side of Gorton Hill. From near the end of the road climb WNW to reach the
col north of Easter Rynechkra (no path) and continue as described above.

## 202  Dulsie to Tomatin by the River Findhorn
*21km/13miles         OS Sheets 27 and 35.   Start 933 418.   Finish 789 320*
From the road junction just north of Dulsie, take the minor road for 9km
up the Findhorn valley to Drynachan Lodge and Daless. From there the route
follows a vehicular track across to the south bank of the River Findhorn by an
easy ford at map ref 860 381 and continues upstream to Ballachronin, and
then by a path to a point opposite Shenachie. The rope and pulley system
used to cross the river there is kept locked, and the alternative to wade across
at a ford is only possible if the river is low. If this is done, continue up the
north bank by a track to Ruthven and then by a minor road to join the A9 road
2km north of the Freeburn Hotel, Tomatin. If the River Findhorn cannot be
safely waded, it is preferable to follow its north bank for the whole way, taking the track which rises SW from Daless farm and going on to the ruins at
Kincraig (not shown on the OS Landranger map). From there minor paths are
followed along the river bank, becoming steep and narrow with a short
scrambly section 1km below Shenachie. Easy ground follows and the route
joins the track leading to Ruthven.

## 203  Boat of Garten to Tomatin by General Wade's Military Road
*18km/11miles         OS Sheets 35 and 36.   Start 913 188.   Finish 810 291↑*
Start at the main road junction 2km west of Boat of Garten and take the
private road under the railway and cross the A9 road, taking great care of the
high-speed traffic. Immediately after crossing, turn right to follow the Military
Road in a north-westerly direction through forest. In 5km cross the narrow
public road south-west of Carrbridge and continue downhill to the River
Dulnain, which is spanned by the splendid stone arch of the Sluggan Bridge,
originally built across a ford on Wade's road by Caulfeild in 1764 and rebuilt
in 1769 after it had been destroyed by floods. A surfaced cycle track follows
the line of the road to just before Insharn, then leaves the right of way and
swings north. To stay on the Military Road, go W from Insharn for about 200
metres across a small stone arch bridge and turn right through a gate into the
forest. Go uphill along a good track and in ½km emerge onto the open hillside. Continue N along the track by the edge of the forest to reach the railway. Go under it and continue along its east side to join the old A9 road and
follow it into the defile of the Slochd Mor, where the railway, old A9 and new
A9 share the narrow pass. Cross the new A9 at Slochd Summit and follow the
(signed) Military Road NW across the moorland to the north-east of the road,
gradually descending to cross the River Findhorn at Raigbeg less than 1km
from Tomatin.

## 204  Tomatin to Whitebridge

*50km/31miles*          *OS Sheets 34 and 35.  Start 803 288.   Finish 487 153*
This is a long expedition through the heart of the Monadhliath, much of it
road walking along the narrow and very unfrequented public road in
Strathdearn.   Start from Tomatin and go for many miles up this road on the
north-west side of the River Findhorn past old shooting lodges - Glenkyllachy,
Glenmazeran and  at the end of the road Coignafearn.

Continue up the private road to Dalbeg , and then a  track and path up
the River Eskin to the narrow pass (650m) where the path ends at a barely
usable bothy. Continue through to the head of  Glen Markie and down the
Glenmarkie Burn. The best going is mainly on the north bank, but occasionally
on the south bank. At a ruin at map ref 563 080 a path is reached which leads
to Stronlarig Lodge. From there a private road goes NW for 2km to a locked
gate, from where the narrow public road goes for 9km by Loch Killin to
Whitebridge.

## 205  Carrbridge to Aviemore by the River Dulnain

*26km/16miles*          *OS Sheets 35 and 36.  Start 906 229.  Finish 896 124*
This is a much shorter route than the previous one, but very pleasant
nevertheless, through the north-east corner of the Monadhliath. From the centre
of Carrbridge take the narrow public road SW for about 3km to the point
where Wade's Military Road, route 203, crosses it.   Follow this route NW
across the Sluggan Bridge and then W to Insharn. There, instead of continuing
N along Wade's route, turn S then SE along a track across the moor to the
monument above the left bank of the River Dulnain.

An alternative and shorter way to this point which misses the Sluggan
Bridge is to continue up the public road for 1km beyond its meeting Wade's
Road, then cross the Dulnain by the private bridge to Inverlaidnan. 300 metres
beyond the bridge (just before crossing a small burn) go SW across a field and
through pinewoods by a pleasant grassy track to the monument.

Follow  the track and path along the NW bank of the river upstream for
5km to a bridge at map ref 813 166, and cross it to climb SE up the estate road
over the north-east shoulder of Geal-charn Mor and go down to Lynwilg.
Cross the new A9 road and take the older road for the last 2km to Aviemore,
from where it is possible to return to the starting point in Carrbridge by train or
bus.

## 206  Kingussie to Tomatin by the River Findhorn

*43km/27miles*          *OS Sheet 35.  Start 756 006.  Finish 803 288*
This is another very long walk through the rolling hills and long glens of
the Monadhliath.   From the centre of Kingussie take the road up the east side
of the Allt Mor through the golf course and across the burn at Pitmain Lodge,
where one must walk past the front of the lodge and round its west side.
Continue NW by the track which goes between Carn a' Bhothain Mholaich
and Carn an Fhreiceadain to the col at map ref 717 070.

From there go WNW across the north slopes of Carn a' Bhothain Mholaich (no path, difficult in mist, use a compass) making a slightly rising traverse across three small streams flowing NE to form the infant Dulnain. A fourth stream flows out of a narrow grassy valley. Follow it upstream SW to a tiny lochan (which disappears in dry weather) and go over the col (760m), where there is a derelict boundary fence, to reach the Allt Glas a' Charbaid. Go down the west bank of this burn to the start of a new estate track at map ref 681 109 (not shown on the OS Landranger map) which leads down the west side of the Elrick Burn across two fords to Coignafearn Lodge.

Alternatively go down the east side of the Allt Glas a' Charbaid along an indistinct path to reach the confluence of a smaller stream with the Elrick Burn at map ref 687 117. Ford the smaller burn and continue along a path beside the Elrick Burn, crossing to its west bank by a bridge downstream, thence to Coignafearn Lodge.

From the lodge follow the private road down the River Findhorn; it becomes a public road at Coignafearn Old Lodge 19km from Tomatin. This route is marked as a road in Roy's map of 1755.

### 207  Kingussie to Laggan
*22km/14miles*                              *OS Sheet 35.  Start 756 006.  Finish 615 944*

Leave Kingussie by the B970 road to Ruthven, turn right to Knappach, cross under the A9 road and after 300 metres recross it (stile and gate) to a roadside parking place with a right of way sign. Follow the track SW along the line of General Wade's Military Road across the moor past Luibleathann bothy and Phones Lodge to Etteridge. Cross the A9 road and the railway at map ref 682 922, then go N across the River Truim to Crubenbeg farm. From there continue past a holiday centre to its north side, pass through a gate and climb W across a field, then go N along the west side of a wall to the public road at map ref 678 943 near Mains of Glentruim. Continue W along the quiet country road to Catlodge on the A889 road, 3km from Laggan.

### 208  Newtonmore to Laggan by Glen Banchor
*16km/10miles*                              *OS Sheet 35.  Start 716 992.  Finish 615 944*

From Newtonmore take the narrow public road up Glen Banchor for just over 2km to its end at the Allt a' Chaorainn. Continue across this burn and along the track to Glenballach and then by the footpath on the north side of the River Calder. The crosing of two burns, the Allt Ballach and the Allt an Lochain Duibh, may be difficult if they are in spate, and beyond the latter there is no path for the last few hundred metres to a bridge and bothy at the Allt Madagain (map ref 648 984). From there follow a good track S through Srath an Eilich and across the moor to Cluny Castle, 3km east of Laggan.

It is possible to go direct to Laggan by leaving the track at the south end of Srath an Eilich and bearing SW just below the steep slopes of Stac Buidhe across grassy moorland with no continuous path to finish through fields where cattle and sheep graze above the village.

**209 Laggan to Whitebridge**
*35km/22miles          OS Sheets 34 and 35.   Start 615 944.  Finish 487 153*
    From Laggan village follow the road W on the north side of the River
Spey for 4km to the Spey Dam, then go N up the track in Glen Markie for
almost 5km until past the Piper's Burn.  Cross the Markie Burn, which may be
difficult if in spate, and head NW up the ridge on the north-east side of
Lochan a' Choire, over the flat plateau of Geal Charn and down to Lochan na
Lairige.  Continue N down the Crom Allt on smooth grassy streamside flats for
2km to the Chalybeate Spring.  From there a path leads on down the burn to
map ref 546 060 where the end of a track is reached going to Sronlarig Lodge.
There route 204 is joined for the last 11km to Whitebridge.

**210  Laggan to Fort Augustus by the Corrieyairack Pass**
*40km/25miles          OS Sheets 34 and 35.   Start 615 944.  Finish 379 091*
    The Corrieyairack road was made by General Wade in 1731 as a contin-
uation of the road from Crieff to Dalnacardoch which continued across the
Drumochter Pass to Dalwhinnie, where it divided, one branch going by
Aviemore to Inverness (see route 203) and the other by Laggan to Fort
Augustus.  There was an older road between these two points before Wade's
time; it is shown on a map of 1725 in the British Museum.  It was by the
Corrieyairack that Prince Charles Edward Stewart marched south after raising
his standard at Glenfinnan.  J.B.Salmond, in his *Wade in Scotland* (1938),
quotes the Hon. Mrs Murray's description of her crossing by coach in 1798.
Today much of the route is within sight of an overhead electricity transmission line.
    Although the usual eastern starting point of the route nowadays is Laggan
village, going from there W along the north side of the River Spey, the original starting point was 2km west along the A86 road on the south side of the
river. The two variants join at the bridge over the Spey 3km west of Laggan.
Continuing W, the route goes across an aqueduct at map ref 553 932, where
a track coming north from Kinloch Laggan joins the Wade road, providing an
alternative and slightly shorter start.  About 9km west of Laggan the road
passes the old barracks and former inn at Garvamore, recrosses the Spey by
Garva Bridge ( a Wade bridge) and continues a further 6km to Melgarve at the
end of the public road.  A short distance up the burn just east of Melgarve,
another old Wade bridge is hidden in the forest.
    At Melgarve (where route 211 branches off  SW) the Corrieyairack track
leaves the Spey and begins the climb WNW along the Allt Yairack to the pass,
the last steep ascent in twelve zigzags.  The 775m summit provides magnificent views, and there is a steep descent on the west side to the Allt Lagan a'
Bhainne bridge, which has recently been carefully restored to its original
state.  Continue down Glen Tarff high on the west side of the deep tree-lined
gorge of the River Tarff to Culachy, and on reaching the public road go right
then first left to Fort Augustus.

**211  Laggan to Roy Bridge or Glenfintaig Lodge (Spean Bridge) by Leckroy**
*48km/30miles or 48km/30miles*
*OS Sheets 34 and 35.  Start 615 944.  Finish 270 814 or 223 863*
Follow the Corrieyairack route described above (route 210) from Laggan as far as Melgarve.  The route to Roybridge and Spean Bridge crosses the Allt Yairack (bridge down) and goes W along the north bank of the Spey past Loch Spey and across the low pass (350m) into Glen Roy.  Go down the River Roy for about 7km to Leckroy where there are good views of the famous Parallel Roads.  A short distance further on, the route splits.

(a)  For Roybridge keep going along the track on the right bank of the River Roy across Turret Bridge to Brae Roy Lodge and continue all the way down the glen along the narrow public road.  Below Achavady there is a viewpoint with information about the Parallel Roads, which are the levels of a series of ice-dammed lochs that existed during the last Ice Age.

(b)  For Spean Bridge go just over 1km past Leckroy and turn N up Glen Turret.  Cross the River Turret by a footbridge and go W along the narrow glen of the Allt a' Chomhlain (path indistinct) to the col (357m).  Cross the fence there by a stile and go down the head of Glen Gloy into the forest to the start of a track leading to Auchivarie. From there continue 10km down the glen by a private road to Glenfintaig Lodge and an old Wade bridge beside the A82 road, 6$\frac{1}{2}$ km from Spean Bridge.

This is one of the old highways of the Highlands, once the main route between Speyside and Lochaber.  It is shown on Moll's map of 1725 as going from Ruthven Barracks to Mucomir at the south end of Loch Lochy, from where a road went south to Fort William and another one north to Kilcumein (Fort Augustus).  The Wade road from Fort William to Fort Augustus was made in 1726.  Routes 210 and 211(b) are shown as roads on Roy's map of 1755.

# SECTION 19
# Rannoch to Lochaber

### 212 Dalwhinnie to Feagour (Strath Mashie)
*10km/6miles          OS Sheets 35 and 42.     Start 636 862↑.   Finish 570 905↑*
   This route, which is nowadays not much frequented, may well have been used by drovers or soldiers of the 18th century as it gives an obvious shortcut from the south end of the Corrieyairack to Drumochter Pass. Leave the A889 road 1km north of Dalwhinnie and follow a private road leading NW to the stalker's house. Take the track below the house and go down to the Allt an t-Sluic, then continue along an intermittent track beside this stream for 2km. On reaching an electricity transmission pole at map ref 610 870 bear NNW up the hillside to a flat boggy col at map ref 607 876 and from there bear NW past the corner of a forest fence and across the wide grassy hollow of the Allt Tarsuinn, aiming for the corner of another forest at map ref 594 892. Cross a stile there and go downhill along the edge of the forest, cross the Allt Tarsuinn and continue (still heading NW) through a clearing to reach the River Mashie.
   If possible cross the river, then go WNW along the forest edge for 600 metres and just inside the forest fence join a made path, following it down to Feagour; or alternatively, continue along to a gate (map ref 576 903) and then down a birch-filled ride leading to a concrete aqueduct which also leads to Feagour. However, should the River Mashie be impassable follow it downstream to the A86 road and Feagour.
   *Walking this route in either direction requires some basic navigational skills.*

### 213 Loch Rannoch to Dalnaspidal
*16km/10miles          OS Sheet 42.     Start 637 592↑.   Finish 645 733↑*
   This route starts from the B846 road on the north side of Loch Rannoch at Annat, 2½km west of Kinloch Rannoch. From there follow a track which goes N up the east side of the Annat Burn for about 1½km, then cross it to continue W then NW for about 2km to the Allt a' Chreagain Odhair. There the track coming up from Craiganour Lodge is joined and the direction is then due N along the track round the east side of Gualann Sheileach to Duinish. From there the route crosses a new bridge across the Allt Shallainn and continues N across wet ground, which can be avoided by keeping up the hillside on the west, to the south end of Loch Garry. There a track is reached and followed along the west side of Loch Garry for 5km to Dalnaspidal, which as the name indicates was at one time a hospice or inn. Dalwhinnie is 13km north along the A9 road, but no one should consider walking along this very busy stretch of highway.
   Roy's map of 1755 shows two routes, one leaving Loch Rannoch near Annat and the other starting from Aulich near Craiganour Lodge, the two joining 3km northwards.

## 214  Loch Rannoch to Dalwhinnie by Loch Ericht

*35km/22miles*                    *OS Sheet 42. Start 506 577. Finish 637 848*
From a point on the B846 road 300 metres north of Rannoch Lodge at the west end of Loch Rannoch, a track goes NW through a small wood and a path continues along the east side of another area of forest. The track resumes N along the west slopes of Meall Liath na Doire Mhoir and goes down to the south-west corner of Loch Ericht and the bridge over the Cam Chriochan. From there go N along the west side of the loch (path for about 2$^1$/$_2$ km) to the Alder Burn and Benalder Cottage, which is an open bothy and may be a useful stopping point on this long walk.

Continue along the lochside by a very narrow and in places non-existent path which clings to the steep lower slopes of Beinn Bheoil along the water's edge to reach the waymarked path by-passing Ben Alder Lodge. From there a private road goes for the final 9km to Dalwhinnie.

This route is marked on Roy's map of 1755.

### 215  Loch Rannoch to Kinloch Laggan

*40km/25miles*                    *OS Sheet 42. Start 506 577. Finish 554 898*
This is another very long route from Loch Rannoch northwards through the heart of the Ben Alder group of mountains to reach the north-east end of Loch Laggan. Follow route 214 as far as the Alder Burn, cross it and  follow the path NW from Benalder Cottage to the Bealach Cumhann (660m). At the bealach continue to follow the path NE on an almost level traverse below the western slopes of  Ben Alder to reach the Bealach Dubh (725m), the prominent pass between Ben Alder and Aonach Beag. Descend the path along the Allt a' Bhealaich Dhuibh and the Allt a' Chaoil-reidhe, passing Culra Lodge, to reach Loch Pattack. Go round the east side of the loch and follow an estate road N down the River Pattack past the Linn of Pattack and the Falls of Pattack to Gallovie. A short distance further the A86 road is reached 1$^1$/$_2$ km east of Kinloch Laggan.

An alternative route is to climb N from Benalder Cottage past the site of Prince Charlie's Cave to the Bealach Breabag (830m) and descend to the south end of Loch a' Bhealaich Bheithe. Continue along the east side of this loch and descend N towards Culra Lodge where the preceding route is joined. This variation involves a little more climbing, but saves a few kilometres of distance, and the splendid scenery of the east face of  Ben Alder rising above Loch a' Bhealaich Bheithe makes this the finest route from Loch Rannoch to Kinloch Laggan.

### 216  Corrour Station to Dalwhinnie or Kinloch Laggan

*37km/23 miles*
*OS Sheets 41 and 42. Start 356 664↑. Finish 637 848 or 554 898*
From Corrour Station on the West Highland Line, go E along the private road on the south-east side of Loch Ossian to Corrour Lodge. Continue by  the path to cross the Uisge Labhair and go upstream for 7km to the Bealach Dubh, where route 215 is joined. Descend the path along the Allt a' Bhealaich Dhuibh and the Allt a' Chaoil-reidhe, passing Culra Lodge. Cross the river just beyond

there and take the path across the moor to reach the road to Ben Alder Lodge and Dalwhinnie. This long walk not only goes through splendid mountain scenery, but also has the advantage that it goes from one railway station to another.

An alternative ending to this route is to go N from Loch Pattack down the River Pattack to reach the A86 road 1 1/2 km east of Kinloch Laggan, from where on the next day you can cross the Corrieyairack Pass to Fort Augustus.

### 217  Rannoch Station to Loch Ossian and Corrour Station
*18km/11miles        OS Sheets 41 and 42.  Start 446 578↑.  Finish 356 664↑*

From Rannoch Station go E along the B846 road for 2 1/2 km to Loch Eigheach and take the track which goes NW. This track is part of The Road to the Isles and it leads in 3km to a crossing  of the Allt Eigheach. Beyond there follow the path NW across the lower slopes of  Carn Dearg and past the stark ruins of Corrour Old Lodge, which after it ceased to be used as a shooting lodge was for a few years an isolation hospital. No more isolated place can be imagined.

Follow the path as it swings N towards Loch Ossian and before reaching the plantation above the loch turn W to descend to the head of Loch Ossian, where the youth hostel of the same name stands on a promontory by the lochside. Corrour Station is a further 1 1/2 km along a road and from there one can return to the day's starting point by train – check timetable.

### 218  Corrour Station (Loch Ossian) to Fersit (Glen Spean)
*20km/12 1/2 miles        OS Sheets 41 and 42.  Start 356 664↑.  Finish 350 782↑*

From Corrour Station follow the private road along the south-east shore of Loch Ossian to Corrour Lodge. Continue N along the road down Strath Ossian past Strathossian House and then follow the path which climbs N round the shoulder of Meall Dhearcaig and continues W along the upper edge of the forest. Cross a stile into the forest and follow rides firstly NW to a ruin, then W to rejoin the original path leading to Fersit. The route through the forest is not very clear, especially when going from west to east, but it is waymarked. At Fersit the end of a narrow public road is reached. It can be followed for a further 3 1/2 km down to the A86 road in Glen Spean at a point 1 1/2 km from Tulloch Station.

### 219  Corrour Station (Loch Osssian) to Fort William by Glen Nevis
*33km/20 1/2 miles        OS Sheet 41.  Start 356 664↑.  Finish 113 743*

This is a very fine walk through the heart of the highest mountains in Lochaber. It can be done from one youth hostel to another (Loch Ossian to Glen Nevis), or from one railway station to another (Corrour to Fort William).

From Corrour follow the path and then the track beside the West Highland Railway down to the head of Loch Treig, and round to Creaguaineach Lodge. From there go up the Abhainn Rath by the path on the north side (by either side is a dangerous section of the route if the weather is or has been wet and is not advisable) as far as Luibeilt, where the crossing of the Abhainn Rath may also be impassable. Continue for a further 2 1/2 km to the watershed at Tom an Eite, where the going is often wet and boggy.

*Looking west along Glen Affric (route 256)*

*Bealach an Sgairne, the high pass on the route from Glen Affric to Loch Duich (route 256)*

*The Black Cuillin from the path above Loch Scavaig (route 279)*

*Heading up Glen Elchaig towards Iron lodge (route 257)*

Once past Tom an Eite the path goes along the north side of the Water of Nevis past the ruin of Steall Cottage and across the meadow below Steall Waterfall to reach the Glen Nevis gorge. Here the river rushes through a narrow ravine over waterfalls and polished rocks, and the path clings to the steep right bank along ledges and through fine old pine trees to reach the end of the public road, where there is a carpark. The walk continues down the road in the glen past Achriabhach to reach the youth hostel, 29km from Corrour. It is a further 4km along the road down Glen Nevis to Fort William.

## 220  Corrour Station (Loch Ossian) to Spean Bridge
*25km/15½miles*          *OS Sheet 41.  Start 356 664↑.  Finish 221 815↑*
Follow route 219 for its first 6km as far as Creaguaineach Lodge. From there go NW then N by the path on the west side of the Allt na Lairige through the Lairig Leacach. (In spate conditions it may be better to cross the Allt na Lairige by the bridge at map ref 308 693 and continue up the east side of the burn.)  At the Lairig Leacach bothy a track is reached which leads over the watershed and down the Allt Leachdach, through a short section of forest and down to Corriechoille at the end of the narrow public road on the south side of the River Spean. Finally walk for 4km along this quiet road to Spean Bridge. Like the preceding one, this route goes from one station to another on the West Highland Railway.

This route is part of the old drove road from the Great Glen southwards. From the confluence of the Allt na Lairige and the Abhainn Rath, the old route went south to Kingshouse Inn, crossing the shallow glen now flooded by the Blackwater Reservoir. Lairig Leacach means pass of the flagstones.

## 221 Corrour Station (Loch Ossian) to Kinlochleven
*23km/14miles*          *OS Sheet 41.  Start 356 664↑.  Finish 193 620↑*
From Corrour Station go NW along the path and track as far as the south end of Loch Treig (1km before Creaguaineach Lodge). From there turn SW up Gleann Iolairean, following the path up the Allt Feith Chiarain, which is the line of the old drove road from Spean Bridge to Kingshouse Inn. Pass Loch Chiarain and continue SW across a level watershed along a path which goes on the north-west side of the Allt an Ruadha Dheirg and the Allt an Inbhir to reach the Blackwater Reservoir, 1km east of the dam. Finally, follow the path along the north side of the River Leven down a very attractive wooded glen to reach Kinlochleven.

## 222  Kinlochleven to Spean Bridge
*29km/18miles*          *OS Sheet 41.  Start 188 623. Finish 221 815↑*
From the north-east corner of Kinlochleven take the path which climbs steeply NE to join the track leading to Loch Eilde Mor. Go  along this track past the two lochs - Eilde Mor and Eilde Beag - to Luibeilt where route 219 is crossed. Cross the Abhainn Rath (which may be impassable if it is in spate) and continue N by a path up the Allt nam Fang. Cross the bealach between Meall Mor and Stob Ban and descend to the Lairig Leacach bothy, where route 220 is joined and followed over the Lairig Leacach, down to Corriechoille and along the road to Spean Bridge.

An alternative route leading to Glen Spean near Tulloch Station can be done by leaving the Lairig Leacach track a short distance north of the bothy and going NE over a low pass to descend by Coire na Cabaig to Coire Laire This glen is long and rather featureless, but a path eventually appears on the right bank of the Allt Laire, and as the forest at the foot of the glen is reached, cross to the other side of the river and follow a forest road down to Inverlair and reach the A86 road in Glen Spean, 1½ km west of Tulloch Station.

## 223   Kinlochleven to Fort William
*20km/12½ miles*                    *OS Sheet 41. Start 183 623↑. Finish 113 743*
This route is part of the West Highland Way, the final part for those going from south to north. It is also on the line of the Old Military Road that was constructed by General Caulfeild in 1749-50 from Fort William southwards over the Devil's Staircase and across the western edge of Rannoch Moor.

Leave Kinlochleven along the B863 road on the north side of Loch Leven as far as the school. From there follow the path which climbs NW up the wooded hillside, cross the private road to Mamore Lodge and higher up join the track from the lodge that leads W up the north side of the glen of the Allt Nathrach. The track leads unmistakably over a pass at about 330m and descends to Lairigmor. The way to Fort William continues along this track, which swings N and at the derelict house of Blar a' Chaorainn joins a narrow public road leading to Fort William.

As an alternative to reach Fort William many walkers continue from Blar a' Chaorainn by a path which goes to the right and N at first across a little knoll. Then NE through the Nevis Forest and over a col north-west of Dun Deardail to join a forest road descending Glen Nevis (close to the Youth Hostel and camp site). In a further 3km the local public road is joined leading to Nevis Bridge on the outskirts of Fort William.

(Two variations from the route are:

From Blar a' Chaorainn, go W to Lundavra and SW past the head of Lochan Lunn Da Bhra continuing across a flat col (no path for 1½ km) to the edge of the Glenrigh Forest where a road is reached. Follow this road on the true right bank of the Abhainn Righ for 5km until a bridge on the left leads across the river and down to Onich. Alternatively continue along the forest road to Inchree forest car park.

The other variation from the route is from Lairigmor.

A path, which is also a right of way, leads SW over the west ridge of Mam na Gualainn to the bealach and descends S to a marker post near an edge of the wood ahead at map ref 099 617. Then SSE by an old waymarker post continue down the hill to a wall at the bottom. Here turn SW on a track which leads to the right of way sign on the B863 road east of Callert House on the north side of Loch Leven).

# SECTION 20
# Ardgour, Sunart and Moidart

## 224  Bonnavoulin (Morvern) to Liddesdale (Loch Sunart)
*35km/22miles   OS Sheets 40, 47 and 49.   Start 561 537↑.   Finish 783 597↑*
   Start from Bonnavoulin on the Sound of Mull near the end of the B849 road from Lochaline and go uphill by a narrow track to Mungosdail farm. Pass close to the house and follow a track E into the forest and uphill for 1½ km to cross a burn and turn NE onto a path which leads out of the forest. Continue NE over a ridge to map ref 601 550 (no path) keeping to the east of Lochan Chrois Bheinn and descend to enter another forest. Go down a good path through it on the west side of the Barr River to join a track which leads SE for 3½ km to Ardantiobairt at the head of Loch Teacuis.
   Take the road N then NW round the head of Loch Teacuis to Carnliath. Go ENE up the north side of the Allt an Inbhire by a waymarked route to the Bealach Sloc an Eich. Cross this pass and descend through the forest to Glen Cripesdale. (18km/11miles from Bonnavoulin). After crossing the new bridge at map ref 662 593 over the Glencripesdale Burn, there are two choices:
   (a)  Go NW along the private road round the coast overlooking Loch Sunart. At several places on this road, particularly from its northernmost point at Rubha Aird Earnaich, there are fine views across the loch towards the hills of Sunart. The road passes Laudale House and eventually reaches the A884 at Liddesdale, 17km from Glencripesdale. It is a further 9km along the public road to Strontian.
   (b)  This is a shorter route, but it involves more climbing. Follow the track E along the north side of the Glencripesdale Burn for 2km, then leave the burn and follow a path uphill through the forest to reach the open hillside near Lochan Dhonnachaidh. From there a forest track leads down the wooded hillside above Loch Sunart to the lochside road described above near Laudale House. Of interest are the stone benches beside the path on the way up from Glen Cripesdale to Lochan Dhonnachaidh; they were the resting places for those who walked this path many years ago. The forest in this area has been clear felled and several new tracks made, but navigation is now assisted by waymarkers.

## 224X  Drimnin to Doirlinn
*11km/7miles            OS Sheets 47 and 49.   Start 556 540.   Finish 606 586*
   This short walk goes round the western tip of Morvern along an old track built in 1880 as a poor relief project. It passes some old settlements which were inhabited at that time, but are now long-since deserted.
   From the end of the public road at Drimnin go N along a track and fork right in 200 metres  to reach another track which is followed N for ½ km to another junction.  Keep right past Drimnin House and continue past Auliston and Portabhata and drop down through wooded slopes to reach Doirlinn at the isthmus separating Oronsay from the mainland.

The track ends here and at present it is necessary to return to Drimnin by the same way. It is planned to create a way SE from Doirlinn along the shore of Loch Teacuis and through the forest to the bridge over the Barr River where route 224 will be joined. When this is done, it will create a pleasant circular walk starting and finishing at Drimnin or an alternative start to route 224 between Drimnin and Ardantiobairt.

### 225  Sallachan (Ardgour) to Strontian
*20km/12¹/₂ miles*              *OS Sheet 40.  Start 978 627↑.  Finish 815 617*
Start from Sallachan on the A861 road at the foot of Glen Gour. An alternative start from Corran Ferry involves 4km of walking along the road to Sallachan.  From there go W up Glen Gour for about 7km along a rough bulldozed track on the south side of the River Gour. Beyond the end of this track at about map ref 912 648 cross to the north side of the river, go uphill in a northerly direction until the old path is found and continue along it to the pass between Sgurr na Laire and Sgurr nan Cnamh. From there go down the pathless and rather boggy north side of the Strontian River for 3¹/₂ km and follow the path which leads to the ruined cottages at Ceann a' Chreagain. If the burn from the mines is in spate, go up its east side to a bridge at map ref 863 666 and continue down the old mine road on the west side of the burn. Finally, go SW along the track through the very fine natural woods of the Ariundle Nature Reserve to reach the road 1¹/₂ km north of Strontian.

### 226  Strontian to Glenfinnan by Glen Hurich
*28km/17¹/₂ miles*              *OS Sheet 40.  Start 815 617.  Finish 924 794↑*
This is a fine cross-country expedition with an interesting section across the rugged hills between Glen Hurich and Cona Glen. From Strontian go N by the narrow public road past Scotstown, Bellsgrove Lodge and the old lead mines. The road crosses a col at 342m and descends steeply to Kinlochan at the head of Loch Doilet. Continue NE by the forest road up the north side of Glen Hurich. Just beyond Resourie bothy there is a hairpin bend in the forest road. From it go E on a short section of old road to the forest fence, cross a stile and climb steeply N then NE up the corrie between Teanga Chorrach and Meall Daimh, then traverse round the head of Coire an t-Searraich to reach the Bealach an Sgriodain, where an old iron gate stands in isolation on the pass. This part of the route is rough and pathless, and requires accurate navigation in bad weather.
Descend NE down easy slopes into the head of Cona Glen, cross the river and go ENE up to the pass west of Meall nan Damh. Continue NE along the path by the Allt na Cruaiche to Callop and across the Callop River to reach the A830 road 2km east of Glenfinnan.

### 227  Strontian to Glenfinnan by Loch Shiel
*35km/22miles*              *OS Sheet 40.  Start 800 614↑.  Finish 924 794↑*
This is an alternative to route 226. Start 1¹/₂ km west of Strontian at Ardnastang and go NE past the Free Church up a narrow road, becoming a path.  In 2¹/₂ km turn left up a path heading NW along the Allt nan Cailleach,

cross the north-east ridge of Beinn a' Chaorainn at about 400m and descend N past the disused Corantee lead mines into the forest in Coire an t-Suidhe. The descent, which is liable to be very wet and boggy but is now waymarked, goes down the right bank of the Allt Coire an t-Suidhe to reach the narrow public road at the west end of Loch Doilet.

This point can also be reached from Strontian by following route 226 as far as Kinlochan (see above) and continuing along the road on the south side of Loch Doilet.

Continue along the road to Polloch and westwards for a further 1½km to the shore of Loch Shiel. The second half of this route goes NE along the forest road on the side of Loch Shiel for many kilometres. At the north end of the loch it is not feasible to cross the River Callop where it flows into the loch, so a diversion has to be made upstream for 2km to a bridge to reach the A830 road.

### 228  Aryhoulan (Ardgour) to Strontian by Glen Scaddle
*34km/21½miles      OS Sheets 40 and 41.   Start 019 684↑.   Finish 815 617*
From Corran Ferry go 6km N along the A861 road to Aryhoulan. From there walk up the track and path in Glen Scaddle for 10km to the point where the glen divides in three below Sgurr Dhomhnuill. Continue along the northern glen, Gleann an Lochain Dhuibh, where the path through newly planted trees near Lochan Dubh is now waymarked. Continue down Glen Hurich by a path on the north side of the river to reach the end of the forest road near Resourie bothy. At this point route 226 is joined and is followed in reverse down Glen Hurich to Kinlochan and then by the narrow public road to Strontian.

An alternative to this route provides a shorter way to Strontian, but it does involve a fairly steep climb and descent. From the point where Glen Scaddle divides in three, go up the southern glen, Gleann Mhic Phail. Its upper reaches are narrow and steep-sided where the burn flows through a rocky ravine. Continue up to the col (495m) between Sgurr a' Chaorainn and Sgurr na h-Ighinn and descend steeply SW to the Strontian River where route 225 is joined and followed down to Strontian.

### 229  Aryhoulan (Ardgour) to Glenfinnan
*26km/16miles      OS Sheets 40 and 41.   Start 019 684↑   Finish 924 794↑*
The start of this route is the same as the previous one. Go 6km N from Corran Ferry to the bridge over the River Scaddle and up the track on the north side of the Cona River. This track goes for about 12km nearly to the head of Cona Glen, and from its end climb NW by a path to the col west of Meall nan Damh where route 226 is joined. Go NE by the path down the Allt na Cruaiche past Callop to the A830 road 2km east of Glenfinnan.

## 230  Ardmolich (Loch Moidart) to Lochailort by Glen Moidart

*16km/10mls*                    *OS Sheet 40.  Start 713 721.  Finish 765 815*
From Ardmolich at the head of Loch Moidart go up the River Moidart to the end of the public road at a junction before reaching Glenmoidart House. Continue along the right-hand road on the south-east side of Loch nan Lochan and the River Moidart for 2km to cross the river by a bridge at map ref 755 733. Rejoin the path on the west side of the river and follow it N, however it disappears completely before reaching the ruined cottage of Assary. From there climb due N up steep grassy slopes to the Bealach an Fhiona (705m) and descend steeply N into Coire a' Bhuiridh and go down the west side of the Allt a' Bhuiridh. In due course a path appears and leads NW then W through a little col on the south side of Tom Odhar and down to Glenshian Lodge Hotel and Lochailort.

## 231  Kilchoan (Ardnamurchan) to Acharacle

*40km/25miles*          *OS Sheets 40 and 47.  Start 489 638.  Finish 676 684*
Take the road from Kilchoan NW in the direction of Achnaha and leave it at map ref 474 675, 200 metres north of the bridge over the Allt Uamha na Muice. Climb a stile over the deer fence and follow the waymarked path NNE which joins up with a track coming from the road at map ref 469 678. Continue NE along this signposted path across a circular plain about 4km in diameter surrounded on almost all sides by low gabbro hills, which are the only visible remains of a once great volcano across whose crater the path goes. Reach Glendrian and at map ref 475 692 go N to within ½ km of the coast, then turn E to Fascadale. Continue E by a minor road to Achateny, then along a track to Kilmory. It is possible to go S from either Achateny or Kilmory to reach the B8007 road where there is a bus service.

To continue to Acharacle, go E from Kilmory by a road to Ockle, then by a good path over rough terrain, passing Gortenfern and through the forest to Gorteneorn. Finally, go along the track on the south side of Kentra Bay to Arivegaig from where it is 2km to Acharacle.

# SECTION 21
# Loch Eil to Glen Shiel

**232 The Dark Mile (Loch Arkaig) to Invergarry or Loch Garry**
*19km/12miles     OS Sheet 34.   Start 176 888↑.   Finish 301 010 or 194 023↑*
Start from the carpark at the Eas Chia-aig waterfalls 2¹/₂ km west of Clunes at the west end of the Dark Mile (Mile Dorcha) on the B8005 road. Climb steeply up the higher path on the east side of Gleann Cia-aig through the forest and reach a forest road. Go N along this road to its end and continue by the path which crosses to the west side of the Abhainn Chia-aig. Continue NE along a very faint path to Fedden, which two centuries ago was a much-frequented drovers' stance.

At this point cross the glen NE to reach the path which contours round below the western slopes of Sron a' Choire Ghairbh, and follow this path N then NE. A forested area is reached, and the waymarked path continues down through it to the Allt Bealach Easain at the end of the forest road up the Allt Ladaidh. Go down this road to its junction with another road which goes from east to west through the forest on the south side of Loch Garry. To go to Invergarry, turn right and follow the forest road, which is waymarked, for 7¹/₂ km to the footbridge over the River Garry at Easter Mandally. Alternatively, a left turn leads 3km W to Greenfield and then N across the bridge over the narrows of Loch Garry to the public road on the north side of the loch 4km east of Tomdoun.

**232X  Loch Garry to Laggan Locks**
*15km/9¹/₂ miles                    OS Sheet 34.   Start 194 023↑.   Finish 286 964*
This is probably an old coffin route from the western end of Glen Garry to the old graveyard at Kilfinnan Church. The start is 4km east of Tomdoun at the bridge over the narrows of Loch Garry. Go S along the road to Greenfield and E from there to the Allt Ladaidh. Continue up the road on the east side of this stream to the  road end at the Allt Bealach Easain. Climb SE up the path on the true right bank of this burn and beyond the end of the path continue up to the bealach between Ben Tee and Sron a' Choire Ghairbh. Descend E across some very rough boggy ground where the going is slow and difficult. It is probably best to keep fairly high above the Allt a' Choire Ghlais, bearing very slightly N of E to reach a stile over a high fence at map ref 273 968. From there go SE by a fairly well defined path to descend the grassy hillside directly above Kilfinnan. The end of the walk at Laggan Locks is 1km further.

**233  The Dark Mile (Loch Arkaig) to Laggan Locks**
*16km/10miles                    OS Sheet 34.   Start 176 888↑.   Finish 286 964*
Follow route 232 to within ¹/₂ km of Fedden. From there go E on the north side of the Allt Cam Bhealaich to join the path which contours round the foot of Sron a' Choire Ghairbh. Continue E along this path, over the Cam Bhealach and down the Allt Glas-Dhoire to the forest road going NE along

Loch Lochy to Laggan Locks. The A82 road, with a bus service between Inverness and Fort William is a short distance further.

A more direct, but much less interesting, alternative route starts from Clunes at the east end of the Dark Mile and follows the north-west shore of Loch Lochy by the forestry road along the lochside to Laggan Locks (12km/7¹/₂ miles).

### 234  Fassfern to Banavie by Glen Loy and the Caledonian Canal
*24km/15miles*                OS Sheet 41  Start 022 789↑.  Finish 113 767

This route, which starts and finishes on the A830 road west of Fort William, gives a variety of scenery from the desolate upper reaches of Glen Loy to its forested lower part and the more cultivated landscape along the tow-path of the Caledonian Canal, with splendid views of Ben Nevis on a clear day. Start from the loop road at Fassfern at the foot of Gleann Suileag and walk up the forest road on the east side of this glen. The road ends just before the bridge across the river  and the way continues for 6km past Glensulaig cottage and  over the featureless watershed leading to Glen Loy, the path (such as it is) being on the north side of the glen. At Achnanellan the narrow and very quiet public road is reached and followed down Glen Loy to the B8004 road. Cross the road and walk down a track leading to a tunnel under the Caledonian Canal. Go through it, turn right and in 200 metres reach the tow-path beside the Canal. Finally walk for 8km along the canal to the series of locks which form Neptune's Staircase and reach the A830 road at Banavie station.

### 235  Kinlocheil to Strathan (Loch Arkaig)
*16km/10miles*                OS Sheet 40.  Start 960 793↑.  Finish 988 916

This is a fine trans-mountain route with some fairly steep up and down-hill work in its middle section which in part follows an old route from Fassfern to Strathan. Start from a point 2km west of Kinlocheil on the A830 road at the foot of Geann Fionnlighe. Go N up this glen by a rough road past Wauchan, and a deteriorating track beyond there to the Allt a' Choire Reidh. Cross this stream by a footbridge and go N up the east bank to its head, then climb NE and cross the pass (500m) just east of Gualann nan Osna, the 'Panting Pass'. Descend NW down to Gleann Camgharaidh.

Cross this glen, go up the steep hillside opposite, over the 435rn col on the south-west ridge of Leac na Carnaich, and down the Allt a' Chaorainn to the footbridge just below its junction with the River Pean at map ref 969 907. Once across this bridge it is necessary to go W for about 200 metres before turning right to reach the road in Glen Pean. Go E along this road to Strathan. The end of the public road along Loch Arkaig is 3km further east at Murlaggan.

### 235X  Kinlocheil to The Dark Mile (Loch Arkaig)
*28km/17¹/₂ miles*         OS Sheets 40,41.  Start 960 793↑.  Finish 173 887↑

This is a long route, with fine wooded glens at its two ends but a rather dreary middle section at the head of Glen Mallie. Follow route 235 to the crossing of the Allt a' Choire Reidh, then continue NE up Gleann Fionnlighe and over the long featureless watershed to Glen Mallie. There is only a faint path in this section, but it improves along Glen Mallie and a good track leads past the ruins of Glenmallie house to Invermallie bothy through some fine old pine woods. Finally, go along the road on the south side of Loch Arkaig to cross the River Arkaig at its outflow a few hundred metres west of the carpark at the Eas Chia-aig waterfalls.

### 236  Glenfinnan to Strathan (Loch Arkaig)
*14½km/9miles*                    *OS Sheet 40.  Start 906 808↑.  Finish 988 916*
Start from the car park on the west side of the A830 road bridge over the River Finnan. Go up the private road on the west side of Glen Finnan under the arches of the West Highland Railway viaduct, passing below Corryhully Lodge to reach Corryhully bothy. Continue along a rougher track which goes for a further 1½km, and climb NE up the glen to the narrow pass (471m) between Streap and Sgurr Thuilm. Beyond there descend NE by an intermittent path on the right bank of the Allt a' Chaorainn to the bridge over the River Pean, where route 235 is joined for the last 1km to Strathan.

### 237  Strathan (Loch Arkaig) to Loch Morar and return by Glen Pean and Glen Dessarry
*28km/17½miles*                    *OS Sheet 40.  Start and Finish 988 916*
This is an outstanding expedition through one of the wildest and roughest corners of the western highlands. Few of the routes described in this book are as rough as this one.

From Strathan at the west end of Loch Arkaig 3km from the end of the public road at Murlaggan,   cross the River Dessarry and go W along a forest road up Glen Pean for 3km and its continuation to Pean bothy at the west edge of the forest. Beyond the bothy cross to the south side of the River Pean, which may be difficult if it is in spate. Continue by rough and pathless going along the south  side of Lochan Leum an t-Sagairt, cross the pass at a tiny lochan and descend to the head of Loch Morar, along a path for the last 2km. Oban bothy is about ½km further west.

Continue round the head of Loch Morar, traversing some very steep ground at the promontory of Sron a' Choin to cross the Abhainn Ceann-loch-morar, possibly with some difficulty. Having reached the ruins of Kinlochmorar, follow the path on the north side of the burn up Gleann an Lochain Eanaiche through a very narrow and steep-sided pass between Carn Mor and Sgurr na h-Aide. 2½km beyond Lochan Eanaiche the head of the glen is reached and  beyond the col it is less than 1km down to the top of the forest in Glen Dessarry. Go E to join a path on the south side of the River Dessarry and follow it down to a bridge at the junction of the Allt Coire nan Uth.

From there a forest road goes down Glen Dessarry on the south side of the river past A'Chuil bothy to return to Strathan.  Alternatively, at the bridge mentioned above, one can cross the Dessarry and go up a rough path through the forest by the Allt Coire nan Uth to join the path on the north side of the glen. This is the traditional right of way from Loch Arkaig to Inverie, and it leads past Upper Glendessarry and Glendessarry Lodge to Strathan.

### 238  Strathan (Loch Arkaig) to Inverie (Loch Nevis)
*27km/17miles*                    *OS Sheet 40.  Start 988 916.  Finish 766 000↑*
   This is one of the best cross-country routes in the western highlands, leading through the heart of the wild mountainous country on the southern border of Knoydart. It can be combined with route 236 to give a splendid two-day expedition from Glenfinnan to Inverie, where the boat may be taken to Mallaig to get the train back to Glenfinnan. Overnight shelter for this long walk can be found at either Pean or A' Chuil bothy.
   Start from the end of the public road at Murlaggan 3km from Strathan near the west end of Loch Arkaig and go up the private road on the north side of Glen Dessarrv past Glendessarry Lodge and Upper Glendessarry. Take the path above the forest to cross the Allt Coire nan Uth and continue to the top of the pass, the Bealach an Lagain Duibh (310m), about 8km from Strathan.
   Continue W along a very rough path to reach Lochan a' Mhaim in the narrow defile of the Mam na Cloich' Airde and then by a better path down to Sourlies bothy at the head of Loch Nevis. The path descending to the head of Loch Nevis was well constructed and at one place was even paved. It is probable that it was built at the time of the herring boom on the north-west coast when Loch Nevis was an important fishing ground, and the path was used by ponies carrying barrels of herring to the markets further south.
   From Sourlies go along the flat sandy shore at low tide, or over the headland at high tide, to reach the grassy flats at the outflow of the River Carnach, and cross the river by a suspension bridge near the ruins of Carnoch village. From Carnoch climb steeply NW by a good path to a high pass, the Mam Meadail (550m), go down Gleann Meadail and across the Inverie River to Inverie on Loch Nevis, where there is hostel accommodation and a boat service to Mallaig.
   This route is shown as a road on Roy's map of 1755. On the Ordnance Survey 6-inch map of 1876 it is marked as a second-class road. Those who walk this rough path nowadays can only admire the hardiness of the Highlanders who travelled along it regularly two or three centuries ago.

### 239  Strathan (Loch Arkaig) to Tomdoun (Glen Garry)
*27km/17mls*              *OS Sheets 33 and 34.  Start 988 916.  Finish 157 011*
   For about half its length this walk goes down Glen Kingie, a truly remote and desolate glen in the hinterland between Loch Arkaig and Loch Quoich. From Strathan go NE up the path on the south-east side of the Dearg Allt and across the pass, where the path is very indistinct, to Kinbreack in Glen Kingie. The next problem may be to cross the River Kingie to reach the paths on its north side. There is no bridge, and in wet weather or if the river is full it is very dangerous to attempt a crossing near Kinbreack, although a diversion 2km upstream might make a crossing possible. This is, therefore, definitely not a route to be attempted if the rivers are in spate. The old right of way was on the south bank of the River Kingie, but this route is now pathless and not recommended.

Once on the north side of the River Kingie, go down the path below
Gairich for 7km to Lochan, from where there is a choice of routes:
(a) Go due N over the west slopes of Beinn Bheag along a path, often very
waterlogged, to the east end of Loch Quoich and cross by the crest of the
dam to reach the road in Glen Garry 9km west of Tomdoun Hotel.
(b) From Lochan follow the Forestry Commission road which crosses the
River Kingie at a bridge about 3km further downstream and then goes E over
the hill just north of Lochan an Staic, and finally NE to a bridge crossing the
River Garry to the road 2½km west of Tomdoun.

## 240  Inverie to Inverguseran and return
*22km/14mls*                                    *OS Sheet 33. Start and finish 766 000↑*
Inverie is reached by mail boat from Mallaig (check sailings). From the
village go N by the estate road over the Mam Uidhe (140m) to Gleann na
Guiserein and down this glen to Inverguseran. Returning to Inverie go SW
(the crossing of Abhainn Inbhir Ghuiserein is likely to be problematic if the
river is in spate) and keeping near the coast avoid the path blocked by
forestry. Finally, from Airor go by the road to Inverie.

## 241  Loch Quoich to Inverie (Loch Nevis)
*32km/20miles*                              *OS Sheet 33. Start 985 036. Finish 766 000↑*
This route, which has three variations, traverses the incredibly wild and
rugged country in the eastern half of Knoydart between lochs Quoich, Nevis
and Hourn. It is an area which well deserves its name - The Rough Bounds
of Knoydart - and equally well, bearing in mind its rocky peaks and high rainfall, it can aptly be described as a land of the mountain and the flood.
Although the crow-flight distance from the starting point beside Loch Quoich
to Inverie is 22km/14miles, the actual walking distance through the tortuous
glens and over high passes is much longer, and with several turbulent burns
to cross these are not routes for wet weather. However, in good conditions
they are among the finest cross-country walks in Scotland.
Start from the public road on the north side of Loch Quoich at map ref
985 036 and go along the north shore of the loch, which is pathless but the
going is not difficult. The first big stream is the Abhainn Chosaidh, and at this
point two ways are possible. One route, which avoids the need to cross this
stream, goes W along its north side, climbing slightly to Loch an Lagain
Aintheich. Cross the watershed just north of this loch and descend the length
of Glen Barrisdale. For most of the way there is a path on the north side of the
River Barrisdale. At the foot of the glen, just before reaching the stalker's cottage, turn left across the river and go SSW up a good path to the Mam
Barrisdale (450m). On its west side descend the path, then a rough road past
Loch an Dubh-Lochain and down the Inverie River to the village of Inverie on
the shore of Loch Nevis.
The other two variations of this route cross the Abhainn Chosaidh and
continue along the remains of an old track to the small dam at the west end
of Loch Quoich. From the south end of the dam follow a path downhill to
Lochan nam Breac and continue along this path above the north side of the

loch. The most straightforward variation at this point is to keep going along this narrow but quite well defined path as it climbs WNW to the Bealach Unndalain (530m). From there continue along the path down Gleann Unndalain below the north face of Luinne Bheinn to reach the path from Barrisdale to the Mam Barrisdale and follow the way described in the preceding paragraph to Inverie.

For the third variation, leave the path above Lochan nam Breac near its west end and go down towards the outflow of the River Carnach from the loch. Descend on the north side of the river through a rough and narrow glen for 2km until a path on the right bank is found. Follow it down to the ruins of Carnoch village and at that point join route 238 for the climb up the winding path to the Mam Meadail (550m) and the long descent of Gleann Meadail to Inverie.

### 242  Kinloch Hourn to Inverie (Loch Nevis)
*24km/15miles*          *OS Sheet 33. Start 950 066↑. Finish 766 000↑*
    This is another fine walk which combines the wild mountain scenery of Knoydart with the fiord-like upper reaches of Loch Hourn. Start from the end of the public road at Kinloch Hourn and go along the fine lochside path for 2km to Skiary. Beyond there the path climbs above the loch for 2km and returns to sea-level just beyond Runival. Look out for the herons circling their heronry on Eilean Mhogh-sgeir 200 metres offshore. Continue W along the path which rounds a point and reaches the sandy flats of Barrisdale Bay. Just beyond the stalker's cottage at Barrisdale join route 241 for the climb to the Mam Barrisdale and the long descent by Loch an Dubh-Lochain and the Inverie River to the village of Inverie.

### 242X  Kinloch Hourn to Arnisdale (Loch Hourn)
*14km/9miles*          *OS Sheet 33. Start 950 066↑. Finish 844 104*
    Cross the bridge at Kinloch Hourn, go through the grounds of Kinloch Hourn House, passing on its right into the woods behind the house, and climb steeply up a path to a pass at about 270m. 400 metres beyond the pass fork left down to the Allt a' Choire Reidh, which is crossed near Lochan Torr a' Choit. From this lochan keep NW along the path which climbs a little for 1km and then descends into Gleann Dubh Lochain. Go down this glen on the north side of the Dubh Lochain and continue along Glen Arnisdale to Corran and Arnisdale village on the shore of Loch Hourn.

### 243  Kinloch Hourn to Glenelg
*26km/16miles*          *OS Sheet 33. Start 950 066↑. Finish 814 195*
    The first part of this route follows 242X as far as the path junction at map ref 910 102 in Gleann Dubh Lochain, from where there are two ways to Glenelg:
    (a) Continue NW up the Allt an Tomain Odhair to the Bealach Aoidhdailean and descend NNW at first down the Allt Ghleann Aoidhdailean, on the north-east side of the burn, to reach a track at the head of Gleann Beag. From that point either go down the glen by this track past Balvraid and the

well preserved remains of Pictish brochs to reach the road beside the Sound of Sleat 1½km south of Glenelg, or go N to cross the Glenmore River by a bridge ½km east of Suardalan bothy and go down Glen More to Glenelg. The final part of this route is along the line of an Old Military Road and past the ruins of Bernera Barracks, built in Hanoverian times.

(b) Alternatively, from the path junction at map ref 910 102 continue NW for only a short distance, then turn NNE up the Allt a' Choire Odhair for 1km and climb N to the Bealach a' Chasain, the pass between Druim na Firean and Spidean Dhomhuill Bhric. Descend NW then N along the E side of headwaters of the Glenmore River to reach Bealachasan and follow route 245X to Glenelg.

Beware from the start of taking the route by the Bealach a' Chasain. If the weather is or has been wet the Allt Grannda may be in spate condition and not possible to cross.

It is unfortunate that the pylons of the electricity transmission line from Glen Garry to Skye march alongside the route from Kinloch Hourn to Gleann Beag over the Bealach Aoidhdailean. They make it impossible to lose the way, but are totally out of keeping with the wild landscape.

## 244  Arnisdale to Glenelg
*20km/12½ miles*                   *OS Sheet 33.   Start 844 104.   Finish 814 195*
Extensive forest felling and replanting with associated fence building in the area south of Eilanreach has made the direct routes between Glenelg and Arnisdale described in the previous edition of this guidebook very difficult to follow. An alternative route goes from Arnisdale for a short distance up Glen Arnisdale, and then up the steep zigzag path into Coire Chorsalain on the south side of Beinn nan Caorach. From the col at the head of this corrie climb N to the Bealach Aoidhdailean, at which point route 243(a) is joined and can be followed by either of its two finishes down Gleann Beag or (a few kilometres longer) down Glen More to reach Glenelg.

## 245  Glenelg to Shiel Bridge by Totaig
*18km/11 miles*                    *OS Sheet 33.   Start 820 199.   Finish 935 189*
From the Free Church at the road fork go NW for 400 metres to the Allt Mor Ghalltair, then NE by path and track across the ridge and through a forestry plantation. Continue until the track drops towards Ardintoul and leave it to descend rightwards to the Allt na Dalach where at map ref 839 237 there is a footbridge across the burn and a stile over the forest fence. The next section of the route through the forest to the broch called Caisteal Grugaig is at present very difficult to negotiate and it requires to be waymarked. Until such time as this is done, proceed with caution. Once the ruined broch is reached there are no more problems as a path leads to the end of the narrow public road at Totaig. Finally go 7km along this road to Ratagan Youth Hostel and 2½km further to Shiel Bridge.

An alternative route goes round the shore from Kylerhea Ferry, joining the above route beyond Ardintoul. The path, which begins at the old ferry house, goes to the electricity transmission line and becomes a rough muddy path along the hillside, beyond which a track goes along the shore round the Garbhan Cosach promontory and along the sandy shore of Camas nan Gall to Ardintoul.

## 245X   Shiel Bridge to Glenelg
*17km/11miles*                    *OS Sheet 33.   Start 938 186↑.   Finish 814 195*
From the camp site at Shiel Bridge take the path along the east side of the Allt Undalain for 600 metres and cross the footbridge to the west side. Follow a good path up the glen for 2km and then climb steeply up this path to Loch Coire nan Crogachan below the south side of Sgurr Mhic Bharraich. Continue along the path over the bealach west of the loch and descend on the north side of the Allt a' Ghleannain to the ruins of Bealachasan. The bridge over the Allt Grannda is dangerous and crossing may not be possible in spate conditions. Go along the forest road to Moyle where the public road is reached and followed pleasantly down Glen More to Glenelg, as in route 243(a).

## 246   Kinloch Hourn to Achnagart (Glen Shiel)
*12km/7¹/₂miles*                    *OS Sheet 33.   Start 950 066↑.   Finish 971 140↑*
Take the road from Kinloch Hourn uphill for about 1¹/₂km to the north end of Loch Coire Shubh. Cross to the E bank of the stream, possibly with difficulty, and follow the path which traverses the hillside N and goes up Coire Sgoireadail to Loch Bealach Coire Sgoireadail. Descend into Wester Glen Quoich, cross the burn and climb NW to the Bealach Duibh Leac (721m), the pass between Creag nan Damh and Sgurr a' Bhac Chaolais. In misty conditions it may be difficult to find the true bealach (look for marker post) as there is no path up the last part of Wester Glen Quoich, however it is important to do so as the only reasonable descent NW is from the lowest point of the bealach. Descend from the pass down a steep slope where the zigzags of the path are now rather indistinct. Lower down, after crossing the Allt Coire Toiteil, a good stalkers' path leads down to the A87 road in Glen Shiel, about 2km from Achnagart and 7km from Shiel Bridge.
This route is marked on Roy's map of 1755. Prince Charles Edward Stuart, in his wanderings in 1746, escaped through a cordon of Hanoverian soldiers just south of Kinloch Hourn and, after hiding in Coire Sgoireadail, crossed the Bealach Duibh Leac in darkness to reach Glen Shiel where he found refuge at Achnagart

## 246X   Kinloch Hourn to Shiel Bridge
*15km/9¹/₂miles*                    *OS Sheet 33.   Start 950 066↑.   Finish 938 186↑*
This route from Kinloch Hourn to Glen Shiel provides a more direct way to Shiel Bridge, but it is rougher and does not follow paths as does the preceding one. From Kinloch Hourn follow route 242X for 2km and take the right-hand path which crosses the Allt a' Choire Reidh and heads N towards the Allt Coire Mhalagain. When the corrie steepens, bear NE to reach the Bealach Coire Mhalagain (696m) between Sgurr na Sgine and The Saddle. From the bealach make a descending traverse NE below a dry stone dyke across rough slopes below the Forcan Ridge of The Saddle to reach the col

between this ridge and Meallan Odhar. From there go NNW down the Allt a'
Choire Chaoil and at its junction with the Allt a' Coire Uaine cross this burn
to reach the path on its W side (which forms part of route 245X). Follow this
path down to Shiel Bridge.

## 247  Glen Garry to Achnagart (Glen Shiel)
*22km/14miles        OS Sheets 33 and 34.  Start 113 018↑.  Finish 971 140↑*
This route starts about 5km west of Tomdoun Hotel in Glen Garry and
finishes near Achnagart in Glen Shiel, 6km up the glen from Shiel Bridge.
Take the path NW up the Allt a' Ghobhainn and go N over the Mam na Seilg
and NW down to the River Loyne. Cross the river and go W along the path on
the north bank. (If the river is in spate and a crossing is not possible, then continue W along the south side). 1 km east of the watershed, the path joins a
track which is followed to Alltbeithe. There turn NW and follow another track
for 2km, and continue along the path up Wester Glen Quoich to join route
246 over the Bealach Duibh Leac to Glen Shiel. (See the comments for route
246 as regards route finding on the bealach)
The walking distance can be considerably reduced by starting from the
Glen Quoich Bridge (map ref 015 041), 16km west of Tomdoun. From the
west end of the bridge go N by a private road alongside the loch to Alltbeithe
and join the route there to continue to Shiel Bridge.
The section of this route from Glen Loyne to Glen Quoich is shown on an
18th-century map in the British Library as part of an old route from
Aberchalder on Loch Oich to Glenelg.

## 248  Glen Garry to Cluanie Inn
*19km/12mls        OS Sheets 33 and 34.  Start 113 018↑.  Finish 079 117↑*
Starting from a point on the road in Glen Garry 5km west of Tomdoun
Hotel, follow route 247 to the River Loyne. Cross the river, then go NE and up
the Allt Giubhais to join the old public road, now closed, which goes N then
NW round the foot of Creag a' Mhaim and descends to join the A87 road 300
metres east of Cluanie Inn.
This route is not possible if the River Loyne is in spate.

## 249  Fort Augustus to Invergarry
*15km/9½mls            OS Sheet 34.  Start 377 097.  Finish 296 012*
Take the public road from Fort Augustus to Auchteraw and continue SW
by a forest road towards the Invervigar Burn. The bridge shown on the OS
1:50,000 map at map ref 336 056 across this burn has been swept away, so
go W along the road on its north side. It ends at a small stream and from there
go SW through a clearing in the forest to a gate in the boundary fence leading to Achadh-nan-darach. Cross the Invervigar Burn by a bridge and continue SW by a path to join a track which is followed SW past Loch Lundie and
down the Aldernaig Burn until it enters the forest near a small dam. At that
point follow a footpath due S down to Invergarry.

## 250  Fort Augustus to Achlain or Torgyle Bridge (Glen Moriston)

*12km/7½ miles   OS Sheet 34.   Start 377 097.   Finish 282 124↑ or 309 129↑*
This short but strategic connection between Fort Augustus and Glen Moriston has a long history.  It is the line of a very old track that was shown in Moll's Atlas of 1725; at that time it was the road to Skye and for that reason Bernera Barracks had been built at Glenelg in 1719-20. In 1750 and the following years it was reconstructed as a Military Road and was marked on Roy's Map of 1755 as 'Great Road of Communication between Bernera and Fort Augustus'. Johnson and Boswell in their journey to the Highlands and Western Islands travelled this way from Fort Augustus to Anoch (Ceannacroc) in Glen Moriston on 31st August 1773. Nowadays the route is a useful connection for long-distance walkers between the north-west end of the Corrieyairack Pass and the long ways through glens Affric and Cannich to the north-west.

Leave Fort Augustus along the road to Jenkins Park and in about 1km turn right up the Old Military Road, climbing in a series of zigzags. The track becomes more level and leads W then NW through the Inchnacardoch Forest for 4km to emerge on the open hillside above Glen Moriston, and a good path continues to the Allt Phocaichain. The route to Achlain, which is the line of the Old Military Road, continues W gradually downhill above the forest where it continues along a broad swathe through the trees crossing some old stone bridges that must have been part of the early road. Having passed below the electricity transmission line, continue along the path until within about 100 metres of the A887 road where a waymarker indicates a right turn directly down to reach the road about 150 metres east of Achlain.

The route to Torgyle Bridge leaves the Old Military Road on the east side of the Allt Phocaichain by a path which is difficult to discern. Go N to the forest and descend the clearing under the western of the two transmission lines. A short distance through the forest take the road which makes a long traverse W before turning NE down to Torgyle Bridge.

# SECTION 22
# Glen Affric, Strathfarrar and Kintail

**251 Torgyle Bridge (Glen Moriston) to Tomich (Strathglass)**
*18km/11miles   OS Sheets 25, 26 and 34.    Start 316 319↑.   Finish 310 275*
This right of way is the logical continuation of route 250 from its ending at Torgyle Bridge northwards over the high moorland to Strathglass. It was along this route that Prince Charlie travelled southwards in August 1746 to hide near Loch Arkaig after learning that the boat he hoped to board at Poolewe to take him to France had sailed without him.

Start 1km E of Torgyle Church on the A887 road, by a signposted path leading on to a track known locally as Eve's Road. Follow this track, which goes under the electricity transmission line all the way over the ridge between Beinn Bhan and An Suidhe, past Loch na Beinne Baine and down towards Guisachan Forest. From the upper edge of the forest two routes are possible. One goes N down the forest road to Hilton Cottage and the road going NE by Balcladaich to Tomich. The other goes NE following the forest fence to the north side of the Allt Bail a' Chladaich, then down this burn to the forest road and thence by the farm road past Guisachan steading to Tomich.

**252 Ceannacroc Bridge (Glen Moriston) to Tomich (Strathglass)**
*25km/15½miles  OS Sheets 25, 26 and 34.  Start 227 106↑.  Finish 310 275*
This route, which is a claimed right of way, is a rather long continuation of route 250 from its Achlain ending in Glen Moriston to Tomich in Strathglass or equally well to Glen Affric. Ceannacroc Bridge is about 5½km west of Achlain along the A887. From there go N along the private road past Ceannacroc Lodge and up the right bank of the River Doe for about 4½km to map ref 197 135, where the river is fordable in reasonably dry conditions. Once across the river, strike due N up the path across the west side of Meall Damh to the bealach (490m) west of Meallan Odhar. Beyond the bealach descend NE along the path on the left bank of the Allt Riabhach to enter the Guisachan Forest, where a forest road leads down to Cougie. From there a private road leads for a further 10km down the strath past Garve Bridge and Hilton Lodge to Tomich, from where there is a bus service to Cannich and Inverness.

**253 Cluanie Inn to Glen Affric**
*25km/15½miles  OS Sheets 25, 33 and 34.  Start 092 120↑.  Finish 201 234*
From a point 1 km east of Cluanie Inn at the west end of Loch Cluanie, go N along a track up the east bank of the Allt a' Chaorainn Mhoir for 3km. Continue N along the path through the pass and down to the River Affric. If the going is very wet, drier ground may be found by keeping higher up along

the hillside on the east of the path. Cross the River Affric by the bridge opposite Alltbeithe Youth Hostel. The public road is a further 13km down the glen, just beyond the east end of Loch Affric.

An alternative route is by the stalker's path which starts 3km east of Cluanie Inn and goes up to the Bealach Choire a' Chait (725m) which is boggy and pathless. From the bealach a path goes down Gleann na Ciche on the east side of the Allt na Ciche to reach a forest road leading to Athnamulloch at the west end of Loch Affric. From there the end of the public road is 7km away at the other end of Loch Affric, and may be most easily reached by continuing along the forest road on the south side of the loch.

## 254  Corrimony (Glen Urquhart) to Tomich  (Strathglass)
*10km/6mls*                    *OS Sheet 26.  Start 378 303.  Finish 310 275*
The little village of Corrimony is reached from the A831 road at the head of Glen Urquhart. From there a track, which was declared to be a right of way by the Court of Session in 1888, used to go SW in a direct line, keeping south-east of Carn Bingally, passing Loch Caoireach and then turning W downhill to Tomich. Recent reports describe this route as something of an obstacle course, with deep peat bog, no visible path and two high deer fences  without stiles, so it cannot be recommended.

An alternative route from Corrimony goes SSW along the track to the RSPB Corrimony Nature Reserve on the north-west side of the River Enrick and on past Loch Comhnard for about 4km to a ford. Continue along a rather obscure path by the riverside for150 metres and then turn W uphill into the forest on the south slopes of Druim na h' Aibhne. Although now partly overgrown by heather, the next 3km have obviously been part of a track which was well constructed many years ago and still shows signs of regular use by walkers. As it crosses the ridge, an impressive view of the Glen Affric mountains opens up. A gravel road is reached at Loch na Beinne Moire and the descent to Guisachan and Tomich is straightforward.

## 255  Tomich to Glen Affric
*15km/9¹/₂ miles*          *OS Sheets 25 and 26.  Start 310 275.  Finish 201 234*
This is the original route through Glen Affric which fell into disuse when the present public road on the north side of the River Affric through Chisholm's Pass was made in the 19th century. The route described here goes from Tomich to the carpark at the end of the public road in Glen Affric, from where the way westwards to Kintail is described as route 256

Cross the bridge at the south-west end of Tomich village and follow the track SW along the west bank of the Abhainn Deabhag for 2km to a junction at map ref 285 256. From there the original route continued SW by Loch an Eang, but the way from there to Loch Pollain Buidhe and beyond is now impassable. Instead, from the junction take the track W over the hill to join the forestry road along the south side of Loch Beinn a' Mheadhoin, and follow it to the bridge across the short section of river between lochs Affric  and Beinn a' Mheadhoin. The carpark at the end of the public road in Glen Affric is just across this bridge.

An alternative route, about 5km longer, goes from Tomich along the private road on the south-east side of the Abhainn Deabhag past Guisachan, Hilton Lodge and Garve Bridge to reach Cougie. Continue W by a forest road to a flat col, then follow a path across the Allt an Laghair and along a ridge to the Allt Garbh, and go down this burn to reach a forest road near a white cottage. Turn E along the road for almost 2km to the bridge at the east end of Loch Affric and the carpark at the end of the public road.

## 256  Glen Affric to Morvich (Loch Duich) by the Bealach an Sgairne
*27km/17miles*          *OS Sheets 25 and 33.  Start 201 234.  Finish 961 211*
With or without the initial 15km of route 255, this right of way through one of the most beautiful of Highland glens is among the great cross-country walks in Scotland. Starting from the carpark at the end of the public road up Glen Affric, two ways are possible to the west end of Loch Affric, one along the road to Affric Lodge followed by the path on the north side of the loch, and the other along the forest road on the south side of the loch to Athnamulloch. The two join 1km west of the head of the loch and the way continues along a track on the north side of the River Affric to Alltbeithe Youth Hostel, approximately half way to Morvich.

From there one way goes W along a path on the north side of Gleann Gniomhaidh to the south end of Loch a' Bhealaich, and then climbs to the narrow pass, the Bealach an Sgairne (515m), between Beinn Fhada and A' Ghlas-bheinn. Descend steeply along a good path down Gleann Choinneachain to the head of Strath Croe and continue along the south side of the Abhainn Chonaig to the bridge over the River Croe 1km from the National Trust for Scotland visitor centre at Morvich.

This route can be linked with routes 257, 262 or 265 by following the river which flows N from Loch a' Bhealaich for 5km to the Falls of Glomach. From there a steep and narrow path leads down the west side of the great chasm of the Allt a' Ghlomaich to Glen Elchaig.

The alternative route from Alltbeithe Youth Hostel is to go SW up the Fionngleann along the path past Camban bothy. In 4$^1$/$_2$ km from Alltbeithe the watershed is crossed and the path descends through the magnificent gorge of the Allt Grannda between the steep slopes of Beinn Fhada and the north ridge of Saileag. Below the gorge, Gleann Lichd opens out and a track continues on the south side of the River Croe to Morvich.

The route over the Bealach an Sgairne is shown on Moll's map of 1725, which marked it 'to Bealach Pass'. On Roy's map of 1755 it is called 'Road from Kintail to Inverness', and is shown continuing from Tomich along the south-east side of the River Glass to the Beauly Firth. The route was also known as St. Dubhthach's Pass, as the Irish missionary St. Dubhthach in the 11th century travelled this way regularly between his parishes in Kintail and Tain. Possibly the name St. Dubhthach's Pass refers to the Bealach an Sgairne, which is the key to this route.

## 257  Loch Mullardoch Dam to Killilan (Loch Long) by Glen Cannich
*32km/20miles*                    *OS Sheet 25.  Start 220 316.  Finish  940 303*

Depending on your transport, this long cross-country walk may have to start with 15km of road walking up  Glen Cannich from Cannich village to the Loch Mullardoch dam, and end with 9km more walking along the side of Loch Long from Killilan to the A87 road at Loch Duich, making a total length of 56km/35miles

From the Loch Mullardoch dam go along the north shore of the loch. The raising of its level in the 1950s submerged most of the original lochside path, but a new imtermittent path and a variety of sheep tracks have developed along the north side, in places rather rough and difficult to follow, especially between the Allt Mullardoch and the Allt Taige.  From there a well-defined track for the next 3km goes to the Allt Socrach, which is bridged at a fank.

Beyond the lodge go S and round a spur about 90m above the loch and keep along the lochside to the Allt Coire Lungard and the start of a rough track leading W to Iron Lodge. Continue along this track past the mud-flats which disfigure the landscape when the water-level of the loch is low, and go along the north side of the glen to the summit (330m) close to Loch an Droma. Descend 1 km to the bridge at Iron Lodge, from where a private road goes down Glen Elchaig to Killilan. From there a narrow public road continues beside Loch Long to Loch Duich.

This route is shown on Roy's map of 1755 as part of the road from Strathglass to Plockton at the mouth of Loch Carron.

As an alternative to going all the way down Glen Elchaig to Loch Long, cross the River Elchaig by a footbridge about 4 km below Loch na Leitreach, then follow the south bank of the river to Camas-luinie and from there go W by a path over a pass and down the River Glennan to Bundalloch, 1 km NE of Dornie.

From the SW end of Loch na Leitreach it is possible to cross the River Elchaig and climb the steep and narrow path to the Falls of Glomach, and from there follow route 265 in reverse over the Bealach na Sroine to Croe Bridge and Loch Duich. This is the shortest way of reaching Loch Duich, but the steep climb at the end of a long day's walk is likely to be a disincentive.

## 258  Glen Affric to Loch Mullardoch Dam by the Bealach Coire Ghaidheil
*35km/22miles*                    *OS Sheet 25.  Start 201 234.  Finish 220 316*

This route is a connection between the upper reaches of Glen Affric and the head of Loch Mullardoch, and for most of its length it is a combination of parts of the two previous routes. From the carpark at the end of the public road up Glen Affric, take the path going W on the north side of Loch Affric, passing the head of the loch, and go up the River Affric for about 2 km to the bridge over the Allt Coire Ghaidheil. Then go N up the stalkers' path on the east bank of the Allt Coire Ghaidheil, over the Bealach Coire Ghaidheil (715m) and down the east side of Gleann a' Choilich. Cross to the west side of the glen before reaching Loch Mullardoch, turn W above the loch and go round the mud flats at its head to reach the path on its north side and go E along the whole length of the loch to the dam at its east end.

### 259  Glen Affric to Loch Mullardoch Dam by the Allt Toll Easa
*13km/8miles*                    *OS Sheet 25. Start 216 242. Finish 220 316*
Start from the carpark in Glen Affric at map ref 216 242 and head up the track, becoming a path, in Gleann nam Fiadh for 4km. Turn off NW to climb another path, steeply at first, up the Allt Toll Easa. From the pass (860m) at its head go E over Toll Creagach (1053m) and descend ESE to the col at map ref 210 280 (795m), then head NE down the slope on the east side of the Allt Fraoch-choire by a discontinuous path directly towards the Loch Mullardoch dam. At the south end of the dam, descend a flight of steps and follow the road below the dam to the public road, along which it is a further 15km to Cannich village.

This variation of the route described in earlier editions of this guidebook avoids the need to walk along the south side of Loch Mullardoch, where the going through the old pinewoods may be very scenic, but is also pathless, rough and tiring.

### 260  Liatrie (Glen Cannich) to Struy (Glen Strathfarrar)
*21km/13miles*                *OS Sheets 25 and 26. Start 253 327. Finish 395 406*
From Liatrie in Glen Cannich (10km west from Cannich village) go N up the Liatrie Burn by a narrow path, at first on the west side of the burn and then, crossing at map ref 252 345, on the east side to the ruins of a shieling. This point can now be reached more easily by a track starting just east of the Liatrie Burn and going directly uphill through two deer fences with gates. Climb N from the shieling up open moorland to reach the saddle between An Soutar and Meallan Odhar. Continue down the E side of the Allt Innis na Larach to a footbridge at map ref 263 383 over the River Farrar, 600 metres upstream from Ardchuilk. From that point there is a walk of 15km down Glen Strathfarrar along a private road through magnificent scenery to reach the public road at Struy.

This route between Glen Cannich and Strathfarrar is part of the old road from Poolewe and Wester Ross to the Corrieyairack and the south. The crest of the ridge between An Soutar and Meallan Odhar  was the furthest north point on the mainland reached by Prince Charlie in his wanderings after Culloden, and it was there that he received the unwelcome news that the boat that he hoped would take him to France had sailed without him.

------------

Routes 261 to 264 all involve access along the private road up Glen Strathfarrar from Struy to the Monar Dam. This road is a right of way, so pedestrian and cycle access is always available. Vehicular access, which can save walking about 22km along the tarred road to the dam, is available subject to an agreement between Scottish Natural Heritage and the various landowners involved, at the following times:
In summer (last weekend of March to 31st October) the gatekeeper, whose house is beside the locked gate at Inchmore, will unlock the gate for cars on

Mondays to Saturdays (except Tuesdays) during the hours 0900 to 1300 and 1330 to 1700, with last exit by 1800. Access is also available from 1330 to 1700 on Sunday afternoons, but there is no access for cars on Sunday mornings and Tuesdays.

In winter (1st November to the last weekend of March ) vehicular access is available, if the gatekeeper is at home, by prior arrangement. Phone (Struy) 01463-761260.

### 261  Struy (Strathglass) to Strathcarron
*59¹/₂ km/37mls*          *OS Sheets 25 and 26. Start 395 406. Finish 943 422*
From Struy go for 22km up the private road in Glen Strathfarrar to the east end of Loch Monar. It is possible to drive to the dam, see the note above, but the walk up the glen is full of interest and beauty, some might think that it is the most attractive part of this long walk, and you are not likely to be disturbed by much traffic. From the Monar Dam continue along the north shore of the enlarged Loch Monar, the last 5km to the west end of the loch being pathless.

Continue W over the Bealach an Sgoltaidh (545m) between Bidein a' Choire Sheasgaich and Beinn Tharsuinn, and go down to Loch an Laoigh. Follow the path on the east side of the loch to Bendronaig Lodge, and continue along the track towards Attadale for about 2km to map ref 995 386 where an old iron gate stands to the north of the track. From there head W across the open moor towards Bealach Alltan Ruairidh (395m), a clear notch in the skyline, and pick up a path below the bealach which continues over it, past Lochan Fuara, over undulating moorland past Loch an Fheoir and down to Achintee near Strathcarron Hotel and station.

An alternative finish to this very long route which saves a few kilometres can be made from the Bealach an Sgoltaidh by descending W to cross the Abhainn Bhearnais at the north end of Loch an Laoigh, not far from Bearnais bothy, map ref 021 430. This crossing will not be possible if there is much water in the river. Climb W uphill from the head of Loch an Laoigh to reach the path which goes from Bearnais bothy to Strathcarron over 8km of wild, rocky and undulating moorland. In places the path is difficult to find, but it is fairly continuous.

### 262  Inchvuilt (Glen Strathfarrar) to Killilan (Loch Long) by Glen Elchaig
*40km/25miles*          *OS Sheet 25. Start 230 387. Finish  940 303*
Reach Inchvuilt far up Glen Strathfarrar on foot or by car as described above for route 261. It may be possible to cross the River Farrar by a ford there, but this should only be done with great caution as river levels can change suddenly owing to discharges from the Monar Dam. There is also a footbridge, but it seems to be rather dilapidated. From there follow the track up the Uisge Misgeach for 6km to a small power station. Alternatively this point can be reached by car by driving up to and across the Monar Dam. There is apparently no objection to this.

From the power station continue W for 3¹/₂ km along a track and stalker's path, then strike NW over the col (no path) between Meallan Odhar and Meallan Buidhe  and descend NW across the north slopes of Meallan Buidhe to cross the Allt Riabhachan by a bridge at map ref 125 392. Go down a track to Pait Lodge and continue along the track going SW from there below the slopes of Beinn Bheag, keeping east of several lochs. In 5km from Pait go S up the Allt Coire nan Each and past Loch Mhoicean, then SW down to Iron Lodge. From there go down Glen Elchaig to Killilan as in route 257 to reach the head of Loch Long, 9km along the public road from Loch Duich.

### 263  Inchvuilt (Glen Strathfarrar) to Loch Long by Bendronaig Lodge
*38km/24miles*                *OS Sheet 25. Start 230 387. Finish 934 306*
    Follow route 262 to Pait Lodge. There cross the stream by the bridge beside the lodge and go W uphill (path indistinct and heavy going) for about 1km, then bear WSW round the foot of Meall Mor and Lurg Mhor to the north side of Loch Calavie, about 8km from Pait. Beyond the loch cross a flat col and descend E to Bendronaig Lodge. From there follow the track to Attadale for about 7km to map ref 957 366 and turn S along a forest road which in 1km reaches the edge of the forest. Continuing S, a path drops gradually to Glen Ling and leads along the west side of the River Ling to the head of Loch Long, from where a 9km walk along the public road leads the A87 road at Loch Duich.

### 264  Struy (Strathglass) to Craig (Glen Carron)
*45km/28mls*          *OS Sheets 25 and 26. Start 395 406. Finish 040 493*↑
    Follow route 261 to the west end of Loch Monar. Just beyond the head of the loch turn NW up the path, which peters out after 1km, to the Bealach Bhearnais. Then go NE down another path for 2km to a footbridge over the Allt a' Chonais. Continue down the glen below the steep rocky face of Sgurr nan Ceannaichean and through the forest lower down by a road which reaches the A890 in Glen Carron at Craig, where Forest Enterprise have provided a carpark, 4km east of Achnashellach.
    This route is marked on Roy's map of 1755 as 'Road from Loch Carron to Inverness'.
    An alternative route diverges from the previous one about 10km along the north shore of Loch Monar. Go N from there up the Abhainn Srath Mhuilich past Loch Mhuilich to the col on the north side of Bidean an Eoin Deirg, then down An Crom-allt on its north-west side. At map ref 113 468 bear WNW across rough peaty ground towards a small plantation, from where a track goes WSW over the watershed to the Allt a' Chonais and down the glen to Craig.

### 265  Croe Bridge (Loch Duich) to the Falls of Glomach
*9km/5½ miles*          *OS Sheet 25 or 33. Start 955 216. Finish 016 257*
    Go up Strath Croe by the private road past Ruarach and Lienassie to the clearing at Dorusduain. This point may also be reached from Morvich by crossing the bridge over the River Croe at Innis a' Chrotha and following the footpath to the left of the house for 2km on the south side of the Abhainn Chonaig to cross a footbridge in a little gorge just below the clearing. Continue up a forest road and on entering the forest turn left up a more substantial road.

Shortly this joins the main forest road leading N up the glen, crossing the burn at map ref 984 232 and ending just before the bridge across the Allt an Leoid Ghaineamhaich. Cross and climb up the path on the north side of this stream to the Bealach na Sroine (517m). Descend the path on the north-east side of this pass to the River Glomach, which a short distance downstream makes a sheer drop of over 100m into a deep gorge. It is possible by scrambling carefully down a rocky path to get an excellent view of the Falls of Glomach. The return may be made down Glen Elchaig, see routes 257 and 266.

### 266 Dornie (Loch Duich) to the Falls of Glomach

*17¹/₂ km/11mls*                    *OS Sheet 33. Start 883 264. Finish 016 257*
    This is far from being the shortest approach to the Falls of Glomach, but it is a good walk through fine country. Taken with route 265 it gives an excellent expedition, both ends of which are on (or very close to) the bus route along the A87 road beside Loch Duich.
    From Dornie go along the east shore of Loch Long to Bundalloch, then by path up the bank of the River Glennan and over the pass at its head to Camas-luinie in Glen Elchaig. Continue up the south side of the glen for 2km to a footbridge at map ref 967 277 and cross the river to the private road. An alternative route is by the public road along the west shore of Loch Long to Killilan, where cars should be parked. Continue by the private road, which is a right of way, up Glen Elchaig to Loch na Leitreach. Just below this loch cross the River Elchaig by a footbridge (the A.E.Robertson Memorial Bridge) and continue up a path along the Allt a' Ghlomaich, which is crossed by a second footbridge. Follow the steep path for about 1km up the west bank of the great chasm to reach the top of the Falls of Glomach. The path approaching the falls is narrow in places and may be slippery when wet, so be careful.

### 266X  Inverinate (Loch Duich) to Camas-luinie (Glen Elchaig)

*9km/6miles*                    *OS Sheet 33. Start 910 227. Finish 947 283*
    This is a direct path over the hills from Loch Duich to Glen Elchaig which can be used  with either route 265 or 266 for going to or from the Falls of Glomach. Start from the A87 road 1km north-west of Inverinate by climbing steeply up the old road over the Carr Brae, and stay on it until the bridge over An Leth-allt. Continue for about 300 metres to a farm building in the field above the road and take the path across this field to a gate in its north-east corner. A good path continues along the north-west bank of An Leth-allt to old shielings in Coire Dhuinnid at map ref 932 249, and it then turns N up the slope to a broad col, across which it is cairn-marked. Beyond the col the path descends NE on the north side of the Allt Mor  to Camas-luinie. At map ref 939 283 an alternative and better path  diverges NNE to reach  the public road in Glen Elchaig about 1km from Camas-luinie.

### 267 Loch Long to Attadale (Loch Carron)

*11km/7miles*                    *OS Sheet 25. Start 934 306. Finish 924 387*
    It is possible to drive the first 9km from Dornie to the head of Loch Long, however the walk along this quiet road above the lochside is very pleasant.

Leaving the public road ½ km before the bridge over the River Ling, go along the private access road to Nonach Lodge. Go past the lodge and its estate buildings to take a path across a field which is left by a gate at its top corner. The path continues above the west bank of the River Ling. At map ref 940 314, just before going under power lines, the path forks. Take the right-hand path and continue up the river to cross the Allt Loch Innis nan Seangan by a footbridge close to its junction with the River Ling. Bear uphill through a gate before continuing parallel to the river along the face of the slope for another 1km. Turn N at a ruined cottage to go uphill, roughly parallel to but just west of the power lines, passing a small loch ½ km east of Loch an Iasaich. Enter the forest and follow a track downhill for 1km to join the private road from Bendronaig Lodge to Attadale. Follow this road for 5km down to Attadale and the A890 road, 4km from Strathcarron Hotel and Station

This route, with some variations, is shown on Roy's map of 1755.

### 268   Stromeferry to Loch Long and Dornie
*15km/9½ miles*          *OS Sheets 24 and 25.   Start 864 344.   Finish 934 306*
Starting from the A890 road, 300m south from Stromeferry, or from a second forest entrance near Achmore at map ref 869 333, go on forest road to head east along the north side of Srath Ascaig. After crossing the bridge at map ref 887 328, go round the south side of Carn na Creige, then NE up the Allt Gleann Udalain to the edge of forest at map ref 903 330.

The route previously left the forest here and led E to meet the Allt Loch Innis nan Seangan but a deer fence further on now impedes progress. Another route (much drier) is possible by continuing on the forest track to its end at map ref 915 336 and E along a ride, out into open ground, meeting the forest fence at a new stile at map ref 930 339. From here it is better to hold due E, descending gradually to join the path beside the Allt nam Bacanan (map ref 942 340). This path leads S to cross the Allt Loch Innis nan Seangan and down to Nonach Lodge at the head of Loch Long. It is a further 9km by public road to Dornie.

### 269   Muir of Ord to Struy (Strathglass)
*21km/13miles*          *OS Sheet 26.   Start 527 503.   Finish 402 404*
From Muir of Ord go W by the narrow public road for 5km to Aultgowrie Bridge. This point may also be reached along the minor road from Marybank on the A832 road. Go uphill WSW along a well-defined track through Achedersen, ignoring a left turn after 4km, and continue between two lochans to the end of the track at map ref 431 486. Turn S down to the burn and the remains of a footbridge at Tighachrochadair. From there go S along a path to join a track leading to an intake sluice on the Allt a' Chrochadair at map ref 436 473. The traditional and direct route from there goes S across flat boggy ground, a logical line but not one which is visible as a path. A more obvious but longer route follows the track NE, E then S past Loch Ballach. The two alternatives join at about map ref 438 450, and from there the track is followed for abut 5km past Erchless Cottage to the A831 road 1km north-east of Struy Bridge.

## 270  Strathpeffer to Lochluichart
*23km /14¹/₂ miles        OS Sheets 20 and 26.  Start 477 574.  Finish 323 626*
Much of the walking on this route is along minor public roads in the lower reaches of Strathconon, an area of forest and small rocky hills in which there are many attractive paths, tracks and quiet public roads. From the south-west end of Strathpeffer take the road to the houses at the north-east corner of Loch Kinellan and the track from there along its north-west side to enter the forest north of Contin. From the west end of Loch na Crann go S towards Contin and before reaching the village look for a path on the right which leads down to a Forest Enterprise carpark. From there go along the main road past the Achilty Hotel and opposite it take the minor road on the left to Loch Achilty and the power station below the Loch Luichart dam. From there, two routes are possible to the head of Loch Luichart:

(a) Continue along the road for 1km to the Loch Luichart dam, cross to its west end and head N through birchwoods  and along the steep west side of Loch Luichart where the old path was flooded when the level of the loch was raised. Beyond the ruins of Arrieleitrach traces of a path may be followed to the head of the loch, where the River Grudie is crossed by the railway bridge 800 metres west of Lochluichart station.

(b) From the power station follow the road past Little Scatwell to the Loch Meig dam, cross it and continue along the road up Strathconon to Bridgend. ¹/₂ km further on strike NW uphill along a track through Strathconon Wood to map ref 303 567 and then fork right along a path going NNW past Loch an Eilein and over to Loch Luichart, joining route (a) about 1km east of the head of the loch.

## 271  Strathpeffer to Achanalt (Strath Bran) by Strathconon
*32km/19miles        OS Sheets 20, 25 and 26.  Start 477 574.  Finish 232 612*
Go as in route 270(b) to Strathconon Wood and continue NW along the track for a further 2km to its end near the head of the Allt Bail a' Mhuilinn. Go N across the col to the east of Carn Garbh and descend NW to Loch Achanalt, where the path continues W to a small patch of forest. A road continues through it to a bridge over the River Bran and a railway level crossing to reach the A832 road 3km west of Achanalt Halt.

## 272  Strathconon to Achnasheen
*10km/6¹/₂ miles              OS Sheet 25.  Start 226 519↑.  Finish 147 562↑*
The public road in Strathconon ends at a carpark about 1km east of Scardroy Lodge. From it go W towards the lodge for ³/₄ km to a junction of tracks at map ref 217 520 and follow the right-hand track WNW up the Scardroy Burn. Beyond the end of the forest, where the track ends, continue along a path over the watershed on the south side of Carn Mhartuin and down the Allt Mhartuin to Inver and the A890 road 3km from Achnasheen.

This route is marked on Roy's map of 1755 as 'Road from Loch Carron to Dingwall'. At that time there was no road through Strath Bran.

### 273 Muir of Ord to Inverchoran (Strathconon) by Glen Orrin

*28km/17¹/₂ miles*          *OS Sheets 25 and 26.   Start 527 503.   Finish 260 507*

This walk goes up Strath Orrin from its lower reaches where the River Orrin flows through the beautifully wooded country to the west of Muir of Ord to the desolate head of the strath where there is no human habitation, the only remaining cottage, Luipmaldrig, having been deserted long ago. From Muir of Ord take the road west for 5km to Aultgowrie, or alternatively start from Marybank, thereby saving 3km of walking. Go along the private road on the south side of the River Orrin for 3km, cross the river and continue up Glen Orrin by the track on the north side of the river for a further 5km to the dam on the Orrin Reservoir.

The old path beyond that point has been submerged and there are 10km of rough tiresome walking along the north bank of the reservoir by intermittent deer tracks.   Towards the head of the reservoir, at map ref 346 491, signs appear of the old path which may be followed for 4km along the River Orrin to Luipmaldrig, with a diversion at the Allt a' Choir' Aluinn to avoid boggy ground. Leave the glen and go WNW up a path past Loch Airigh Lochain and over the broad ridge to descend through a small forest to Inverchoran in Strathconon.

To extend this route westwards, go 4km along the road beside Loch Beannacharain to the carpark at the end of the public road and from there follow route 272 to Achnasheen, a total distance from Muir of Ord of 45km/28miles. The return to Muir of Ord can be done by train, and if you want to take 2 days for this walk, Luipmaldrig cottage will give shelter for the night.

### 274 Inverchoran (Strathconon) to Loch Monar (Glen Strathfarrar)

*16km/10miles*          *OS Sheet 25.   Start 260 507.   Finish 203 394*

The access road to Inverchoran is 7km up Strathconon from Milton. Go for ¹/₂ km along the road to the farm and from there go SW up Gleann Chorainn by a track, which becomes a path, crossing and recrossing the burn and leading to the bealach at the head of the glen. There the left-hand path is taken down to Loch na Caoidhe in the upper reaches of Glen Orrin. 1¹/₂ km beyond the head of this loch, where the floor of the glen changes from flat boggy meadow to rising ground, cross the River Orrin and follow the path along the crest of a moraine to the foot of the steep hillside to the south. The path becomes harder to follow, but at first is on the right of twin burns, crossing to the left about three-quarters of the way up. Cross the ridge above at map ref 208 450 where the path is lost among various deer tracks, but it reappears at the Allt a' Choire Dhomhain. Continue along the path, now well defined, down the west bank of this stream to reach Loch Monar. Turn E along the path through the Creag a' Chaobh defile to Monar Lodge from where the Monar Dam is 1km away.

See the note on pages 141 & 142 regarding access by car to the Monar Dam.

## 275  Strathconon to Craig (Glen Carron)

*24km/15miles*                    *OS Sheet 25.  Start 226 519.  Finish 040 493*

From the carpark at the end of the public road in Strathconon at Loch Beannacharain,  go to the head of the loch and keep on the left-hand road to Scardroy. Continue SW along the track to Corrievuic and onwards by the path on the north bank of the River Meig up a long and featureless glen for 12km to Glenuaig Lodge. This involves crossing several side burns which normally present no difficulty. In spate conditions, however, for example when snow is melting on the hills above,  the Allt na Criche in particular can be treacherous. From Glenuaig Lodge a track leads over the col to the Allt a' Chonais and down this river to Craig in Glen Carron, 4km east of Achnashellach.

# SECTION 23
# Skye

## 276 Kinloch (Isleornsay) to Kylerhea

*12km/7¹/₂ miles      OS Sheets 32 and 33.  Start 693 165↑.  Finish 788 209↑*

This route is thought to follow part of an old drove road from the Sleat district in Skye to Kylerhea, where the cattle were forced to swim across the narrows to reach the mainland near Glenelg before resuming their long journey southwards.

This short section of that route starts from the A851 road between Broadford and Isleornsay at map ref 693 165, just south of a roadside phone box. Follow a forest road across the Abhainn Ceann-locha and then go SE to a carpark and behind the Kinloch Lodge Hotel for about 2km to map ref 712 154. At that point a newly made path branches off E uphill. Follow this good path for 2km to map ref 732 160 where it turns downhill, and continue NE by a fainter path  which traverses through clearings in the forest  to emerge at map ref 747 172. For the next 2km the path is visible, though in a bad state of repair; it  passes through more recent plantations where the path has been left clear of planting, then comes 1¹/₂ km gradually descending across more open ground through the top of an old natural wood. Finally there is a 2km section where the path has seriously deteriorated, in places lost in the dreadful bog. It may be better to go down to the shore for this part of the route. Finally, reach a footbridge over the Kylerhea River ¹/₂ km from the end of the public road in Kylerhea.

## 277 Luib to Torrin and return

*17km/10¹/₂ miles                    OS Sheet 32.  Start and finish 564 277↑*

This circular low-level route through the Red Hills of Skye starts and finishes either at Luib or Torrin. From Luib go S between Glas Bheinn Mhor and Beinn na Cro past Lochain Stratha Mhoir, and down Srath Mor to the B8083 road at the head of Loch Slapin. Walk along the road for 2km to Torrin village and take the path which goes N through Srath Beag between Beinn na Cro and Beinn Dearg Mhor. On the north side of the pass go down beside the Allt Strollamus until, about 400 metres before reaching the A850, follow an old road NW then W round the hillside back to Luib.

## 278 Sligachan Hotel to Glen Brittle

*13km/8miles                    OS Sheet 32.  Start 486 299↑.  Finish 413 205↑*

From Sligachan Hotel follow the A863 road towards Drynoch for 700 metres, then go SW along the private road to Alltdearg House. Continue behind the house and up the path on the north-west bank of the Allt Dearg Mor to the Bealach a' Mhaim. Go down the path on the north side of the Allt a' Mhaim and alongside the forest fence to reach the road in Glen Brittle. Finally, go down this road to your destination at the youth hostel, the climbers' hut or the camp site beside the beach.

## 279  Elgol to Sligachan Hotel
*17km/10½miles*                    *OS Sheet 32.  Start 520 139↑.   Finish 486 299↑*

Take the path from Elgol which goes N at a height of about 100m above sea-level across the steep west face of Ben Cleat. There are superb views of the Black Cuillin across Loch Scavaig from this part of the route. The path drops down to sea-level at the foot of Glen Scaladal and continues just above the shore to Camasunary. This beautifully situated spot on the machair above Camus Fhionnairigh can also be reached from Kilmarie on the B8083 road (map ref 545 173) by a track across the Strathaird peninsula.

From Camasunary the direct route to Sligachan goes N by the path up Srath na Creitheach, over the pass at only 85m at Lochan Dubha and down Glen Sligachan on the east side of the river to reach the hotel.

A much more interesting and scenic route goes W from Camasunary for 700 metres across the machair to the Abhainn Camas Fhionnairigh. There is no bridge and the crossing will be difficult, maybe impossible, if the river is full or the tide is high. Once across this stream, continue along the path below the steep southern perimeter of Sgurr na Stri and round the Rubha Ban to Loch nan Leachd, an inner pool of Loch Scavaig. On a fine day the views across the loch to the Cuillin are magnificent. The Bad Step is reached where the path approaches a slabby rock buttress dropping sheer into Loch Scavaig. The only difficult part is where one has to scramble up a narrow ledge across a slab directly above the sea. There is an easier alternative at a higher level which is reached by a well marked scramble. Beyond the Bad Step there are no difficulties; the path drops to sea-level and crosses a little promontory to reach the outflow of Loch Coruisk.

The continuation to Sligachan does not cross the River Scavaig, but goes NE up a rough path and slabs past Loch a' Choire Riabhaich and over the Druim Hain ridge at about 310m. Beyond there descend for about 2½km by a path to join the main route between Camasunary and Sligachan near Lochan Dubha.

## 280  Glen Brittle to Loch Coruisk and Sligachan Hotel
*24km/15miles*                    *OS Sheet 32.  Start 413 205↑.   Finish 486 299↑*

This is a difficult walk by normal standards, and should only be attempted by those with some scrambling ability. It may not be possible to cross some of the streams, for example the Scavaig River, if they are in spate, so it is also an expedition for reasonably dry conditions, which some might think are rather rare in Skye.

From the camp site at Loch Brittle take the path E upwards towards Coire Lagan for about ½km and then follow another path going ESE across a small stream towards the foot of Sron na Ciche. Cross the Allt Coire Lagan and follow a lower path which passes below the mouth of Coir' a' Ghrunnda.

Beyond there the path is not very clear, but it continues traversing at a height of about 220m ESE below Coire nan Laogh and the screes of Garsbheinn, gradually climbing to about 300m to the tiny lochan (map ref 476 176) at the source of the Allt an Fraoich.

300 metres past this burn, the route turns N and continues for about 1km

along a shelf, marked by cairns, as far as the Allt Coir' a' Chruidh. Cross this burn above a waterfall and continue contouring at about 300m above the sea until a large crag appears on the left. Then start descending towards the shore, crossing the Allt a' Chaoich, the Mad Burn, which may be very difficult or impossible in spate as the stream is then a foaming cascade. Go round the head of Loch na Cuilce at sea-level past the climbers' hut and along a path to the outflow of Loch Coruisk.

Cross the river by stepping stones, which may be submerged when the water level is high. Once across, the Bad Step variation of route 279 is joined and followed NE by a path to Loch a' Choire Riabhach, over the Druim Hain ridge and down Glen Sligachan to the Sligachan Hotel. The scenery throughout this route, particularly at Loch Coruisk, is magnificent

## 281  Strath Suardal to Boreraig and Suisnish
*13km/8miles*                    *OS Sheet 32.  Start 620 208↑.  Finish 594 202↑*
This walk starts from the road in Strath Suardal not far from Broadford and goes to the long-since deserted crofting township of Boreraig, then returns round the coast to Kilbride near Torrin. Start from the B8083 road in Strath Suardal 4km from Broadford, only a few hundred metres from the old church and graveyard of Cill Chriosd, and follow the path S past Loch Lonachan and down the Allt na Pairte to Boreraig. The path passes close to some old marble quarries, and when they were in production many years ago a narrow-gauge railway, known as the Broadford Express, ran from there to the pier at Broadford. Traces of this old railway can still be seen. Continue W from Boreraig along the shore of Loch Eishort by a cliff path, indistinct in places, to Suisnish. From there go N along a track well above the shore of Loch Slapin, with good views across the loch to Bla Bheinn and its satellite peaks. The track leads to Kilbride on the B8083 road near Torrin and only 3km away from the starting point of the walk.

## 282  The circuit of Idrigill Point from Loch Bharcasaig
*20km/12½miles*                    *OS Sheet 23.  Start and Finish 257 426↑*
This is a circular route in the southern tip of the Duirinish peninsula which gives some good views of the steep cliffs and wild coastline of northwest Skye.

From the A863 road just south of Dunvegan, drive or walk down the minor road past Orbost to Loch Bharcasaig and start from there. Climb W up the broad grassy ridge of Healabhal Bheag, the higher of the two prominent hills called Macleod's Tables. At a height of about 300m, as the ridge becomes steeper just below the summit of the hill, make a level traverse SW across the grassy hillside to the Bealach Bharcasaig. It is also possible to climb Healabhal Bheag, but the final slopes to the top are quite steep and rocky. From the bealach descend W into the head of Glen Dibidal and go down this glen as far as the flat ground about 60m above sea-level. Continue SE along the top of the sea-cliffs with a good deal of climbing up and down, following traces of a path in places, past Glen Ollisdal and Glen Lorgasdal towards Idrigill Point. It is worth going to the promontory 700 metres west of Idrigill Point to get a fine view down to the sea-stacks called Macleod's Maidens.

From Idrigill Point return N along a good path past some old sheilings at Idrigill and across the undulating hillside to reach a forestry plantation. Go through it by a road which leads to the head of Loch Bharcasaig a short distance from the starting point.

*At Loch an Eoin on the path between Coulags and Torridon (route 286)*

*The path from Corrie Hallie to Shenavall, looking towards Beinn Dearg Mor (routes 297 and 298)*

The path along the southern flank of Ben Mor Coigach above Loch Broom (route 313)

Spidean Coinich, the south-eastern peak of Quinag, above the Bealach a' Chornaidh (route 317)

# SECTION 24
# Wester Ross

### 283  Kishorn to Applecross
*18km/11miles                    OS Sheet 24.  Start 808 404↑.  Finish 711 445*
    To avoid the enclosed area of the former oil rig construction yard at the head of Loch Kishorn, the recommended starting point for this walk is at map ref 808 404 on the Bealach na Ba road from Kishorn to Applecross, where there is limited space for car parking. From there descend SSW across boggy ground to reach the shore of Loch Kishorn beside the mouth of the Allt a' Chumhaing, and cross the burn by the footbridge there. Continue SW parallel to the shore to Airigh-drishaig over rough ground, the old path having disappeared, but the best route follows the line of the electricity pylons.
    From Airigh-drishaig the most direct path to Toscaig goes inland. Start by climbing approximately along the line of pylons, then a clear path is found which continues past Loch Airigh Alasdair and Lochan an t-Sagairt and down near the Toscaig River. The alternative is round the coast by a rough and in places precipitous path to Uags then a better one from there for 2km N to some shielings, and finally to Toscaig by an intermittent path visible in some parts and marked elsewhere by a few cairns.
    The last part of this walk goes along the normally very quiet road from Toscaig past the little villages of Camusterrach, Camusteel and Milton to Applecross. There are superb views from many points on this walk across the Inner Sound to Skye.

### 284  Applecross to Kenmore or Inverbain
*16km/10miles   OS Sheet 24.  Start 711 445.  Finish  754 576↑ or 787 549↑*
    From Applecross village go round the head of the bay and take the private road, which is a right of way, up the north-west side of the River Applecross past Hartfield. Follow the road past two plantations to its end and continue along the left-hand path, which turns N and goes in an almost straight line across the desolate interior of the Applecross peninsula to Kenmore.
    An alternative finish to this walk, which is 2km shorter, is to take the right-hand path from the road end and go NE to Inverbain.
    Both these paths are, as cairns indicate, old coffin routes which were used in time past by burial parties going to the church at Applecross.

### 284X  Leacanashie (Loch Carron) to Achintraid (Loch Kishorn)
*5km/3miles                    OS Sheet 24.  Start  851 356↑.  Finish 840 388↑*
    This is almost certainly part of an old route leading N from the disused ferry at Strome, and its final section is along a coffin road. It goes through a pleasant mix of forest and open moorland with magnificent views across the head of Loch Kishorn to the hills of Applecross.
    From a small carpark at Leacanashie take a path steeply uphill through mature forest to join the forest road above. Go W along this road for about

120 metres, then take a footpath uphill on the right of the road and follow this over a ridge and downhill to join a forest road above the Reraig Burn. Follow it ENE until just beyond the junction with another road, and there go NE up the burn. Although the path is easy to follow, it is rather boggy and soon emerges from the forest through a gate in an old fence. A little further on reach an old burial ground at map ref 852 377 and from there go NW over a ridge and descend to Achintraid by a well made coffin road.

### 285  Loch Carron or Strathcarron to Shieldaig or Annat (Loch Torridon)
*20km/12¹/₂ miles*
> *OS Sheets 24 and 25.   Start 922 422.   Finish 815 540 or 894 544↑*

The start of this route is on the A896 road at the head of Loch Carron, midway between Lochcarron village and Strathcarron Station. Go along the private road to Tullich and before reaching it make a diversion over a stile round the west side of the gardens to reach the old path behind the house. Continue up this path beside the Abhainn Bhuachaig, cross the Bealach a' Ghlas-chnoic and descend on the north side of the Allt a' Ghiubhais.

At the point where the path turns SW towards Glasnock, leave it and cross the level strath to Ceann-loch-damh. From there two possible routes continue northwards:

(a) Cross the river flowing into Loch Damh from Loch Coultrie to reach the A896 road and follow it N to Shieldaig.

(b) Cross the Abhainn Dearg and follow the path along the east side of Loch Damh. In 4km a track is reached which continues along the lochside and reaches the A896 road midway between Shieldaig and Annat.

From that point the last few kilometres to Shieldaig go along the road. The most attractive way of reaching Annat is to cross the A896 and go down a private road towards the little bays of Ob Gorm Beag and Ob Gorm Mor and along the wooded fringe of Loch Torridon to the Loch Torridon Hotel.

The route along the east side of Loch Damh is shown on Roy's map of 1755 as the 'road' from Lochcarron to Shieldaig, with a branch going east to the head of Loch Torridon.

### 286  Coulags (Glen Carron) to Annat (Loch Torridon)
*15km/9¹/₂ miles     OS Sheets 24 and 25.   Start 958 451↑.   Finish  894 544↑*

This is one of three fine routes which cross the passes between Glen Carron and Torridon. A feature of them are the splendid mountains of the Achnashellach and Coulags forests, bare rocky peaks of Torridonian sandstone and quartzite penetrated by rough stony paths.

Start from the A890 road 4¹/₂ km north from Strathcarron Station at the bridge over the Fionn-abhainn and follow the well-defined path N past the new Coulags Lodge and up the east side of the river. In 2km the river is crossed and in another 1km Coulags cottage is passed. 1km further on there is a junction of paths. The most direct way continues N up the glen past Loch Coire Fionnaraich to the Bealach na Lice (420m) and then NW down to Loch an Eion.

A longer route, but finer scenically, is to take the left-hand path 1km north of Coulags cottage and climb W to the col between Maol Chean-dearg and Meall nan Ceapairean. Descend the path to Loch Coire an Ruadh-staic, which is in a fine setting below the steep north face of An Ruadh-stac, and continue along it on a level traverse round the foot of Maol Chean-dearg to Loch an Eion, where the previous path is rejoined. From the loch an easy walk of 4¹⁄₂ km down a good path leads to Annat at the head of Loch Torridon.

## 287 Achnashellach (Glen Carron) to Annat (Loch Torridon)
*16km/10miles        OS Sheets 24 and 25. Start 003 484↑. Finish 894 544↑*

This is a very fine walk up Coire Lair into the heart of the Achnashellach mountains. Start from the A890 road at the private road leading to Achnashellach Station, go up to the station, cross the line and proceed up a narrow track through rhododendrons to a junction of forest roads. Take the road on the left (signposted) for ¹⁄₂ km, then follow a short path on the left by a small burn to a gate in the deer fence which leads to the path on the north bank of the River Lair. Follow this path uphill through the pine woods and after leaving the forest climb more steeply towards Coire Lair, with the huge sandstone buttresses of Fuar Tholl on one's left.

In about 2¹⁄₂ km the path levels off and continues WNW up Coire Lair between the dark cliffs of Sgorr Ruadh on the left and the grey quartzite screes of Beinn Liath Mhor on the right. After crossing the Bealach Coire Lair (650m) at the head of the corrie, the path drops about 100m and then continues W on a level traverse for ¹⁄₂ km to the Bealach Ban (550m). From there the path descends SW below Meall Dearg to join route 286 on the ascent to the Bealach na Lice. Continue along that route to reach Annat.

Alternatively, one can return to Glen Carron by reversing route 286 past Coulags bothy, and thus make an almost circular walk through the mountains and back to the A890 road in Glen Carron, 6km from the starting point at Achnashellach.

## 287X Coulags or Achnashellach (Glen Carron) to the Ling Hut (Glen Torridon)
*14km/9miles    OS Sheet 25. Start 958 451↑ or 003 484↑. Finish 960 569↑*

This route is a variation of the two preceding ones, leading to the Ling Hut in Glen Torridon instead of Annat. Follow either route 287 up Coire Lair or 286 with a diversion over the Bealach Ban to reach a point (map ref 952 519) on the path midway between Bealach Coire Lair and Bealach Ban. From there descend due N by a faint but cairned path for 1km to reach the upper end of a good path which continues N down to Glen Torridon, with fine views of Liathach and Beinn Eighe across the glen. The path reaches the Ling Hut and goes round the east end of Lochan an Iasgair to reach the A896 near the carpark at the foot of Coire Dubh Mor.

## 288 Craig or Achnashellach (Glen Carron) to Glen Torridon
*14km/8¹⁄₂miles  OS Sheet 25. Start 029 490↑ or 003 484↑. Finish 002 581↑*

This classic route across the Coulin Pass is the most straightforward way from Glen Carron to Glen Torridon. The traditional way, as used by James Hogg, the Ettrick Shepherd, in 1803, is the Old Pony Track which starts between Achnashellach and Craig in Glen Carron at map ref 029 490 and goes fairly directly uphill through the forest to meet the forest road 500 metres south of the Coulin Pass. An alternative start is from Achnashellach Station (as for route 287) to a junction of forest roads, then NE up the road on the right for some 2km to join the Old Pony Track. Continue along the road over the Coulin Pass and down into Glen Torridon for 3km to the bridge over the Easan Dorcha.

This bridge can be reached by a quite different route from Achnashellach Station by following route 287 up Coire Lair as far as the junction of paths at map ref 990 503. Follow the right-hand path NNE below the steep face of Beinn Liath Mhor and down the Easan Dorcha, past the 'tea house' where the gentry from Coulin Lodge may have relaxed after a hard day's stalking.

Continue down the private road along the River Coulin for 1³/₄km and cross the glen to Torran-cuilinn. The direct route to Kinlochewe, and the line of the old right of way, goes NW for 200 metres, then N along a path which climbs through the forest, across the west side of Carn Loisgte and down through another forest to reach Glen Torridon 2km south of Kinlochewe. This route is difficult to follow and in some places is impassable through the thick forest, and at several places the original track has disappeared. It is not recommended.

It is better to continue from Torran-cuilinn along the path on the north-east side of Loch Coulin to join the private road near the outflow of the loch. From there go along the east side of Loch Clair, from where one has the classic view of Liathach, to reach the A896 road in Glen Torridon 5km from Kinlochewe.

### 289  The Low-level Traverse of Liathach
*12km/7¹/₂ miles        OS Sheets 24 and 25.  Start 959 569↑.  Finish 869 577↑*

Start from the carpark beside the A896 road in Glen Torridon near Lochan an Iasgair and follow the path N through Coire Dubh Mor between the dark sandstone buttresses of Liathach on the left and the vast scree slopes of Beinn Eighe on the right. In about 4km the highest point of the walk is reached and the way turns W along a well reconstructed path on the north side of a string of little lochs - Lochan a' Choire Dhuibh and Loch Grobaig.

On this part of the walk there are (on a clear day) superb views of the great northern corries of Liathach, the finest being Coire na Caime backed by the high pinnacled ridge of the mountain. The path continues downhill along the Abhainn Coire Mhic Nobuil, with Beinn Alligin's cliff-lined Toll a' Mhadaidh on the right, and finally passes through a small pine wood to reach the road between Torridon and Inveralligin.

### 290  Loch Torridon or Glen Torridon to Bridge of Grudie (Loch Maree)
*17km/10¹/₂ miles or 14km/8¹/₂ miles*
*OS Sheets 19, 24 and 25.  Start 869 577↑ or 959 569↑.  Finish 963 678*

This is another fine walk which goes through the heart of the Torridon mountains, and with a short diversion one can visit the finest of the Torridonian corries - Coire Mhic Fhearchair on the north side of Beinn Eighe.

Start from the carpark on the road between Torridon and Inveralligin at the foot of Coire Mhic Nobuil (the finishing point of route 289). Go up the path beside the Abhainn Coire Mhic Nobuil almost to the watershed near Lochan a' Choire Dhuibh, and then go E for a few hundred metres to join the path which contours round the base of Sail Mhor.

An alternative and shorter approach to this point can be made from the carpark in Glen Torridon at the start of route 289 and up the path through Coire Dubh Mor.

Follow the path round Sail Mhor to reach Loch Coire Mhic Fhearchair. Beyond the head of this lochan the great Triple Buttress forms the headwall of the corrie, the most impressive example of mountain architecture in Torridon.

To continue to Loch Maree, return down the path for a few hundred metres until below the waterfalls on the Allt Coire Mhic Fhearchair, then follow a faint path NNE downhill across this stream and back across it much lower down to reach at map ref 946 630 the start of the path down Glen Grudie on the west side of the river. This path leads in 5km to the A832 road near Bridge of Grudie.

## 291  Glen Torridon to Kerrysdale (Gairloch)
*20km/12¹/₂miles*
OS Sheets 19 and 25.  Start 959 569↑.  Finish 857 720 or 894 712

Start from the carpark in Glen Torridon as for route 289 and follow the path N through Coire Dubh Mor to Lochan a' Choire Dhuibh.  From there strike N through the col between Sail Mhor and Carn na Feola, the east peak of Beinn Dearg.  Go past Loch nan Cabar and the south-west side of Lochan Carn na Feola, then bear NW for about 3km across a very featureless tract dotted with several small lochans to reach Poca Buidhe bothy near the head of Loch na h-Oidhche.  From there follow the path along the east side of the loch and down the Abhainn a' Ghairbh Choire, then on the north-east side of Meall a' Ghlas Leothaid to reach the A832 road at map ref 857 720 between Loch Maree and Kerrysdale.

An alternative finish to this route can be made by leaving the path 1km north of the north end of Loch na h-Oidhche and going NE along the left bank of the stream down to Loch Garbhaig and round the shore to the loch's outlet.  From there take the land rover track down the west side of the Abhainn Garbhaig leading to a forest road that joins the A832 road near Victoria Falls. ?km NW along the A832 is the start of route 294 from Slattadale to Poolewe, and the addition of this makes a splendid long cross-country walk, 30km/19miles, from Glen Torridon to Poolewe.

## 292  Loch Torridon to Shieldaig (Gairloch) by the hills
*20km/12¹/₂miles*     OS Sheets 19 and 24.  Start 869 577↑.  Finish 808 724↑

Start as for route 290 from the carpark on the road between Torridon and Inveralligin and go up the footpath in Coire Mhic Nobuil for 1¹/₂km.  After crossing the river continue N along the deteriorating footpath up the Allt a' Bhealaich into the deep glen of the Bealach a' Chomhla between Beinn Alligin and Beinn Dearg.  From the cluster of lochans at the bealach bear NW on a descending traverse towards the north-west end of Loch a' Bhealaich, keeping above the very rough peaty ground near the lochside.  From there follow the path past Loch Gaineamhach (where, since the bridge over the river outlet is no longer in place, crossing may be a problem in wet weather) and Loch Braigh Horrisdale to reach Shieldaig Hotel on the B8056 road 6km from Gairloch

### 293  Torridon to Badachro by the coast
*34km/21miles  OS Sheets 19 and 24.  Start 883 570↑.  Finish 781 736*
This long route follows the footpath round the north shore of Loch Torridon  from Torridon village to Badachro on Loch Gairloch. Some sections of it can be done along the narrow public roads at both ends, and the distance between the road ends at Diabaig and Red Point  is only 12km/7½ miles. Start from Torridon along the coastal path which goes below Torridon House to Inveralligin.

The right of way follows the estate road past Torridon House towards Rechullin, and it is not necessary to divert along the shore.  From Inveralligin one can either walk along the road to Diabaig or follow the path which goes first to Alligin Shuas and then round the rocky coast well above sea-level to Port Laire and Diabaig.

Continue along the good footpath which goes high above the lochside NW then N to Craig Youth Hostel, and from there along the path at a lower level to Red Point where the public road is reached.  Between there and Badachro it is possible to avoid the road by following a path across the hillside to South Erradale and another path from there to Badachro past Loch Clair. (An old 'road' in use in 1755).

### 294  Slattadale (Loch Maree) to Poolewe
*11km/7miles                    OS Sheet 19.  Start 888 714↑.  Finish 860 790↑*
Leave the  A832 road in the Slattadale Forest and go N for ¾km to a carpark.  Go N along a path through the forest by the side of Loch Maree and climb to a viewpoint overlooking the loch.  Further north the path leaves the forest and climbs NW up a glen on the south side of Creag Mhor Thollaidh to cross a pass at 250m.  Continue down a narrow glen on the north side  of the pass to reach the A832 road 2km south of Poolewe.

The next five routes are in the Letterewe and Fisherfield forests between Loch Maree and Loch Broom.  This is one of the finest wilderness areas in the Highlands, a region of remote mountains and lochs, penetrated only by a few paths, some of them old rights of way.  There are no permanent habitations in the interior of this area, and the only shelters to be found are the bothies at Carnmore and Shenavall, which should not be used in the stalking season. Those who venture into this area should be fit, well equipped and self-reliant, but for those who do so the rewards are great.

## 295  Incheril (Kinlochewe) to Poolewe

*31km/19¹/₂ miles*               *OS Sheet 19.  Start 030 625↑.  Finish 858 808↑*

This is a classic and historic walking route of the Highlands, alongside one of the most beautiful of Scottish lochs.  It is, however, not to be undertaken lightly, for not only is it long, but the going in places is very rough and there are no hostelries on the way.  This is an old route to Poolewe from the south, linking with the Coulin Pass from Loch Carron.  The route across Creag Tharbh on Loch Maree was also the way used about 1850 by the postman travelling from Dingwall to Poolewe, as recorded by Osgood Mackenzie in his book, *A Hundred Years in the Highlands*.  Those who walk this route today will gain a high respect for the postmen of 150 years ago.

Kinlochewe is the starting point for expeditions into the Letterewe and Fisherfield wilderness from the south.  There is a car park 1km east of the village at Incheril at the end of the public road from where the long walks start, either NW along Loch Maree or NE up to the Heights of Kinlochewe.  The route to Poolewe goes NW along the path on the north side of the Kinlochewe River to reach the head of Loch Maree and continues along the loch.  In places it climbs about 100m above the shore and goes by Furnace to Letterewe.  Any attempt from there to walk along the lochside to Ardlair is difficult and requires great care to negotiate the crags of Creag Tharbh (the Bull Rock) which drop steeply into Loch Maree.  A detour of this margin of the loch is necessary to avoid these dangerous crags.

The viable alternative from Letterewe is to follow the path which climbs N beside the Allt Folais and crosses this stream in about 1km to go along the path parallel with Loch Maree for a further 1¹/₂km until the watershed is reached at about map ref 941 735 where the path swings N.  Continue N by this path which goes over the col and down Srathan Buidhe to the low ground at the foot of the pass.  There, turn NW round the base of Beinn Airidh Charr and go past Loch an Doire Chrionaich and down the Allt na Creige, along a path which has been improved, to reach Kernsary.  From there a private road goes past Inveran and along the River Ewe to Poolewe.  This route is shown on Roy's map of 1775 and also on Arrowsmith's map of 1807.

An option (which is not advised) between Letterewe and Kernsary, is to leave the path at map ref 941 735 and bear W climbing to about 350m.  Then go NW at this height continuing with caution above Creag Tharbh for some 4km to descend warily through crags to the lochside at Ardlair.  From there follow a path which in 2km strikes N away from Loch Maree and goes by the west side of Loch Tholldhoire to Kernsary to continue as described to Poolewe.

## 296  Incheril (Kinlochewe) to Corrie Hallie (Dundonnell)

*29km/18miles*               *OS Sheet 19.  Start 038 625↑.  Finish 114 851↑*

From the carpark at Incheril go up the private road to Heights of Kinlochewe.

Take the left-hand track which goes N up Gleann na Muice, and beyond its end continue along a path up the glen to the south-east end of Lochan Fada. From there bear NE towards Loch Meallan an Fhudair and beyond there continue N on a level traverse to the Bealach na Croise.

There is a path of sorts on the north-west side of the stream flowing NE from the bealach, and lower down cross to join the path on its east side. Go N along the east side of Loch an Nid and down the path beside the Abhainn Loch an Nid until it joins a track near Achnegie. Follow this track uphill and across high moorland to Loch Coire Chaorachain, beyond which the track drops down through birch woods to reach the A832 road at Corrie Hallie, 4km from Dundonnell Hotel.

### 297 Poolewe to Corrie Hallie (Dundonnell)

*36km/22¹/₂ miles*          *OS Sheet 19. Start 858 808↑. Finish 114 851↑*

This is the finest and longest of the routes which cross the wild mountain land between Loch Maree and Loch Broom. Its grandest feature is the succession of splendid mountains in whose shadows one walks - Beinn Airigh Charr, Beinn Lair, A' Mhaighdean, Beinn Dearg Mor and finally, grandest of them all, An Teallach. For nearly its entire length the route follows good paths, but there are at least two river crossings which in spate conditions are likely to be very difficult if not impossible, so this is a walk which should be done in good weather.

From Poolewe, go up the private road along the River Ewe to Kernsary, and from there follow the recently remade path up the Allt na Creige and past Loch an Doire Crionach to the foot of Srathan Buidhe. After a short diversion up this narrow glen, continue E along the path to the head of Fionn Loch, and cross the causeway between it and Dubh Loch. At that point one is in the heart of the Letterewe wilderness under the great crags of Carn Mor and Sgurr na Laocainn.

Go E then NE up the path past Lochan Feith Mhic-illean, across the watershed and down Gleann na Muice Beag and Gleann na Muice to Larachantivore in the shadow of Beinn Dearg Mor. The crossing of Strath na Sealga to Shenavall is possibly the most problematical part of this long walk, as the two rivers - Abhainn Gleann na Muice and Abhainn Srath na Sealga - may be easy to cross when conditions are dry, but they are the opposite during and after wet weather. The easiest crossing may well be where the combined rivers flow into Loch na Sealga.

From Shenavall follow the path which climbs E from the bothy up a little glen to reach the high moorland at the foot of Sail Liath, and continue NE to join the track near Loch Coire Chaorachain where route 296 is joined 3km from Corrie Hallie.

### 298 Gruinard to Corrie Hallie (Dundonnell)

*24km/15miles*          *OS Sheet 19. Start 962 912↑. Finish 114 851↑*

Start from the A832 road 1km south of Gruinard House near the bridge over the Gruinard River and walk for 9km along the private road up the river to the boathouse at the foot of Loch na Sealga. Continue along the path on the south west side of the loch, at one point climbing about 30m above it to traverse across a steep craggy section. From there on the going is easier along the remains of an old track to the head of the loch.

The crossing of the Abhainn Srath na Sealga may cause problems or even be impossible if the river is in spate. Shenavall is reached 1½km up the strath from the loch, and from there route 297 is followed E then NE past Loch Coire Chaorachain to Corrie Hallie.

### 299  Incheril (Kinlochewe) to Loch a' Bhraoin (Braemore)
*23km/14½ miles     OS Sheets 19 and 20.   Start 038 625↑.   Finish 162 761↑*

From the carpark at the end of the public road at Incheril go along the private road to Heights of Kinlochewe and take the left-hand track up Gleann na Muice, as for route 296. From the end of the track at map ref 070 667 take the path which climbs N out of the glen on its east side. In less than 2km the path forks at a small shelter, and at that point take the left-hand path N then NE for 1½km to its end at the stream high up in Gleann Tanagaidh.

Climb NNE on the west side of the burn flowing down from the Bealach Gorm, and on the north side of this pass go down to the path 1½km upstream from Lochivraon bothy.   Go E along this path, past the bothy and along the north shore of Loch a' Bhraoin to the ruined house at its east end.   From there a track leads in 1km to the A832 road 6km from the A835 at Braemore junction.

### 300  Achnasheen to Incheril (Kinlochewe) by Loch Fannich
*25km/15½ miles  OS Sheets 19, 20 and 25.   Start 199 599.   Finish 038 625↑*

This walk across the hills south of Loch Fannich and down the many dreary miles of Srath Chrombuill is not one that can be strongly recommended, and the initial problem of gaining access at the start may be a sufficient deterrent to those wanting to explore this unfrequented corner of the Highlands.

The start is 4km NE of Achnasheen at the edge of the Strathbran Plantation, and access to the private road leading N to Loch Fannich is at present blocked by a high locked gate and barbed wire fence.   Once these obstacles are overcome, go along the road to Loch Fannich and 2km W along the lochside  to the pipe track leading SW then W along Srath Chrombuill. Leave this track at about map ref 140 637 and keep going W, gradually dropping down to cross the Abhainn Bruachaig to find an old fence which leads to Leckie.   From there follow the road all the way down the glen past Heights of Kinlochewe to Incheril and Kinlochewe.

### 301  Grudie (Loch Luichart) to Loch a' Bhraoin (Braemore)
*29km/18miles                     OS Sheet 20.   Start 312 626.   Finish 162 761↑*

Start at Grudie on the A832 road 1½km west of Lochluichart Station and go up the private road beside the River Grudie to Loch  Fannich and along its north shore to Fannich Lodge.   Continue along a track to the west end of the loch and follow the path N up the Allt Leac a' Bhealaich to the pass, the Bealach Breabag, at 550m between Sgurr Breac and Sgurr nan Clach Geala.

Go down the path along the east side of the Allt Breabag to a footbridge at map ref 163 747 to reach the outflow of Loch a' Bhraoin. From there a track leads in 1km to the A832 road   6km from its junction with the A835 at Braemore.

There is a link between routes 300 and 301 which is not shown on the OS 1:50,000 map. Follow route 300 from the A832 to the south side of Loch Fannich and W along the lochside for 2km. A short distance further, at map ref 177 650, a recently made road is reached which leads NW about ½km above the lochside to the Abhainn a' Chadh Bhuidhe. On the north side of this stream leave the new road  (which continues W), and follow an old grassy track round the head of Loch Fannich and cross the Abhainn Nid to join route 301 at the foot of the Allt Leac a' Bhealaich.

## 302  Dundonnell to Ullapool

*9km/5½ miles*                     *OS Sheet 19.  Start 094 878.  Finish 115 930*
Start from the A832 road at Dundonnell and take the farm track to the river opposite Eilean Darach. The track continues further than shown on the map. Cross by the suspension footbridge and follow the private drive beyond the houses to join the minor public road. Go uphill by this road which swings left and gradually climbs  N high above the head of Little Loch Broom. At the crest of the ridge leave the road, which descends W to Badrallach, and follow a track NE downhill, gradually at first then steeply to Allt na h-Airbhe (Alltnaharrie). There is a passenger ferry from there to Ullapool, but as it may not operate at all times and in bad weather, it would be wise to check before leaving Dundonnell.

## 303  Dundonnell to Inverbroom

*12km/7½ miles*          *OS Sheets 19 and 20.   Start 094 878.  Finish 178 840*
From Dundonnell follow the farm track and cross the footbridge over the Dundonnell River as for route 302. Go past Eilean Darach to the minor public road and turn right along it up Strath Beag for 2km.  After passing Dundonnell House turn left off the road just before the bridge at Brae (map ref 114 856) and take the path to the right, away from the farmhouse (home of Frank Fraser Darling in the early 1930's) and leaving it soon, climb steeply to join a well-defined track.  This rises to 400metres before passing the north end of Loch an Tiompain and crosses an old stone dam (map ref 166 845). The descent to Croftown is less well defined, gradual at first then steeply to a zig-zag beside a wood and exits beside cottages to a minor road at Inverbroom, 1km south of the head of Loch Broom, and a few hundred metres from the A835 road.

# Easter Ross

### 304  Dingwall to Strathpeffer and Garve
*20km/12¹/₂ miles        OS Sheets 20 and 26.  Start 554 586.  Finish 395 614*
A feature of this walk is that it goes from one railway station to another one, so it might be worthwhile to consult the train timetable before setting out.  From Dingwall station go through the town due W up the road past Knockbain to Knockfarrel, and along the crest of the ridge with Loch Ussie on one's left.  Continue along the track downhill past Cnocmor Lodge to the A834 road at the youth hostel 800 metres south-west of Strathpeffer town centre.

To continue to Garve, take the single track road opposite the youth hostel past Kinellan farm to the houses at the east end of Loch Kinellan and go along a track on the north side of the loch. Continue W then NW into the forest and through it towards Loch na Crann to reach a road which is followed S for a few hundred metres. At the next intersection of roads, turn NNW past the Rogie Falls, which can be viewed by taking a path downhill on the left. The forested area between Loch na Crann and Black Water has several roads, tracks and paths, and care is needed to follow the right ones. Continue along the forest road on the east side of the Black Water past Rogie, then W under the railway and through the forest on the north side of Loch Garve past Strathgarve Lodge to reach Garve.

An alternative route between Strathpeffer and Garve, which follows in part an old track shown on Roy's map of 1755, is to follow the route described above to the point a few hundred metres south of Loch na Crann and instead of turning NNW towards the Rogie Falls, continue S towards Contin as far as map ref 456 570 where a path on the right leads down to a carpark. From there go along the main road across the Black Water and past the Achilty Hotel, then take the minor road W to Loch Achilty and along the north side of the River Conon to the Loch Luichart dam.  The way continues N through woods along the east side of the loch for 1¹/₂ km and then NE under electricity transmission lines across a col following traces of a path and an old track to reach the A832 road 1km south of Garve.

### 305  Evanton to Inchbae Hotel (Garve)
*28km/17 miles        OS Sheets 20 and 21.  Start 608 664.  Finish 400 694*
From Evanton go W by the public road along the north side of the River Glass to cross it by a bridge at Eileanach Lodge and follow a private road along the south-west shore of Loch Glass to Wyvis Lodge. Continue W along the south side of the Abhainn Beinn nan Eun for 3km to reach the Allt Bealach Culaidh which flows down from Loch Bealach Culaidh. Go SW up exceedingly boggy ground on the west side of the Allt Bealach Culaidh to the loch. Continue along the lochside by a rough, steep and bouldery slope some 20 metres or more above the water.  This is an unpleasant section of the route which might

be avoided by taking a higher line well to the north-west of the way just described, passing Feur-lochan.

From the head of Loch Bealach Culaidh  go SW on the line of a path shown on the OS map, but barely discernible on the ground, until the col  near map ref 431 709 is reached.  The path becomes more evident at this point and bears WSW along the line of an old fence above the forest until a gap in the plantations at map ref 416 704 is reached.  From there follow the faint line of an old right of way down to the A835 road 400 metres east of Inchbae Hotel.

An alternative route, avoiding the bad section described above, is possible from a stile at map ref 457 734.  Go S up a well used zigzag path climbing onto Carn Gorm, then descend SW by a poor but recognisable path towards Meallan Donn and go W on the north side of the forest to join the preceding route at map ref 416 704 and continue down to the A835 road. This may be the line of an old right of way.

### 306  Garve to Aultguish Inn
*12km/7¹/₂ miles*                        *OS Sheet 20.  Start 395 614.  Finish 351 704*
To avoid walking along the busy main road, leave Garve by the minor road across the Black Water and go NW past the Home Farm to Little Garve. Follow the road W round to its junction with the realigned A835 road.  Cross it and go up the verge to the concrete planks over the ditch and climb steeply to rejoin the original path at a stile.  Go NW through the forest along a good track for 2km and continue N out of the forest on the west side of  Creagan an Eich Ghlais and past Lochan nam Breac.

The route continues NNW across a col, drops to cross the Allt Bad an t-Seabhaig and then goes NW along a path through recently planted mixed trees. After crossing the next burn, the Allt Glac an t-Sidhean, make a gradual descent across very boggy ground in which only traces of the path are visible, and reach the Allt Giubhais Beag just above Aultguish Inn.

This route was part of the old road used for carrying fish from Ullapool, as shown on Arrowsmith's map of 1807.  It was replaced by the new road in 1840.  At one point about 400 metres uphill from Aultguish Inn the remains of an old bridge across the Allt Giubhais Beag are still evident.

---

The next six routes traverse the glens and straths of Easter Ross between the Dornoch Firth and the head of Loch Broom.  Most of the routes follow long private roads giving access to remote lodges and bothies far up these straths, and they converge at the tiny village of The Craigs at the head of Strathcarron along which a narrow public road goes  for 12km to Ardgay at the head of the Dornoch Firth. There is a station there and Bonar Bridge is 1¹/₂ km away along the A9 road. Of particular historical interest in this area is Croick Church, 2km up Strath Cuileannach from The Craigs.  When the inhabitants of these glens were being brutally cleared from their homes, many of them had to shelter in Croick Church and some of them carved their names and messages on the glass of the east window, still to be seen.

### 307  Aultguish Inn to Ardgay (Dornoch Firth)
*43km/27miles*  OS Sheets 20 and 21. Start 373 708. Finish 600 904
   The start of this route from the A835 road is about 2km east of Aultguish Inn at Black Bridge. Follow the private road N up Strath Vaich on the east side of the Abhainn Srath a' Bhathaich past Lubriach and the plantation just beyond there. The track goes over a little knoll from where there is a fine view up Loch Vaich. Go along the east side of the loch past the ruins of Lubachlaggan and beyond the head of the loch climb gradually to the pass on the east side of Meall a' Chaorainn and descend to Deanich Lodge in Gleann Mor. Continue down this very long glen past Alladale Lodge to The Craigs and finally go along the quiet public road in Strathcarron to reach Ardgay.

### 308  Alness to Ardgay (Dornoch Firth)
*23km/14½ miles*  OS Sheet 21. Start 645 736. Finish 600 904
   The start of this route may be made at the cross-roads 5km north of Alness near Dalnavie. Go NW past Ardross along the narrow public road to its end at Braeantra. From there follow a path which goes N, at first through a pine wood then up the open hillside to a prominent boulder. Pass a deer fence and gate to another prominent boulder beyond the crest of Creag Braigh an t-Sratha. From there climb to Clach Goil and descend gradually N towards the headwaters of the Wester Fearn Burn along a typical wide drove track. From Garbhairidh bothy a path leads downstream on the south-east side of the burn, with a slight climb across the lower slopes of Meall Doir a' Chuilinn before descending again to cross the Wester Fearn Burn by a footbridge at Garvary.
   From there northwards for 2 or 3km the route becomes much rougher and more difficult. After crossing the Wester Fearn Burn go N up a forest ride, crossing two forest roads and the upper deer fence to reach Cnocan Ruigh Ruaidh (map ref 596 868), 600 metres from Garvary. Then go just E of N for 1km, the path at this point being almost lost in mossy and waterlogged moorland, but it appears again at map ref 597 877. Follow it across the moorland between Church Hill and the Glas-choille plantation and on down through open woods to join the minor road ½ km south of Kincardine, from where it is 1km north-west along the A9 to Ardgay.
   An obvious alternative to the route from Garvary to Kincardine described above is to go down the private road on the right bank of the Wester Fearn Burn to reach the A9 road near Fearn Lodge.

### 308X  Aultnamain to Dalnaclach via Strath Rory
*7km/4½ miles*  OS Sheet 21. Start 667 778↑. Finish 733 763↑
   This route was part of a network of old drove roads leading to Milton. Today it makes a pleasant walk through Strath Rory to Dalnaclach, at one time a rest stop for drovers. The start is signposted from the A836 road about 3½ km south of Aultnamain Inn. The track goes E through a plantation for a short distance until the Strathrory River is reached. Then a path, wet in places, follows the river, passing below Cnoc an Duan, an example of a vitrified fort, to Dalnaclach (signposted) on the Scotsburn road.

The Lairgs of Tain was another old drovers' road, by-passing Tain and avoiding the Struie road where the tolls were high in droving times. From Edderton on the A9 road, 6km north-west of Tain, the minor road signposted to Edderton Mains is followed and continues as a track round the west side of Edderton Hill through the Morangie Forest. At Culpleasant (map ref 743 797) the track divides and the three possible routes to the Scotsburn road are signposted: NE to Rosehill, E to Quebec Bridge and SE to East Lamington.

### 309  Alness to Oykel Bridge
*46km/29miles       OS Sheets 16,20 and 21.  Start 645 736.  Finish 385 009*
The first part of this walk is the same as   route 308 as far as Braeantra. From there continue up Strath Rusdale by the private road on the north side of the Abhainn Glac an t-Seilich.  Cross the col at the head of the glen to reach Lochan a' Chairn and continue NW along the track beside the Salachie Burn for 2km before bearing W over a col at 437m to descend quite steeply into Glen Calvie.  Go down this glen past Glencalvie Lodge to The Craigs in Strathcarron.

Turn NW along the road past Croick Church and up the track in Strath Cuileannach  for 8km to Lubachoinnich.  Leave the track about 1km beyond there opposite a ruined sheep fank (at map ref 407 958) and climb NW on a rising traverse across the grassy hillside, trying to follow the original path which is now almost completely overgrown, to map ref 395 969. There the path reappears and leads NNW across two deer fences (by stile and gate) to reach the ridge west of Cnoc nan Caorach.  Finally descend by various paths which converge about 1km south of Amat,  from where it is about 1½ km across the River Einig to Oykel Bridge.

### 310  Inverlael (Loch Broom) to Ardgay (Dornoch Firth)
*50km/31miles       OS Sheets 20 and 21.   Start 182 853.  Finish 600 904*
This is a very fine walk which goes from coast to coast - Loch Broom to the Dornoch Firth - at one of the narrowest parts of Scotland. It is not a walk to be undertaken lightly or in bad weather conditions, as it crosses wild mountainous country to the north of Beinn Dearg.  Glenbeg bothy is a possible overnight shelter.

From Inverlael at the head of Loch Broom, go up the River Lael by the forest road to Glensguaib and continue E steeply uphill by a path onto the Druim na Saobhaidhe.  In 2km this path crosses the Allt Gleann a' Mhadaidh and continues E up a wide glen to reach several lochans in Coire an Lochain Sgeirich. 1km beyond the last lochan the path peters out on a broad col. Descend E then SE down Gleann Beag where there is no path until Glenbeg bothy is reached.

From the bothy go along the south side of the Abhainn a' Ghlinne Bhig for 2km to a bridge where a track starts.  Follow this track down the glen to Deanich Lodge where route 307 is joined  for a further 15km down Gleann Mor to The Craigs and 12km more to Ardgay along the public road in Strathcarron.

Two other ways across the mountainous western part of this route are possible, but they should only be attempted by experienced mountain walkers. Both go up the forest road to Glensguaib and continue SE along the path on the north side of the River Lael. One route turns off this path near map ref 236 834 by another stalker's path which climbs E towards Lochan a' Chnapaich. Cross the col east of this lochan and descend along the Allt Uisg a' Bhrisdidh to Gleann Beag.

The other route follows the path up the River Lael to its source at a wide col with some lochans. From there descend NE and follow the stream which flows into Loch Tuath and the north end of Loch Prille. Go ENE from there over another col and down the stream on its east side to Glenbeg bothy.

### 311   Inverlael to Oykel Bridge or Ullapool
*29km/18miles or 25km/16miles*
    OS Sheets 16,19 and 20.   Start  182 853.   Finish 385 009 or 131 941
    From Inverlael go up the River Lael, crossing to the north side of the river at the first bridge,  and continue to map ref 206 855 and there strike N up a zigzag path to reach a higher forest road.  Continue N then NE out of the forest up a newer track on the west side of a deep gorge and when above the gorge head E.  At about map ref 230 875 the track peters out on level ground. Continue E then NE  round a hill and drop gradually to the old crofting settlement of Douchary in Glen Douchary near map ref 244 903. From there the two routes go their separate ways:
    (a) Going to Oykel Bridge, a path goes down Glen Douchary on the east side of the river and then NE across a watershed to the head of Loch an Daimh. Follow the track on the north-west side of this loch past Knockdamph bothy and down to Duag Bridge, from where a private road goes down Glen Einig to Oykel Bridge.
    (b) To go to Ullapool, do not follow the path down Glen Douchary but head NNW across a col south-west of Meall na Moch-eirigh and descend to East Rhidorroch Lodge in Glen Achall.  Cross to the north side of the Rhidorroch River and go down the private road past Loch Achall to the A835 road 1km north of Ullapool.  An alternative end to this route can be made by leaving the private road at map ref 155 952 just west of Loch Achall and climbing up the path over the north-west ridge of Maol Calaisceig , then taking the lower path at the bifurcation at map ref 141 949 to descend steeply to Ullapool.
    Inverlael was at one time the centre of the Loch Broom district, Ullapool not being founded until 1788.  On Roy's map of 1755 the route going E over the hills from Inverlael is marked 'Road from Loch Broom to Tain'.  It went over the col to the Allt na Lairige, across Glen Douchary and NE over to Strath Mulzie, then E to Strath Cuileannach and finally down Strathcarron to the head of the Dornoch Firth.
    Two other routes shown on the same map are: (i) east from Inverlael over the hills to Gleann Beag and Gleann Mor (route310), and (ii) the old road to Garve which went SE from Inverlael to the col between Beinn Enaiglair and Iorguill, then down by Loch a' Gharbhrain to Aultguish. The first proper road between Ullapool and Garve was made in 1792-94.

### 312  Ullapool to Oykel Bridge or Alness
*31km/19miles or 75km/47miles*
> *OS Sheets 16,19 and 20.  Start 131 941.  Finish 385 009 or 645 736*
> Go N from Ullapool along the A835 road for 1km, then turn right up the private road on the south side of the Ullapool River and continue up Glen Achall as far as East Rhidorroch Lodge.  Beyond there go along the track which leads to Loch an Daimh, along its north shore past Knockdamph bothy and down Glen Einig to Oykel Bridge.

It is a further 24km to Invershin Station and Carbisdale Castle youth hostel.  For Carbisdale, go E from Amat on the south side of the River Oykel, first by a track and then by the old Strath Oykel road.  This route is shown on Arrowsmith's map of 1807.

The much longer variation of this route goes 1½km down Glen Einig from Duag Bridge and then follows a path on the right which goes E to the Allt nan Caisean.  Continue SE over a low ridge  to reach the end of the track in Strath Cuileannach and follow it past Croick Church to The Craigs.  At this point one can either go down Strathcarron to Bonar Bridge, or up Glen Calvie and over the col to Strath Rusdale, eventually to reach Alness by reversing the southern end of route 308.  This route, from Ullapool to Alness or vice versa, is a splendid expedition across Ross-shire, not likely to be done in a single day except by bicycle.

### 313  Strath Canaird or Ullapool to Achiltibuie
*17km/10½ miles or 28km/17½ miles*
> *OS Sheets 15, 19 and 20.  Start 146 013 or 131 941.  Finish 026 081*
> This is a spectacular walk, not without some difficulty, along the lower slopes of Ben Mor Coigach which drop steeply into the sea at the mouth of Loch Broom.  At the west end of the walk a public road comes by way of Achiltibuie from Strath Canaird as far as Culnacraig, a total distance of 37 km but actually only 10km from the start of the described walk.

The usual starting point is in Strath Canaird where a parking facility has been created adjacent to the A835 road on the south side of the river bridge opposite the narrow road to Blughasary.  Walk the 1km along this road past Blughasary (where, contrary to the indication on some OS maps, there is no public car park) and cross the River Runie by a footbridge to reach the foot of the hillside. Go WSW along a path, muddy in places, for 1½km on the outside of the deer fence which encloses the grazing land to reach the burn which flows down through a narrow gorge from Loch Sgeireach.  50 metres beyond the burn and 50 metres before reaching a gate in the deer fence start climbing steeply uphill by a path marked by cairns and wooden posts. After the initial steep climb, the path bears left on a rising traverse W for 1½km. From the crest of a little spur at map ref 104 012 descend gradually across rough and in places boggy ground, still following cairns and posts until at map ref 091 014 the path, which is very narrow at this point, crosses a steep grassy slope above sea-cliffs with a few metres of scrambling down a rocky step. Great care is needed at this point.

Beyond there the path continues its gradual descent to reach the shore line at Geodha Mor, then traverses the steep lower slopes of Garbh Choireachan just above the sea and finally climbs to the cottages at Culnacraig at the end of the public road. From that point there is a choice of routes, either by road direct to Achiltibuie or seaward by path to Achduart and then by road past Acheninver Youth Hostel.

For those who want to start this walk at Ullapool, the following route goes from there to Strath Canaird.  Leave Ullapool northwards by the A835 road and 2km beyond the bridge over the Ullapool River take the vehicle track which climbs NE over the west side of Creag na Feola and ends at Loch Dubh (presumably the original path was submerged by the damming of the loch).  Go round the west side of this loch along a series of huge flat stones interspersed with bog. After crossing a small dam at the north end of the loch a tarmac road goes past Loch Beinn Deirg and all the way down to Strath Canaird.

This route is shown on Arrowsmith's map of 1807 as the only way in those days from Ullapool to Achilitibuie and was the local postman's walk except for the start of the described walk from Ullapool to Loch Dubh, for which the more accessible fishers' track has been substituted because of large scale water works and community forestry which now block the original path by way of the east side of Creag na Feola.

# SECTION 26
# Sutherland and Caithness

### 314 Inverkirkaig (near Lochinver) to Elphin by the Cam Loch
*22km/14miles*                    *OS Sheet 15.  Start 078 195.  Finish 214 119*
This long cross-country route on the south side of Suilven involves some rough and pathless walking. Starting from Inverkirkaig, a few kilometres south of Lochinver, go E along the road for 1km to the bridge over the River Kirkaig and follow the path on the north side of the river past the Falls of Kirkaig. At map ref 117 177 go N along the path to the shore of Fionn Loch and continue along the path round the west end of the loch and along the north side almost as far as its south-east end. At map ref 144 168 head ESE into an obvious defile past a sheep fank and over the left shoulder of a rock dome to find a faint path by the burn. Further on, at a lone tree, climb out of the defile on its north side onto the open hillside where the path is more evident. Continue along the side of Loch Gleannan a' Mhadaidh in a straight line past the ruined house of Bracklach to the end of Cam Loch. Half way along the north side of this loch the path of route 315 is joined and followed to the A835 road 2km from Elphin. Post Bus service.

### 315  Lochinver to Elphin by Glen Canisp
*22km/14miles*                    *OS Sheet 15.  Start 094 223↑.  Finish 214 119*
This is one of the best long distance walks in Assynt, taking a direct line through Glen Canisp between the splendid peaks of Suilven and Canisp, and following a good path for most of the way. Leave Lochinver by the private road to Glencanisp Lodge; it is possible to drive for 1½km to a parking place near the west end of Loch Druim Suardalain. Continue along the road past the lodge and up Glen Canisp by a fine path past Suileag bothy, along the north side of Loch na Gainimh and through the narrow defile of Ghlinne Dhorcha. Cross the burn at the outflow of Lochan Fada and climb gradually along the bare stony ridge on its south side. Less than 1km beyond the head of the loch, the path turns S along a low ridge and drops to Cam Loch. Finally follow the path SE along the lochside to reach the A835 road 2km from Elphin. Post Bus service.

### 316  Lochinver to Inchnadamph
*23km/14½ miles*                    *OS Sheet 15.  Start 094 223↑.  Finish 251 218*
This route follows good paths in its western half, but the eastern part along the south side of Loch Assynt is rough and pathless for much of its distance and the line is not well defined. Between these two halves the route approaches close to the A837 road at the west end of Loch Assynt, so the walk can be started or ended there. This is an old right of way, and at one time there were isolated habitations on the south side of Loch Assynt, but these have long since been abandoned and that side of the loch is now wild country.
Starting from Lochinver, the first part of the walk goes by the private road and path up Glen Canisp to Suileag bothy, as described above. From there

strike N along a path over the moorland past Loch Crom and Loch an Leothaid, crossing a col just east of Cnoc an Leothaid and descending to the River Inver, where a bridge leads across to the A837 road. To continue to Inchnadamph, do not cross the bridge but go E along a wet and boggy path to two old shielings. Continue in the direction of the Doire Daimh, where a fairly obvious dyke on the north side of the burn is a good line to follow, appearing as a dark ridge among lighter surrounding rocks. Continue along a terrace below the steep slopes of Beinn Gharbh to the top of a small birch wood and from there descend SE, aiming for a prominent oxbow in the River Loanan at map ref 245 216 where the river is crossable unless in spate. Post Bus service between Lochinver and Inchnadamph.

### 317   Loch Assynt to Kylesku over Quinag
*12km/7¹/₂miles*                    *OS Sheet 15. Start 183 267↑. Finish 230 336*

In previous editions of this guidebook this route was described as starting from Lochinver, thereby adding 10km to its length along the first part of route 316 described above plus 3km along the A837 road from Little Assynt to Tumore. The start from Tumore seems more logical, especially as there is some steep climbing over Quinag on the way to Kylesku.

Start 200 metres west of Tumore at a small carpark, where the right of way is signposted to Nedd. Climb up the path, passing through a deer fence before reaching the Bealach Leireag. At that point a large cairn marks the start of the steep climb to the Bealach a' Chornaidh, the col at the centre of the Quinag massif. The ascent to the bealach is less difficult than it appears from below, there being a cairned path which leads up scree and heather to the main ridge of Quinag between Spidean Coinich and Sail Gharbh.

Descend E then SE down steep grass slopes towards Lochan Bealach Cornaidh. A path develops and leads down to the north side of the loch, but its continuation E should not be followed unless it is intended to descend to the A894 road near its highest point. To reach Kylesku, bear ENE from the loch down broad sandstone pavements which ease the walk towards Loch nan Eun and a crossing of the Allt na Bradhan near map ref 237 297 to reach the A894 road 5km from Kylesku. Post Bus service.

### 318   Altnacealgach to Inchnadamph
*20km/12¹/₂miles*                    *OS Sheet 15. Start 296 083↑. Finish 251 218*

This route gives a fine walk which takes one through the heart of the highest mountains of Assynt. The southern starting point is on the A837 road 4km south-east of Altnacealgach Hotel. Go NE along the private road past Loch Ailsh to Benmore Lodge and 2¹/₂km further to the end of the track beside the River Oykel. Continue up the glen for about 4km, then leave the main stream which flows down from Dubh Loch Mor and climb due N to the narrow pass between Conival and Breabag Tarsuinn. Go NW through this rocky defile and descend along the Allt a' Bhealaich, which disappears underground near the Traligill Caves. From that point a good path, becoming a track, leads down Gleann Dubh past Glenbain to the road at Inchnadamph. Post Bus service.

### 319   Kylesku to Inchnadamph by the Eas a' Chual Aluinn

*16km/10miles*                    *OS Sheet 15.  Start 238 285.  Finish 251 218*
    This is a very fine but rough walk through the wild, rocky landscape of the Assynt mountains, visiting one of the finest waterfalls in Scotland. The Eas a' Chual Aluinn is often said to be highest fall in Scotland, however this may be disputed as it is not a single drop, but a series of steep cascades. In very dry weather the falls almost disappear, so they are seen at their best in wet weather or preferably just after wet weather. Either the northern or the southern part of this route can be used as an approach to the falls, the southern being very much longer and rougher.
    Start from a carpark just north of the summit of the A894 road 6km south of Kylesku and follow the path round the south end of Loch na Gainmhich and uphill beside the Allt Loch Bealach a' Bhuirich to reach the Bealach a' Bhuirich. Descend on its east side by a good path and in 1km reach the burn which feeds the Eas a' Chual Aluinn. Of the two paths which go down to the top of the falls, the one on the right bank of the burn is the safer and it leads to a viewpoint at a large rounded boulder on the edge of the escarpment.
    Return to the path junction and continue SE for 1km to a small cairn at another path junction beside two little lochans at map ref 280 270. Follow the right-hand path between the two lochans and climb SW up a rough corrie where the path tends to disappear in places before reaching the bealach between Glas Bheinn and Beinn Uidhe. The ascent of Glas Bheinn from the bealach is only a short diversion. Continue SE along the path on a descending traverse below the screes of Beinn Uidhe to Loch Fleodach Coire, then S across a broad ridge past a ghillie's shelter and finally down a good stalker's path above the Allt Poll an Droighinn to reach Inchnadamph. Post Bus service.

### 320   Kylesku to Altnacealgach round the east side of Ben More Assynt

*30km/19miles*                    *OS Sheet 15.  Start 238 285.  Finish 296 083↑*
    This is a long extension of the previous route which starts 6km south of Kylesku and goes through some very wild and remote country on the east side of the Ben More Assynt range.  Follow route 319 to the path junction at the two little lochans at map ref 280 270.  Continue SE along the left-hand path downhill for about 3km to its end  north-west of Gorm Loch Mor.
    There follows a rough, pathless section along the south-west side of this loch below the steep craggy hillside, then a climb to the outflow of Loch Bealach a' Mhadaidh to reach the start of another path.  Follow this one SE then S round the east side of Ben More Assynt, climbing about 100 metres, then dropping to Loch Carn nan Conbhairean and climbing again over the shoulder of Sron an Aonaich before at last dropping to the River Oykel.  Finally go S along the private road past Benmore Lodge and Loch Ailsh to reach the A837 road 4km from Altnacealgach Hotel. Post Bus service.

## 321  Loch Assynt to Drumbeg
*11km/7miles*                    *OS Sheet 15.  Start 182 267↑.  Finish 123 326*
The southern end of this route, which is a right of way, starts about 200 metres west of Tumore on the A837 road along the north side of Loch Assynt. The northern end is on the very  narrow and tortuous B869 road a few kilometres east of the little village of Drumbeg. Starting from the south, the first 1½km is the same as route 317 as far as the Bealach Leireag. From there follow the path NW down Gleann Leireag along  the right bank of the burn and on the north side of Loch an Leothaid. In places the going is wet and the path faint. Towards its north end the path bears away from the Abhainn Gleann Leireag and reaches the B869 road at map ref 156 314 near a small cairn. Drumbeg village is 3km west along the road. Post Bus service.

## 322  Kylestrome to Achfary
*11km/7miles*                    *OS Sheet 15.  Start 218 345.  Finish 293 396*
Starting from the new car park about 150metres off the A894 along the narrow public road which leads to the north end of the long since closed Kylesku ferry, go 300 metres to the gate of Kylestrome Lodge. From there follow the path on the north side of this road uphill NE then E and in 2km reach flatter ground to continue NE past several small lochans. Alternatively, go along a narrow road from Kylestrome on the north shore of Loch Glendhu for almost 3km, then climb up the path beside the Maldie Burn to  Loch an Leathiad Bhuain and climb N from the loch to join the higher path. Continue NE, climbing a little to reach Bealach nam Fiann. Finally, descend E to go down through the Achfary Forest and reach Lochmore Lodge 1½km southeast of Achfary on the A838 road. Post Bus service.

## 323  Kylestrome to Loch Stack
*10km/6miles*                    *OS Sheets 9 and 15.  Start 200 377.  Finish 265 437*
Start from the A894 road at Duartmore Bridge 4km NW of Kylestrome. Follow a stalker's path NE across the undulating moorland past a succession of secluded lochans, reaching a height of 300m before descending past the foot of Ben Stack to reach the A838 road near Lochstack Lodge at the outflow of Loch Stack.  An alternative finish to this walk, which adds 2km, is to go down Strath Stack on the south side of Ben Stack to reach Achfary. Post Bus service.

The next four routes penetrate into the very remote and rugged mountains of the Reay Forest between Loch Stack and Strath More, the glen which leads from the head of Loch Hope to Altnaharra. The starting and finishing points are a long way from any villages. There are, however, Post Bus services to and from Achfary, Gobernuisgach Lodge and Gualin House.

## 324  Achfary to Strath More by Bealach na Feithe
*20km/12½miles*                    *OS Sheet 9.  Start 297 402.  Finish 462 422*
Start from the A838 road ½ km north of Achfary at the bridge over the river flowing into Loch Stack.  Go along the private road past Airdachuilinn to

Lone cottage and continue E on the path up the grassy glen of Srath Luib na Seilich to reach the Bealach na Feithe (450m). Descend due E on the far side of this pass and reach a track which leads to Gobernuisgach Lodge at the foot of Glen Golly. From there a private road leads in a further 3km to the road in Strath More between Loch Hope and Altnaharra. The latter is the nearest hostelry, but it is 15km away.

### 325  Achfary to Strath More by Glen Golly
*24km/15miles*                    *OS Sheet 9. Start 297 402. Finish 462 422*
This route is a variation of the previous one, penetrating further into the mountains of the Reay Forest. Follow route 324 for its first 3km to Lone cottage. From there continue NE by the path up the Allt Horn to the pass just north-west of Creagan Meall Horn. This pass is in the heart of the Reay Forest mountains, surrounded by the barren stony peaks of Foinaven, Arkle and Meall Horn. Descend E down the steep path to An Dubh-loch, climb a short distance and continue E to Lochan Sgeireach on the watershed at the head of Glen Golly. From there the path goes downhill for 6½ km beside the Glen Golly River, which flows in a deep, birch-fringed gorge to Gobernuisgach Lodge, where route 324 is joined.

### 326  Gualin House to Strath More by Srath Dionard
*25km/15½ miles*                    *OS Sheet 9. Start 310 570. Finish 462 422*
Gualin House is remotely situated beside the A838 road between Rhiconich and Durness. This route follows a straight line which goes SE from there to Gobernuisgach Lodge through Srath Dionard, a long deep glen hemmed in by the steep slopes of Cranstackie and the great north-eastern corries of Foinaven. Leave the road just north-east of Gualin House and go up Srath Dionard by a track on the south-west side of the river. Continue beyond the end of the track, picking the best way up the boggy glen to reach Loch Dionard and go along its east shore. From the south end of the loch climb uphill along a path which leads to the top of Creag Staonsaid and drops slightly to Lochan Sgeireach where route 325 is joined and followed down Glen Golly to Gobernuisgach Lodge.

### 327  Achfary to Gualin House
*25km/15½ miles*                    *OS Sheet 9. Start 297 402. Finish 310 570*
This route is a variation of the previous ones, combining 325 and 326, with a rough and pathless section in the middle. The first half goes from Achfary by route 325 past Lone cottage, then up the path to the pass below Creagan Meall Horn and down to the outflow of An Dubh-loch. From there descend by the Allt an Easain Ghil down a steep and narrow corrie to reach flat ground at the head of Loch Dionard. The second half of the route goes along the east side of this loch and down Srath Dionard, which is boggy and pathless at first until the track lower down the strath on the left bank of the river leads to the A838 road near Gualin House.

## 328  Loch Merkland to Strath More
*15km/9miles*            *OS Sheets 9 and 16.  Start 384 329.  Finish 462 422*
    This is part of an old drove road.  Start near the north-west end of Loch
Merkland on the A838 road between Lairg and Durness. Follow the track
which goes NNE along the east side of the Allt nan Albannach, then NE by the
Bealach nam Meirleach between Meall a' Chleirich and a chain of three small
lochs.  Continue along the track down the glen of the Allt a' Chraois to
Gobernuisgach Lodge and the road in Strath More.

---

    The next four routes cross the vast tracts of undulating moorland and
rounded hills on the eastern border of Sutherland and into Caithness. This
area, and in particular the Flow Country of Caithness which is characterised
by great expanses of wet peat bog, is a complete contrast with the rocky
mountains of west Sutherland described in the preceding pages.

## 329  Lairg to Crask Inn by Loch Choire
*30km/19miles*            *OS Sheet 16.  Start 575 140.  Finish 524 248*
    Start from the A836 road 8km north of Lairg near Dalmichy.  Go E along
a track for 6km to Dalnessie far up the River Brora, then go N along a path up
this river  for 3½ km to a confluence of streams. Continue up the western
stream, the Allt Gobhlach, and keep going N over a flat featureless col and
down the Allt Coire na Fearna to the head of Loch Choire. Turn W and follow
the path on the north side of Loch a' Bhealaich through the Bealach Easach
and over a col to descend W down Srath a' Chraisg to Crask Inn. Post Bus
service to Lairg.

## 330  Crask Inn to Kinbrace
*40km/25miles*            *OS Sheets 16 and 17.  Start 524 246.  Finish 862 317*
    From Crask Inn (Post Bus service) reverse the last part of route 329 through
the Bealach Easach to Loch a' Bhealaich and Loch Choire. Continue along the
lochside to Loch Choire Lodge and then go E along a private road to Gearnsary
and past Loch an Alltan Fhearna and the south end of Loch Badanloch to the
B871 road 6km west of Kinbrace, where there is a station with a rather
infrequent train service. There is also a Post Bus service to Bettyhill.

## 331  Halkirk to Forsinain or Braemore
*33km/21miles or 38km/24miles*
                         *OS Sheets 10 and 11.  Start 129 595.  Finish 073 505*
    These two routes follow minor roads and tracks across the wide landscape
of Caithness. From Halkirk go S for 7km to the B870 road and SW along it for
1km to continue by a minor road to Strathmore Lodge. Keep going in the
same direction along a track past the north end of Loch More almost to the
bridge at map ref 072 464. Just before reaching the bridge go W along a forest
track past several lochans to reach the railway line in 5km. The track leads
SW to Altnabreac Station and past it for a very short distance until just before

the bridge across the Sleach Water a turn W leads across the railway line and along the track signposted 'Station Hill'. Follow forest tracks W across the Flow Country, passing close to the north side of Loch Leir in 4km and join a track going WSW across the south side of Sletill Hill to reach Forsinain, 6km north of Forsinard Station on the A897 road. Depending on the timetable, it may be possible to return almost to the day's starting point by train.

The alternative route from the bridge near the north-west corner of Loch More goes along a track on the west side of the loch and up the Thurso River to Dalnawillan Lodge and Dalganachan, then S to Glutt Lodge, 12km from Loch More. Just before reaching the lodge turn left and go SE along a well made track across the Dunbeath Water to Lochan nam Bo Riabhach. Continue SE by the track to reach Braemore, 9km from Dunbeath along a narrow public road. There is a Post Bus service between Halkirk and Glutt Lodge.

### 332  Trantlemore to Strathy
*37km/23miles*                    *OS Sheet 10.  Start 896 524.  Finish 842 651*
This route starts from a point only about 3km north of the end of the previous route, so the two could be combined  to give a long two-day route through the remoter parts of Caithness and northwest Sutherland, finishing on the north coast. Leave the A897 road in Strath Halladale 2km south of Trantlemore, cross the River Halladale by a Bailey bridge and follow a track SW for 2¹/₂ km to a junction just beyond the gate at map ref 876 501. Take the southern track through forestry plantations leading towards Ben Griam Beg for 7km. Then follow the path W away from the hills and turn N to reach Loch nam Breac after a further 6km.

The next section involves a short pathless section over boggy ground. Go through the obvious gap in the trees to the north and beyond them bear westward to the plantation by Lochstrathy bothy, 3km. After negotiating the deer fence, the track near the bothy can be reached through the pines. The route now turns N down the long open glen of the River Strathy, following the track on the east side of the river. Ignore the branch in 2¹/₂ km which goes W towards Loch nan Clach, but keep on the main track through plantations of young conifers and more substantial forests of mature pines, many of which have now been felled. In 13km from the bothy the track passes Bowside Lodge and 3km further the walk ends at Strathy village.

# Index

Copies of the map showing the routes described in Scottish Hill Tracks may be obtained by sending a stamped self-addressed envelope to:

**Scotways**
**24 Annandale Street**
**Edinburgh EH7 4AN**

Readers of this book are invited to send comments regarding the route descriptions to the Society at the above address. Changes in land use, in particular forestry, can cause changes in access. The Society welcomes information that will assist in keeping this book accurate and up to date.